D0753655

❧ MERE EQUALS

MERE EQUALS

THE PARADOX OF
EDUCATED WOMEN
IN THE EARLY
AMERICAN REPUBLIC

LUCIA MCMAHON

CORNELL UNIVERSITY PRESS
Ithaca and London

Copyright © 2012 by Cornell University

First published 2012 by Cornell University Press

Printed in the United States of America

Library of Congress Cataloging-in-Publication Data

McMahon, Lucia.
  Mere equals : the paradox of educated women in the early American republic / Lucia McMahon.
     p. cm.
  Includes bibliographical references and index.
  ISBN 978-0-8014-5052-5 (cloth : alk. paper)
  1. Women—Education—United States—History—18th century. 2. Women—Education—United States—History—19th century. 3. Women—United States—Social conditions—18th century. 4. Women—United States—Social conditions—19th century. I. Title.
    LC1752.M35   2012
    371.822—dc23   2012009966

Cornell University Press strives to use environmentally responsible suppliers and materials to the fullest extent possible in the publishing of its books. Such materials include vegetable-based, low-VOC inks and acid-free papers that are recycled, totally chlorine-free, or partly composed of nonwood fibers. For further information, visit our website at www.cornellpress.cornell.edu.

Cloth printing   10 9 8 7 6 5 4 3 2 1

To Elizabeth McMahon Kroll and Jackson McMahon Kroll

✺ Contents

❧ PREFACE

Between the 1780s and 1820s, American women acquired education during an expanding but experimental stage when scores of female academies proliferated across the new nation, yet decades before colleges and other institutions of higher education admitted women. The literary public sphere eagerly took notice of women's educational efforts, publishing prescriptive essays on women's education, accounts of commencement ceremonies held at female academies, and numerous examples of educated women founded in both fact and fiction. In the midst of sweeping institutional advancements, the prescriptive literature could not agree about the forms, uses, and effects of women's education; it offered everything from enthusiastic praise of women's intellectual equality to didactic parodies of pedantic women. At the time, even the most ardent supporters of women's education could not resolve the tensions between intellectual equality and sexual difference that informed the era's understandings of women's education. Thus, an author who proudly proclaimed, "Nature has formed the sexes upon an equality in mind," was careful to assure his readers, "I would not have it supposed I am an advocate for female independence."[1]

In *Mere Equals,* I address the issue of women's education in early national America explicitly within the context of an equality versus difference debate. As I argue, the education of women revealed an unanswered conundrum that was at the heart of how notions of gender and society functioned in the early national period: How does a society committed to equality maintain what are perceived as necessary differences? If properly educated women were capable of becoming the intellectual equals of men, how would Americans continue to justify women's formal exclusion from politics and other male-dominated professions? If women achieved intellectual equality, what other forms of equality would they seek? Would educated women, as critics warned, abandon their domestic responsibilities and compete with men for economic and political power? Would women's intellectual equality challenge the very notion of sexual difference—and perhaps more important, the social, political, and economic structures of male power and privilege sustained by gender difference and hierarchy? These questions found various expressions—but no easy resolutions—in the literary public sphere as early national Americans repeatedly debated the place of educated women in the early republic.

The organizing concept for this book—"mere equality"—reflects how early national Americans grappled with the issue of women's intellectual capacity. Mere equality represented an imperfect, paradoxical attempt at compromise—implicit in the *mere* was the persistent notion that women were different from men and, further, that to become *merely* the equals of man would represent a loss of women's influence and power as *women*. The *mere* was underwritten and sustained by notions of sexual difference. At the same time, *equality* was, of course, a powerful concept in the young nation, so powerful that it was not inconceivable that women (and other previously disenfranchised groups) might very well desire some of the social, economic, and political benefits that equality promised. Mere equality attempted to reconcile the persistent belief in gender difference of the era with its more liberating and enlightened ideas about equality. It was a vague, malleable concept that was subject to multiple interpretations. Its positive connotations enabled some women to explore how a sense of intellectual equality could transform their everyday lives. Yet, for many prescriptive writers, mere equality functioned as a constraint, an effort to remind intellectual women that they were still *women,* whose lives remained primarily defined by cultural models of sexual difference. Thus, although mere equality enabled educated women to achieve some measures of personal and social equality, it failed to fundamentally challenge the structural underpinnings of male patriarchy and privilege. Individuals could support the notion of women becoming the mere equals of men without having to cede much ideological, political, or economic ground.

What did educated women gain—and lose—in their pursuit of mere equality? To answer this question, this project goes beyond prescription and examines, through women's own words and experiences, how educated women attempted to live merely as the equals of man. This approach offers a unique contribution to the historiography, exploring the intersections between prescriptions and experiences to uncover how early national women responded to and negotiated cultural aims regarding the forms, uses, and purposes of education.[2] My analysis has been informed by recent scholarship that has mapped the early national literary and educational landscapes. Historians and literary scholars, such as Elizabeth Dillon in her provocative work on gender and the literary public sphere, have explored the prescriptive realms of sexual difference and separate spheres.[3] These studies have focused primarily on how early national models of womanhood served to reify patriarchal systems of male power and privilege. Although such works address how ideological constructions of gender roles and identity functioned in early national America, they typically do not examine the relationship between literary representations and lived experiences.

Others scholars have explored the intellectual lives of early national women. These studies focus largely on women's acquisition of education and subsequent entrance into public careers and spaces. Mary Kelley's path-breaking book, *Learning to Stand and Speak: Women, Education, and Public Life in America's Republic,* details the relationship between women's education and their roles as "makers of public opinion." Kelley demonstrates how educated women strove to transform the public and literary landscape through their teaching, writing, and activism. Their efforts were made possible by the ever-increasing number of educational institutions founded for women throughout the nineteenth century. Margaret Nash's detailed work has examined the rigorous instruction and curriculum offered to female students in academies across the nation between 1780 and 1840. Together, these important studies have demonstrated that radical advancements in women's access to and acquisition of education occurred throughout the first half of the nineteenth century.[4]

Much of the recent historiography on women's education to date has focused primarily on the public and printed aspects of women's education—whether through analysis of the literary public sphere, accounts of accomplished women, or histories of institutional progress. In *Mere Equals,* I take a different approach, focusing on the private and social experiences of educated women.[5] The majority of educated women did not experience their lives exclusively within literary or prescriptive realms, nor did most early national women seek public careers. Most educated women went on to live relatively quiet lives as friends, sisters, wives, and mothers. The issues that framed the prescriptive literature and the lives of public women certainly influenced the lives of more "everyday" women—and throughout this book, I explore that influence. Yet most early national women experienced the effects of education in their private and social lives, not on more public stages.

In this project, I narrate a story about how a generation of young women who enjoyed access to new educational opportunities made sense of their individual and social identities. The women highlighted in this study shared several key defining socioeconomic characteristics. They were white and, for the most part, were members of emerging middle-class or elite families that subscribed to new cultural ideals stressing the importance of education for women. These young women had the ability—and seized the opportunity—to take advantage of new educational possibilities being made available to them. They had both the financial resources and leisure time to attend female academies and/or to devote several hours a day to their studies. Most of these women were born and raised either in the mid-Atlantic or New England. Although I have found and cited occasional evidence from the writings of southern women and men, the evidentiary base for this study is primarily from the northern states. More research is needed on how educated women from the southern and western regions experienced and expressed their intellectual aspirations.

I have chosen a case study model to tell vivid, detailed stories about how particular women and men understood the connections between education, equality, and difference during this era. I focus on individual women's experiences with particular life stages and relationship arcs: friendship, family, courtship, marriage, and motherhood. Studying particular relationships enables me to construct personalized narratives of how individual women and men negotiated cultural and intellectual models of identity and behavior. The primary source base includes both prescriptive and popular writings (including newspapers, periodicals, fiction, and school catalogs and curriculum) and the personal narratives of women's educational and social experiences (as revealed through their diaries, letters, and personal papers). I selected the individual studies based largely on the availability of primary-source collections that could support in-depth narratives of personal experience. The women I focus on are relatively "unknown" historically and have been largely unexplored in other published accounts of early national women's lives. Their stories and experiences are meant to be individual but not idiosyncratic. A case study model perhaps necessarily raises questions about representativeness, but I have found echoes of these individual experiences in a number of personal and prescriptive writings from the era. Each individual narrative is supported by additional primary source evidence and grounded in key historiographical findings. Thus, the individual examples presented lend themselves to some generalization and are representative of a larger emotional and intellectual universe—similar language, preoccupations, and ideals can be found in a variety of early national writings and experiences.

Although I focus on individual relationships, the efforts to construct new forms of social and personal relationships necessarily reflected on early national society as a whole. When educated women attempted to assert their social and intellectual equality with men, they raised fundamental questions about the place of sameness and difference in the young republic. Their efforts took place during a period of flux, when new ideas about gender identity emerged in response to revolutionary political and social changes.[6] Despite its enlightened faith in the principles of equality and independence, the young nation remained committed to sexual difference and other forms of hierarchy. Faced with these constraints, early national women did not press for the full political rights of citizenship; instead, they explored more tentative and personal forms of mere equality. By experimenting with forms of mere equality primarily in their social and personal lives, educated women, perhaps inadvertently, obscured larger questions of their continued legal and political inequality. Women's expressions of mere equality in friendship and love did not require radical reconstructions of early national law or government.

Although early national women did not, as a whole, seek full political equality, their expressions of mere equality suggest some of the complex, even paradoxical ways in which Americans grappled with the possibilities and constraints inherent in their political and social rhetoric. The case studies that follow suggest that everyday experiences provide fruitful avenues for examining the complex relationship among education, equality, and difference that permeated the early American landscape. By exploring how debates about the nature of equality and difference found expression in the both the prescriptions for and experiences of educated women, *Mere Equals* contributes to our understanding about how gender identity continues to inform ideas about social and political organization.

❧ ACKNOWLEDGMENTS

In the space of time it took to see these pages to print, there was much living—and dying. I begin by acknowledging the untimely loss of Robert Takesh's quiet grace, Jim Disbrow's contagious laughter, Teresa Hom's joyful spirit, Ana Margarita Gómez's strong voice, Pearl McMahon's wry humor, Teri DiMatteo's loving kindness, and most of all, Tina McMahon's unconditional love.

Despite the losses, the living has been joyous. All my thanks and love go to my family: Jack, Elizabeth, and Jackson Kroll; John, Joey, and Skylar McMahon; Marie, Steve, Amber, Amanda, and Marilyn Takesh; and Debbie, Rich, Steve, Mike, and Nicole Kramer. You all enrich my everyday life in countless ways. Jack, Liz, and Jax Kroll have lived with this book for a very long time (nearly as long as I have lived with the house renovations). I thank them for their patience and understanding when research and writing took me away from them; I also thank them for taking me away from the past and pulling me back to the present. For their love and laughter, I thank Sandra Auletta, Catherine Gravino, Mark LaSalle, Joey McMahon, Debby and Kate Schriver, Bob and Teri Serafin, Steve Takesh, Sandy Trezza, and especially Marie McMahon Takesh—the best sister on the planet! My deepest gratitude goes to Audrey Brigliadoro, Ellen Pfeffer, and Raji Thron for continually inspiring me through the grace of their yoga practices and communities.

In the midst of living and laughing, as walls were torn down and rebuilt, this book emerged. The book began to take shape in its current form in large part thanks to a National Endowment for the Humanities postdoctoral fellowship, held in residence at the Library Company of Philadelphia. I am indebted to James Green, Connie King, and the entire Library Company staff for providing such a supportive environment for ideas to flourish. I also had the good fortune to share my residence with fellow fellows Will Mackintosh, Jeff Kaja, Peter Reed, and Jonathan Chu.

The strength of this book is reflected in the archival materials I uncovered while conducting research. Ron Becker, Bonita Grant, and the entire staff at the Special Collections and University Archives at Rutgers University have provided years of research support, for which I will always be grateful. I express my appreciation to the staff and librarians at the following institutions, for research assistance and for permission to quote from their collections: American Philosophical Society, Andover Historical Society, American Antiquarian Society, Duke University Library, Historical Society of Pennsylvania, New York Historical Society, Schlesinger Library, Princeton University Library, and Virginia Historical Society. I have incorporated portions of my previously published article, "'Of the Utmost Importance to Our Country': Women, Education, and Society, 1780–1820," *Journal of the Early Republic* 29, no. 3 (fall 2009): 475–506. Funds from the Research Center for the Humanities and Social Sciences Summer Stipend Program at William Paterson University, as well as a sabbatical leave, provided crucial support as I worked on the manuscript.

Both intellectually and personally, I continue to benefit from a wonderful group of early Americanists: Robert Churchill, Sara Gronim, Greg Knouff, Pete Messer, and Serena Zabin. I offer belated, but heartfelt, thanks to Jill Anderson, Jennie Brier, Kim Brodkin, Finis Dunaway, Chris Fisher, Matt Guterl, James Levy, Pat McDevitt, and especially Neil Brody Miller for their support and friendship during my graduate work at Rutgers. At William Paterson University (WPU), I am fortunate to work with a wonderful group of colleagues and friends (consider yourself all included in these acknowledgments!), especially Malissa Williams, who keep me smiling and laughing. And although Michael Innis-Jiménez left WPU, he remains a trusted colleague and friend.

The officers and members of the Society for Historians of the Early American Republic (SHEAR) have created a vibrant intellectual community that serves a model by which all other conferences are judged. Special thanks and praise go to Charlene Boyer Lewis (my long-standing SHEAR ambassador), Rodney Hessinger, Margaret Sumner, Will Mackintosh, and Nick Syrett for providing some of my best SHEAR memories. For their support, encouragement, and good company, I am grateful to Catherine Allgor, Andrew Burstein, Sara First, Kara French, Cassie Good, Katie Jorgensen Gray, C. Dallett Hemphill, Nancy Isenberg, Anya Jabour, Mary Kelley, Catherine Kelly, Susan Klepp, Albrecht Koschnik, James Lewis, Jen Manion, and Peter Onuf.

Michael McGandy at Cornell University Press provided expert editorial assistance. He, along with the two anonymous readers for the press, saw the promise and potential of this project, and their useful feedback helped me to more fully realize my visions for this book. Sarah Grossman shepherded me through the production process with patience, grace, and good cheer.

Debby Schriver and Lisa Purcell both read an earlier draft of the manuscript in its entirety and provided invaluable suggestions and feedback. Janet Dean and crew have provided recurring sources of motivation and encouragement. I gratefully maintain long-standing intellectual debts to Jennifer Jones, Paul Clemens, and Jan Lewis. Without Jennifer to emulate, I would not have wanted to become an academic, and without Paul to advise me, I certainly would not have made it this far. I cannot adequately convey in words how much I have benefited from Jan Lewis's support, guidance, and inspiration.

Finally, in true nineteenth-century fashion, I thank you, Dear Reader. Writing is often a lonely and solitary process, but reading brings us into a community of shared ideas and intellectual expressions that is as meaningful to me today as it was for the subjects of this book two hundred years ago.

🍎 MERE EQUALS

Introduction
Between Cupid and Minerva

In an 1802 essay provocatively titled, "Plan for the Emancipation of the Female Sex," an anonymous author suggested that women "would willingly relinquish that authority which they have so long enjoyed by courtesy, in order to appear formally on the theatre of the world merely as the equals of man." To achieve mere equality, women could "petition the legislature to sanction their emancipation by law." To gain equality, women needed only to ask for it—equality was, in essence, already theirs for the taking because no "gallant man" would allow his wife or mother to "sue in vain." This author recognized the law as one road to female emancipation, but he also underscored the early national connection between education and equality. As part of his "Plan for Emancipation," he proposed that the nation "found a college for the instruction of females in the arts and sciences." The faculty at this college would be women devoted entirely to their careers. "For the better preservation of female rights," he insisted, "the professors should all be enjoined celibacy." In addition to teaching, these "fair sages" would publish works on "the nobler subjects of civil polity or philosophy." Yet female students would be trained not to emulate their professors' public careers but to assume traditional domestic roles: "Young women entrusted to the tuition of female philosophers in this university, may when they become mothers, instruct their children;...and thus a gradual increase of wisdom, and consequently, of happiness, will be diffused throughout the community."[1]

By 1802, when this essay was published, scores of female academies were being established throughout the young nation, yet the idea of a college for women was still outside serious consideration. Indeed, it is difficult to discern if the essay's author was principally serious or sarcastic. If the "Plan for Emancipation" was meant as a parody, its stance on women's education did not contain enough true derision. The author presented the female college and its students in largely positive terms and failed, unlike most critics, to disparage educated women as pedants or bluestockings. As another author noted, "Few men would (I imagine) wish their wives and daughters to prefer Horace and Virgil to the care of their families."[2] Whatever the intentions of this 1802 "Plan for Emancipation," the fluid, nebulous nature of early national ideas about women's education and gender roles made it difficult to distinguish where possibility ended and parody began.

In 1819, less than two decades after the publication of the "Plan for Emancipation," Emma Willard, educator, echoed many of its suggestions and strategies in her "Plan for Improving Female Education." Willard petitioned the New York legislature not for female emancipation as such but, rather, for official improvements in and government support of women's education. Willard insisted that schools for women needed the same "respectability, permanency, and uniformity of operation" that characterized male institutions. As Willard argued, "It is the duty of a government, to do all in its power to promote the present and future prosperity of the nation, over which it is placed. This prosperity will depend on the character of its citizens." Women were citizens, and their proper education was vital to the success of the nation. Yet, according to her nineteenth-century biographer, Willard struggled "to find a suitable name for her ideal institution," and reportedly asserted, "It would never do to call it a 'college,' for the proposal to send young ladies to college would strike everyone as an absurdity." She instead decided upon the term "female seminary," hopeful that such naming "will not create a jealousy that we mean to intrude upon the province of the men." Willard was careful to insist that she had no desire to offer "a masculine education," stressing that education needed to reflect men and women's "difference of characters and duties."[3]

Whether presented as parody or possibility, early national articulations of women's education were marked by this persistent tension between intellectual equality and sexual difference. In essence, proponents of women's education insisted that women were at once equal to and different from men. This paradox found expression in Willard's rejection of "masculine education" for women, as well as in the assertion in the 1802 "Plan for Emancipation" that education would put women in positions *merely* as the equals of man.

Yet it is also striking that both plans proposed legal and educational measures as paths to women's equality. Women in post-Revolutionary America did not achieve substantial measures of equality or emancipation through legal channels. Early national women could not vote or hold office; and once married, women were subject to the doctrine of coverture, which made it challenging for them to hold property or acquire independent wealth. Within the educational landscape, however, progress was well underway. The period from approximately 1785 to 1825 represented a watershed moment in women's institutional access to education.[4] Although colleges remained closed to them, women enjoyed unprecedented access to a variety of new educational opportunities.

As the institutional landscape changed, so did representations of educated women within the literary public sphere. Through a variety of forms—including engravings, poetry, essays, anecdotes, character sketches, and novels—prescriptive writers explored the place of educated women in early national America.[5] Although many supported advancements in women's education, early national Americans were troubled by the idea that women's intellectual equality might disrupt the social, economic, and political frameworks that were sustained by the notion of sexual difference. Understanding how prescriptive writings articulated the tensions between education, equality, and difference is a crucial first step that will inform subsequent explorations of how individual women understood and experienced the boundaries of mere equality within their own lives.

"The Female Mind Shall Equal Prove"

Prior to the American Revolution, as one 1810 essayist recalled, women were "systemically shut out of Minerva's Temple." The young nation sought to expand women's access to education: "Thanks to the liberal and aspiring spirit of the age and country, the genius and education of women are not shamefully neglected." Educators established scores of new academies and seminaries for both women and men, insisting that education was an essential component of nation building. "It must therefore be a pleasure to all who wish for the prosperity and glory of this rising nation," the *Pennsylvania Gazette* reported in 1786, "to observe the zealous and liberal exertions of its citizens, in promoting the cause of literature, and providing for the instruction of youth in every useful and ornamental science." The need for well-educated men reflected political and social ideals about well-informed citizens who would take the lead in matters concerning the political, economic, and literary spheres of the nation.[6] Yet many early national Americans asserted that the proper education of women was equally important. As advocates insisted, women's education involved nothing less than "the most effectual means of establishing, promoting, and securing, on the most solid foundation, the domestic and social happiness of the present and future ages."[7] Education was both a symptom and cause of the commitment of the young nation to liberty, freedom, and independence.

Such enlightened faith in the powers of education was accompanied by an optimistic, and potentially radical, belief in the equality of women's and men's intellectual capacities. Educators asserted that women "were beings endowed with reason," who possessed intellectual capacity and "an equality of mind" with men. As one author contended, women "possess a strength of reason equal to ours... and can attain the knowledge of every thing they are required to do, with at least, an equal facility." Another essay on female education began with a poem that captured the era's optimistic faith in women's intellectual potential: "When'er the female mind shall equal prove.... No longer shall it vauntingly be said / *Her's* is *inferior to the mind of man*."[8] This widespread belief in women's intellectual equality had promising potential, suggesting that women could perhaps live merely as the equals of man. As John Burton, author of *Lectures on Female Education and Manners,* argued, "it cannot be denied, that your sex have given equal proofs with the men, of genius, judgment, taste, and imagination." Burton tantalizingly intimated that women were, in theory, as capable of receiving the same education as men, perhaps for the same ends: "It is not necessary, neither it is expedient for the purpose of civil society, that girls should be educated in the same manner as boys: but were a similar plan to be adopted, the women, without doubt, would be as well informed in the system of human knowledge, as the men."[9] As Burton suggested, women's station in society was a matter of custom and access to education, not due to any lack of intellectual ability. Yet, because it was deemed neither "necessary" nor "expedient" for women to be granted full access to political and economic equality, writers such as Burton repeatedly tempered their celebratory remarks about women's intellectual capacities by evoking prescribed gender roles: "The respective employments of the male and female sex being different, a different mode of education is consequently required. For whatever equality there may be in the natural powers of their minds, which I shall not consider at present, yet the female sex, from their situation in life, and from the duties corresponding with it, must evidently be instructed in a manner suitable to their destination, and to the tasks which they will have to perform."[10]

Despite their enlightened faith in women's intellectual equality, early national Americans continued to believe that men and women were dissimilar beings with contrasting manners, morals, and dispositions—and duties. Although the female mind was capable of intellectual equality, the female body apparently was not fitted for political equality: "'Tis Nature herself that prescribes for them a sedentary life, and devotes them to domestic occupations; 'tis Nature herself that secludes from public offices, the functions of which could not be combined with the duties of a mother and a nurse."[11] The enthusiasm for women's educational accomplishments stopped well short of extending the rights of suffrage and direct political power to women. This tension produced the notion of mere equality that dominated early national discussions of women's education.

The belief that women were indeed mere equals of men, at least intellectually and socially, while at the same time profoundly different in body and station, generated conflicting models of womanhood. To negotiate this thorny realm of equality and difference, early national Americans explored complementary gender roles that celebrated certain elements of equality (intellectual and social) while simultaneously insisting that "natural" distinctions (gender and race) defined the parameters of full political citizenship. Stressing the mutuality of relations between the sexes, writers urged women to find contentment in a model of gender identity that remained inherently hierarchical. "Do not these facts justify the order of society, and render some difference in rank between the sexes, necessary to the happiness of both?"[12] This complementary model of gender relations attempted to square the overriding insistence on prescribed gender roles with a positive characterization of women's intellectual capacities. In the process, the prescriptive literature obscured questions of power and authority inherent in this model of social organization. Although granting women intellectual capacity equal to that of men, prescriptive writers ultimately focused on maintaining a social and political order rooted in sexual difference and male hierarchy.

Discussions of women's education thus revealed a persistent contradiction between women's intellectual capacity (which many agreed was equal to that of men), and the decidedly different uses intended for education in their everyday lives. In essence, once having agreed that women could learn, proponents of women's education could not agree about what women should learn because their universal faith in the capacity of women's intellectual abilities came into conflict with their adherence to conventional gender roles. As one author insisted, "A *good* education is that which renders the ladies correct in their manners, respectable in their families, and agreeable in society. That education is always *wrong*, which raises a woman above the duties of her station." Instead of selfishly acquiring knowledge for their own sakes, women were asked to educate themselves for the benefit of early republican society. "How much better it would be then, were females educated, in order to make useful and ornamental members of society." As John Burton stressed, "the accomplishments, therefore, which you should acquire, are those that will contribute to render you serviceable in domestic, and agreeable in social life."[13] The main purpose of women's education, then, was not to provide women with the means to develop personal autonomy and ambition but, rather, to enable them to serve men and society. As subsequent chapters in this book reveal, access to education dramatically affected how individual women made sense of themselves and the world around them. But such changes in women's identity formation were of little interest to most prescriptive writers. Instead, educated women's roles were defined almost exclusively in relationship to men; they were to exercise moral influence, to provide pleasing conversation, and to serve as attractive companions. Prescriptive writers expressed little regard for the individual aspirations of educated women; rather, they worried about how women's pursuit of education would affect men.

Thus, while recognizing that the acquisition of education could enable women to live as mere equals to men, writers repeatedly warned that too much intellectual "sameness" between men and women would jeopardize domestic and social harmony by creating rivalry and competition. Prescriptive writings asserted that there was "a line of character between the sexes, which neither can pass without becoming contemptible." Women overly interested in the "masculine attainments" associated with certain forms of education and knowledge were accused of selfishness, pedantry, and affectation, traits considered "repugnant to female delicacy, so derogatory to the natural characteristic of her sex." As another author, identified as "Alphonzo," insisted, "A strong attachment to books in a lady, often deters a man from approaching her with the offer of his heart. This is ascribed to the pride of our sex."[14] Implicitly, men did not want women who were smarter than they were, women who would disagree with them, or women who would seek opportunities in the spheres of government and business:

When a woman quits her own department, she offends her husband, not merely because she obtrudes herself upon *his* business, but because she departs from that sphere which is assigned *her* in the order of society—because she neglects *her* duties and leaves *her own* department vacant.... The same principle which excludes a man from an attention to domestic business, excludes a woman from law, mathematics, and astronomy. Each sex feels a degree of pride in being best qualified for a particular station, and a degree of resentment when the other encroaches upon their privilege. This is acting conformably to the constitution of society.[15]

In promoting a separate spheres model, writers insisted that women could not occupy themselves with "masculine" concerns without necessarily neglecting their domesticity and desirability. Accordingly, the prescriptive literature urged women to make themselves "lovely" to men, and as Alphonzo insisted, "to be *lovely* you must be content to be *women;* to be mild, social and sentimental—to be acquainted with all that belongs to your department—and leave the masculine virtues, and the profound researches of study to the province of the other sex." Prescriptive writings stressed the need for educated women to retain their feminine attractiveness and desirability to men, fearful of what might occur if educated women were no longer "content to be *women*"—in other words, if they sought to live *merely* as the equals of man.[16]

"Knowledge, Combined with Beauty"

Part celebratory, part cautionary, prescriptive representations were important tools by which social commentators attempted to teach particular lessons about the proper content, forms, and effects of women's education. The frontispiece of the 1791 volume of the *Massachusetts Magazine* presented an inspirational model of womanhood meant to guide educated women. Surrounded by mythological and material embodiments of education, this representative woman exhibited an aura of intellectual seriousness *and* attractive femininity. The editors offered an "Explanation of the Frontispiece":

> The Fair Daughters of Massachusetts, are collectively represented by the symbolic figure of an elegant and accomplished young Lady, seated in her study, contemplating the various pages of the Magazine. Their general acquaintance with the necessary branches of reading and writing, and the more ornamental ones, of History and Geography, is happily depicted, by those instruments of Science, which adorn the Hall of Meditation. *Minerva,* the Goddess of Wisdom, assisted by *Cupid,* crowns her with a chaplet of Laurel: *Hymen's* burning Torch is displayed aloft—a delicate intimation, that knowledge, combined with beauty, enkindles the purest flames of love.[17]

In this representation, love and learning were coupled seamlessly in that both Cupid and Minerva crowned the achievements of this symbolic figure. "Knowledge, combined with beauty," enabled women to spread happiness

Figure 1. Frontispiece of the *Massachusetts Magazine,* 1791. In this symbolic image, Cupid and Minerva crown an educated woman's achievements while Hymen's torch glows above, all indications that she has achieved the perfect balance of "knowledge, combined with beauty." The Library Company of Philadelphia.

and harmony throughout the young nation. As Daniel Bryan, educator, insisted, "the influence of enlightened Beauty" was "inconceivable." An attractive and intelligent woman, as a student at a female academy remarked, represented the ideal form of womanhood: "I do not know any thing which so nearly approaches the *acme* of human excellence, as a young female of an enlightened understanding, a well-informed mind, and a pure and virtuous heart, united in a fair-proportioned and beautiful form."[18]

An "enlightened beauty" presented no apparent contradiction between love and learning, yet prescriptive thinkers frequently expressed concern about the potentially negative effects of women's education. In an 1809 essay titled, "On Female Education," James Milnor, a trustee of the Philadelphia Academy, aptly described the merits, as well as the possible dangers, inherent in women's pursuit of education. Milnor noted, "that as a polite and well-informed woman is the most welcome companion of the intelligent of our sex, a female pedant is in all respects the reverse." By failing to acquire "useful" knowledge, a pedant was given to affectation and the "ostentatious display of the decorations of her mind." But Milnor also recognized that in the effort to avoid pedantry, educators "may err on the contrary extreme." Young women also had to fear the consequences of a poor education, produced most often by reading novels. "Instead of the evil of pedantry, these are calculated to seduce the unsettled minds of young persons into the adoption of erroneous and immoral principles." Such women entertained "frivolity" and "false views of life" that often led to "disastrous course of conduct."[19]

In his essay, Milnor identified two extremes on a spectrum of ideas about educated women. Education and knowledge were presented as important antidotes to frivolity and coquetry (symptoms of undereducation), but the danger of overeducation (specifically, pedantry) was ever-present. In effect, educated women were asked to perform a delicate balancing act. They constantly risked falling into one or the other of these perceived extremes—extremes that can be thought of as representing either too much love or too much learning. A poorly educated woman was in danger of becoming too coquettish, too sexualized, and too susceptible to seduction. On the other end of the spectrum was the woman with too much education, or more precisely, one who had gained knowledge considered inappropriate for women. Both the undereducated coquette and the overeducated pedant let their level of education interfere with their attractiveness to men—thus threatening compatibility between the sexes. The figures of the pedant and the coquette served as foils against which model republican wives and mothers were measured.[20]

On one end of the spectrum was the pedant. Both supporters and critics of women's education agreed that the pedant was a dangerous figure—a woman who selfishly pursued knowledge to the detriment of her domestic and social duties. "Female pedantry is the object of my ridicule," one author remarked with obvious disdain. When a woman "applied herself to her study" too much, her actions resulted not in "that deference and respect which she had vainly expected" but, rather, "desertion and contemption." Instead of properly preparing herself for participation in early national society, the pedant exhibited behavior that was antisocial, selfish, and vain. It was best, as *The American Lady's Preceptor* recommended, for women to avoid "all abstract learning, all difficult researches, which may blunt the finer edges of their wit, and change the delicacy in which they excel into pedantic coarseness."[21] Even the strongest proponents of women's education were careful to warn about the dangers of overeducating women. As Susanna Rowson, author of several books and founder of a female academy, underscored, "many are the prejudices entertained, and the witticisms thrown out against what are called learned women." Rowson summarized this mind-set in her *Present for Young Ladies:* "The mind of a female is certainly as capable of acquiring knowledge, as that of the other sex; but if an enlightened mind must consequently be a conceited one it were better to remain in ignorance, since pedantry and presumption in a woman is more disgusting than an entire want of literary information, the one often awakens compassion, the other invariably excites contempt."[22]

Pedantry was rooted in conceit and vanity. As John Burton warned, young women needed to avoid becoming "vain enough to imagine, that your boasted merit is held in the same estimation by others." Such affectation, he asserted, implied that women were "so full of their own importance" as to exhibit an "egotism" that was "intolerable." Samuel Whiting, author of *Elegant Lessons,* agreed, remarking, "affectation of learning and authorship, in a woman with very little merit, draws upon itself the contempt and hatred of both sexes."[23]

One of the most striking critiques of pedantry appeared in the guise of a memoir. In 1816, the *Juvenile Portfolio* published an "autobiographical" essay titled, "The Life of a Learned Lady. Written by Herself," by "Eugenia Splatterdash." This fictitious and facetious character single-handedly and self-reflexively embodied the supposed excesses of the female pedant. Eugenia was "born a genius." Her mother, a "domestic drudge," possessed no "superior talents." Her father, a "Grub-street poet," took a superficial interest in her education, passing on his "smattering of French, and also of Latin" to Eugenia. The model of insincerity, Eugenia was able to fool her friends into thinking that she actually possessed knowledge: "By the very judicious use of a few Latin phrases, I have not an acquaintance who does not believe that

I have a thorough knowledge of the Latin language, while at the same time, I do not know enough even to make a lady a pedant."[24]

In admitting that her knowledge of Latin was insufficient to render her pedantic (in the traditional sense of paying undue attention to learning), Eugenia complicated how the pedant was defined. The pedant could also represent the excessive display, rather than the true possession, of knowledge. As Genevieve Fraisse, French historian, argues, the pedant assumes that "the [female] mind dresses up reason, imitates genius, and as a result exists primarily for the sake of appearance."[25] According to Eugenia, a pedant must possess just enough knowledge to make her display somewhat believable, if not sincere. Eugenia further complicated the understanding of pedantry by intimating that she was at once pedantic and fearful of the label. She informed her readers that she "understood Greek and Hebrew, but did not choose to display this knowledge, for fear of being thought pedantic." Thus, Eugenia displayed the knowledge that she did not truly possess and ostensibly kept hidden the knowledge that she had actually acquired. She parodied the pedant, at once embracing and resisting its defining characteristics. Yet Eugenia's advice to other women suggested that she was, at heart, a pedant: "Always pretend to [know] a great deal of knowledge, and you will obtain credit for possessing it."[26]

If Eugenia's contradictory assertions represent a confusing training guide for female pedantry, she already presented quite a disorderly model of womanhood. Yet it was the effects of her pedantry that suggest the real dangers inherent in a woman's excessive attention to education. Eugenia "disdained [domesticity] as unworthy of a genius." She confessed that she "was too fond of literary dust" to "mend my clothes and sweep the house." She assured her readers, however, that her aversion to domesticity was not problematic: "Spiteful people have said that learned ladies never get husbands; but this I can contradict from my own experience." Yet her marriage was a sham. She married a soldier who claimed to enjoy "the pleasure of having an intelligent companion," but Eugenia confessed that he "disappeared with [the dowry] in about a month, and I never heard of him again." She refused to consider her pedantry a cause of his departure: "I still maintained my contempt of all domestic employments. Indeed some people alleged this was the cause of my husband's running away from me; but whether this were true or not I never thought it worth while to inquire."[27] Despite her over-interest in education, Eugenia possessed no useful knowledge and was thus a poor judge of character. She was unable to choose a suitable husband and had no sense of what was expected of her as a wife.

Returning to her father's house after her failed marriage, Eugenia continued to disdain domesticity, and her "poor father was therefore under the necessity of performing the household duties." With her time thus free to devote to literary pursuits, Eugenia wrote poetry, novels, and textbooks and read voraciously. In what is undoubtedly a thinly veiled reference to Mary Wollstonecraft's *A Vindication of the Rights of Woman,* Eugenia began reading a work written by a "champion of her sex's rights." Reading Wollstonecraft, whose reputation, by this time, was thoroughly tarnished and discredited, Eugenia decided that women were "fit to be ministers of state, orators, admirals and generals," a position that caused her to "despise more than ever, all that are called feminine employments."[28]

Eugenia's story ended on an ironic, if seemingly less than tragic, note. She was satisfied with her successful career as an author and a genius, and felt "on an equality with the most learned men."[29] Unapologetic about her unchecked ambition, Eugenia represented the disruptive potential in women's search for mere equality. Ultimately, Eugenia's story is meant to amuse but also to instruct young women, demonstrating how both domesticity and desirability were eradicated by affected displays of learning. Eugenia can be read as the negative foil to the Massachusetts woman presented earlier—she was improperly educated; lacked beauty and desirability; and represented a masculine, indeed absurd, model of womanhood. This was mere equality gone awry.

"The Arts of Coquetry"

If a woman was too engrossed with education, she risked being labeled a pedant. Yet, if a woman's attention to education was too superficial, she could be criticized for that as well. Samuel Whiting, author, warned about the dangers awaiting any "utterly uncultivated" young woman: "What is there to correct her passions, or to govern her practice? What is there to direct her in the choice of companions and diversions; to guard her against the follies of her own sex, and the arts of ours?" As critics warned, the path to coquetry was most often laid "by a false Education, the folly of parents, or the flattery of a corrupted world." Unlike the pedant, who was preoccupied with learning, the coquette neglected her education, afraid that any overexertion might interfere with her beauty and charm. As one author quipped, "useful studies must by no means be attended to, as possibly it might damp Miss's vivacity."[30]

Neglecting useful studies, coquettes instead were more likely to spend countless hours engaged in reading novels. Indeed, novel reading was perhaps the surest path to coquetry. Prone to coquettish behavior, novel readers were ill prepared for the realities of courtship and marriage, preferring instead to inhabit a dreamlike world of their own imagination. Such was the case for

"Melissa," a young woman whose "invincible attachment to novels" turned her into a coquette. Melissa felt herself "well qualified for a heroine, as any, who shine in the page of romance. . . . Indeed she had charms, and her mind was well stored with modern female erudition; (for she had perused numberless novels)." Melissa replaced real education with romantic fancies, and through her voracious novel reading, "the arts of coquetry were . . . carefully studied." Given to affectation and flirting, Melissa rejected many sound marriage proposals, "knowing that once sacrificed at the altar of Hymen, she could no longer enjoy the felicity of coquetry." Instead, Melissa spent her entire life an unmarried woman, and when her charms no longer worked, "she professed herself a *man hater.*"[31]

Whereas the pedant was cast as an unattractive, masculine figure, the coquette represented disorder in the form of excessive female sexuality. The "ultimate aim" of the coquette was to gain "power" over male admirers and the surrounding social scene. Ultimately, however, this power was chimerical: "However flattering it may be to the vanity of the female sex, to make conquests, or to have many admirers, yet it betrays a kind of coquetry by no means admirable." Although coquettes reveled in their ability to attract men, they represented a disruptive form of desirability—one that ultimately led to rejection and embarrassment for men. Expecting to meet heroic men who resembled characters from novels, coquettes hesitated to accept "several offers that would otherwise have appeared highly advantageous and proper." By rejecting marriage proposals from respectable men, coquettes eventually found themselves alone and unwanted. As critics repeatedly warned, any worthy man would come to recognize the insincere flirtations of a coquette and would refuse to consider her as an ideal mate. "How faint and spiritless are the charms of a coquet [sic], with the real loveliness of . . . innocence, piety, good-humour, and truth."[32] By disrupting marital models, coquettes were as problematic as pedants.

Perhaps ironically, the most influential warning about the dangers of coquetry came from a novel. Many early republican readers would have been familiar with Hannah Webster Foster's immensely popular novel, *The Coquette.* Scholars have noted the importance of this novel to the early republican literary landscape.[33] This epistolary novel, based on the real-life experiences of Elizabeth Whitman, tells the story of her fictional counterpart, Eliza Wharton, and her descent first into coquetry and then her seduction, abandonment, and death. Initially, Eliza is presented as a charming figure, whose "elegant person, accomplished mind, and polished manners have been much celebrated." Despite her attention to education, Eliza is prone to coquettish behavior, favoring the attentions of male admirers that her "bewitching charms" seem to attract effortlessly. She is courted by two men: Reverend Boyer, a respectable, worthy gentleman; and Major Sanford, a charming but rakish figure whose intentions are less than honorable. Early in the novel, Sanford discloses his aims to a friend: "I fancy this young lady is a coquette; and if so, I shall avenge my sex by retaliating the mischiefs she mediates against us."[34]

Like Eugenia Splatterdash, Eliza Wharton resists the idea of becoming constrained by the "duties of domestic life." Reading her reluctance as coquetry, Sanford resolves to seduce her. He convinces Eliza that a union with Boyer (who, while virtuous, lacks fortune and gaiety) would cause her "restraint," "confinement," and "embarassments." Professing his sincerity, Sanford gains her trust while simultaneously plotting to break up her relationship with Boyer. Eliza begins to believe the adage that "*a reformed rake makes the best husband,*" but her friends wonder why she "would be willing to risk all upon the slender prospect of his reformation." They repeatedly warn her about Sanford's "vicious character" and urge her to "lay aside those coquettish arts which you sometimes put on." Eliza ignores her friends' advice and continues her relationship with Sanford, even as she becomes engaged to Boyer. Ultimately, Boyer tires of her coquettish behavior and withdraws his suit. Eliza suffers from a "depression of spirits" and eventually enters into an illicit affair with Sanford, who by the time of the actual seduction, has already married another woman for her fortune. Despite her friends' repeated warnings, and despite "her advantages of education," Eliza suffers the tragic fate of seduction. Removing herself from the society of her forgiving family and friends, Eliza chooses to bear the shame of her illegitimate pregnancy alone. Before delivering her stillborn child and then succumbing to death herself, Eliza relates her sad tale. Unlike Eugenia Splatterdash, Eliza Wharton is repentant, and she urges other women to avoid the coquettish behavior that made her more susceptible to Major Sanford's deceptions.[35]

Eliza Wharton's story is instructive, but it also complicates warnings about coquetry. Eliza's problem was not merely that she was a coquette, as suggested by the novel's title. According to Kristie Hamilton, literary scholar, Eliza "is perceived by many as a coquette because she attempts to balance all of her opportunities, sanctioned and unsanctioned, until one should present itself as that which will best satisfy her in her pursuit of happiness." But because Eliza initially is presented as a well-educated, accomplished young woman, she further complicates traditional definitions of coquetry, which typically placed the blame on a lack of education. "A woman of sense and education," as one author insisted, "is above practising the arts of coquetry."[36] Thus, the *ambivalence* that Eliza experiences as an educated woman can be seen as an additional source of danger. Eliza's desire to weigh her various options, rather than settling for expected conventional norms, can be read not only as a symptom of coquetry but also as a problematic effect of her education. Well-educated, Eliza was reluctant to assume the role of an amiable wife without first exploring her identity as an independent woman. She falls a victim not only to seduction but to her desire for mere equality.

"On an Equal Footing"

Through myriad warnings and cautionary tales, the literary public sphere revealed a continued sense of ambivalence about educated women's roles in society. Rather than clarifying the relationship among education, equality, and difference, such prescriptive models may have created confusion for any woman who was relying on them to guide her behavior. As one proponent of women's education rhetorically asked, "How can a pretty woman fail to be ignorant, when the first lesson she is taught, is that beauty supersedes and dispenses with every other quality;... [and] that to be intelligent is to be pedantic?" Women recognized that the charge of pedantry could be used to discredit their intellectual pursuits. Yet, by stressing the need for women to remain desirable and attractive to men, prescriptive writers could be guilty of encouraging coquettish practices. "Shall we blame her for being a coquette," this author continued, "when the indiscriminate flattery of every man teaches her that the homage of one is as good as that of another?"[37]

The censure of both coquettish and pedantic behavior reflected two extremes on a spectrum of fears about the implications of women's education. We never learned, for example, whether Eugenia Splatterdash was a true genius or a pedant; the point, in some way, is irrelevant because both were masculine figures and thus inappropriate for women.[38] As a pedant, Eugenia was ridiculed in terms that criticized not only her ostentatious display of knowledge but also her problematic assertions of equality. The coquette was an equally dangerous figure. She turned fears about educated women's desirability to men on their head by deciding that no man was worth marrying. Eliza Wharton's coquetry was a warning about the ill effects of women's education, especially about what happened when educated women developed heightened expectations about courtship and marriage. Both the pedant and coquette challenged traditional gender roles by insisting on living merely as the equals of man on their own misguided terms.

Eugenia Splatterdash and Eliza Wharton serve as two representative case studies from the literary public sphere. The didactic nature of their tales suggests that it was not educated women themselves but rather early national society as a whole that was unready for women to explore the possibilities of mere equality. The remaining chapters in this book offer examples drawn from lived experiences to illustrate how actual women attempted to craft identities for themselves as learned women in a world marked by persistent ambivalence about their educational accomplishments. As we will see, many educated women resisted representations of the coquette and the pedant, determined to achieve the right balance between Cupid and Minerva. Early national women eagerly embraced opportunities to acquire education and put it to good use. As a student at a female academy in New York insisted, "Since we have the same natural abilities as themselves, why should we not have the same opportunity of polishing and displaying them by the principles of an independent and virtuous education." This young woman rejoiced that enlightened Americans "wish to see the fair sex on an equal footing with themselves, enjoying all the blessings of freedom."[39]

Inspired by this equal footing, educated women began to imagine what it would be like to live merely as the equals of man—at least in their personal and social relationships. In this book, I tell their stories to explore how the concept of mere equality functioned in early national society. In chapter 1, I describe the educational worlds of early national women, juxtaposing prescriptive writings against the lived experiences of young women who attended female academies established throughout the early republic. Female academies inspired women to develop identities that celebrated their intellectual ambitions. Enthusiastic about their studies, young women were determined to defend their ardent interest in education against prescriptive warnings about both coquettish and pedantic behavior.

When they left the safe, nurturing space of the female academy, educated women searched for new ways to enact identities founded in the promise of mere equality. In chapters 2–6, I focus on women's experiences with friendship, family, courtship, marriage, and motherhood. In all stages of their lives, women self-consciously crafted personal and social relationships in which their intellectual achievements were valued, appreciated, and celebrated. Through relationships with like-minded individuals, educated women searched for mere equality, inextricably linking their intellectual, emotional, and social aspirations. In particular, women believed that egalitarian relationships between men and women *were* possible, and to their credit, they found men willing and eager to enact relationships that emphasized shared intellectual and emotional interests.

Despite prescriptive fears about masculine, pedantic women, early national men did not seem troubled by the intellectual women in their lives, nor did early national women reject their domestic roles after acquiring education.

In fact, we could argue that most educated women faced the inverse of the disruptive scenarios envisioned by prescriptive writers: Could they sustain the promise of mere equality when faced with the increasing demands of family life and domesticity? That is, could individual women enact identities and relationships rooted in expressions of mere equality *within* their assigned gender roles? The first generation of educated women did not, as a whole, make larger claims for political equality—they asked primarily for the right to be educated. Accepting the constraints of prescribed gender roles with respect to the law and politics, women who acquired education channeled those energies primarily toward their individual identities and relationships. "Ask those gentlemen of this assembly whose wives have been the best educated whether they find them to be less attentive to domestic concerns," Anna Harrington suggested to the audience of a Ladies' Exhibition held at an academy in Lincoln, Massachusetts. "May not more women be trusted with knowledge, as well as these. Or is there any fear that women shall gain too much influence; and become mistresses of the world in spite of man?" The fear that intellectual equality would lead women to seek "too much influence" was not borne out by the everyday lives of educated women. "When we shall quit our domestic employments, put on offensive armor, and become fond of the art of war," Anna asserted, "then such an event may be feared."[40] While accepting (for the time being) the limited range of such efforts, educated women began to explore—and without "offensive armor"—what the promises of mere equality might entail in their individual lives.

❧ CHAPTER 1

"More like a Pleasure than a Study"

Women's Educational Experiences

In 1801, Violetta Bancker left her home in New York to attend Mrs. Capron's Female Academy in Philadelphia. In a letter to her father, Violetta described her teachers: "you and mama wish to know my opinion of Mrs. Capron: I find her very affectionate and kind. Mrs. Mallon who is the English teacher is a very sensible woman and very capable. . . . the other teachers are all very agreeable." Among her various studies, Violetta expressed particular interest in geography, which as she noted, "is so very pleasing that it seems more like a pleasure than a study." A year and a half later, Violetta remained in Philadelphia. She left Mrs. Capron's school to attend another academy, taught by Mr. Jaudon. "I find my time and the season for learning are fast passing away and cannot be recalled," Violetta reflected. "I fear I have not improved as I ought the many precious and golden hours that have passed, and I think I am resolved to be more diligent and careful in the improvement of *what* may remain." Writing to her mother in December 1802, Violetta expressed growing commitment to her academic studies:

The solicitude which my kind Preceptor expresses for my improvement, and the constant exertion which he uses in directing my studies to the best effect are with me powerful motives to industry; for I think it would be at once foolish and ungrateful to thwart his kind endeavors for my advantage by my own inattention. But the pleasure it will give to my dear parents and friends at New York to hear and know of my improvement in useful and ornamental branches, is another and even a higher motive to stimulate my industry in the pursuit of such acquirements.[1]

Violetta was flattered by her teacher's interest in her academic progress, which inspired her to attend more diligently to her studies. Her parents also clearly supported her intellectual endeavors—they paid for her tuition as well as her living expenses in Philadelphia for nearly three years. Violetta was eager to please her instructor and parents, but she clearly derived personal enjoyment and satisfaction from her studies. As she reflected, her extended stay in Philadelphia provided "the theatre of many scenes of juvenile bliss, wholesome instruction, and salutary advice."[2]

Violetta Bancker's educational journey was representative of larger trends that shaped individual women's access to educational opportunities throughout early national America. The "age of academies" ushered in a new era in women's education that has been well documented by historians of education.[3] Rather than provide a traditional institutional history of female academies, in this chapter I focus on individual women's experiences with education. I have uncovered evidence of female students' educational journeys in a number of primary source materials, including women's private journals and letters, student journals and compositions, and published orations, essays, and school catalogues. Evidence from these various writings suggests that education mattered deeply to those women, who were among the first generations to benefit from changes in the early national educational landscape. Women's writings indicate how they used education and knowledge as tools of self-fashioning, constructing identities for themselves that privileged the importance and worthiness of their educational endeavors.[4] Young women also demonstrated their awareness of the frequent public discourse and debate surrounding women's education. Reluctant to be cast as the coquette or the pedant, women approached education with optimism, determined to fashion positive identities as learned women.

Exploring the interplay between public representations and personal experiences, in this chapter I examine women's educational acquisitions as both individual and social enterprises. What did access to education mean to young women? How did the acquisition of new forms of knowledge shape women's sense of themselves? Did the pursuit of intellectual equality inspire women to live merely as the equals of man?

"An Astonishing Revolution of Sentiment and of Practice"

In May 1813, fourteen-year-old Margaretta Cornell left her family home in Monmouth County, New Jersey, and traveled to New Brunswick, New Jersey, to begin attending Miss Hay's boarding school. "How do you like your present situation?" Maria Cornell inquired of her daughter. "I hope it is favorable for the purposes of study and improvement—and that you will be diligent—make this opportunity the harvest of your mind—which has hitherto been too much neglected." Maria continually urged Margaretta to devote herself fully to her education. "Be cheerful—Let your studies—not home—occupy your mind and be your chief concern."[5] Although Margaretta experienced some initial homesickness, she took her mother's advice to heart. "If you was to come and offer to take me home, I would not accept your offer," she wrote in May 1814. "Time is so precious, I am sure I shall not be able to improve it in a proper manner." Maria was pleased at her daughter's developing devotion to her studies. "To know that you are well happy and contented from home gives a joy... not to be described. Go on therefore in virtue and knowledge," Maria implored her daughter. Margaretta's father also expressed his support, urging his daughter to "attend to the various branches of improvement not as a task—but with a view to advance your future comfort and usefulness in the world."[6]

Margaretta remained at Miss Hay's school for approximately two years, but by May 1815 she was attending the Female Academy of New Brunswick, a school established "for the purpose of giving to young Misses, a more accurate and extensive education than is customary." To compete with Miss Hay's school, the Female Academy employed college-educated male instructors and offered a comprehensive course of study, including "Reading, Writing, Arithmetic, English Grammar, Geography and Composition." Maria expressed renewed enthusiasm for her daughter's new school situation: "I am truly pleased that you are so well satisfied."[7] With her parents' continued support, Margaretta flourished at the Female Academy. In September 1815, she wrote a composition reflecting on her educational journey. When she first began her studies, Margaretta admitted that she dreamed "of being freed from the shackles of a school-life." Yet as she prepared to finish her studies and return home, she discovered that "*All—All* is reversed." Under the care of her "much esteemed Tutor," Margaretta grew to deeply appreciate the educational advantages that had been given to her. Regretting her "former negligence," Margaretta determined to spend her remaining school days devoted "to the improvement of every moment as it flies."[8]

Margaretta Cornell's educational experiences underscore external transformations in women's institutional access to education, as well as the internal transformations women experienced as they acquired new forms of knowledge. Margaretta began her studies at a boarding school, homesick and eager to be free of school. She completed her studies over two years later at a female academy, where she expressed a determination to improve "every moment." Her individual experiences reflected widespread changes to the educational landscape that affected the lives of tens of thousands of American women. As one essayist proclaimed in 1810, "an astonishing revolution of sentiment and of practice with respect to the education of women, has, of late, been accomplished in America." The result was a rapidly changing educational landscape. As a girl, Jane Bayard was sent to a neighborhood school held in a "little cottage"; just a few years later, her younger sisters attended the well-regarded Moravian Seminary for Young Ladies in Bethlehem, Pennsylvania.[9]

Although some eighteenth-century women had found various means to acquire knowledge and to lead deeply intellectual lives, their access to formal educational opportunities remained sparse and idiosyncratic.[10] Boarding schools, such as the one founded by Sophia Hay in New Brunswick, provided basic academic instruction but tended to emphasize genteel accomplishments such as "music, drawing, and dancing." Throughout the early national period, boarding schools came under increased attack for failing to provide a serious academic environment. As figure 2 suggests, boarding schools were seen as training grounds for frivolous behavior and conduct. "I cannot feel altogether satisfied with the plan of sending them to Miss Hay," Catherine Frelinghuysen wrote to her sister Maria Cornell in 1813, "she has even considered herself incompetent to teaching Grammar and Geography." As a concerned aunt, Catherine was "very much interested for the girls, and wish a well grounded education to them."[11] Her doubts about Miss Hay's abilities reflected rising standards and expectations for women's education that prevailed throughout the early national period.

The experiences of Rachel Van Dyke, New Brunswick resident, lend support to Catherine Frelinghuysen's concerns. Rachel was a student at Miss Hay's school for several years before enrolling in New Brunswick's Female Academy in 1807, then under Mr. Preston's direction. "A new world opened to me; and I improved more in one quarter under his tuition, than I had done for many years with Miss Hay." Rachel regarded the Female Academy as far superior to Miss Hay's school and regretted "the time I wasted at Miss Hay's school," where she attended to her studies "like a parrot—without understanding what I recited."[12] Rachel continued her studies at the New Brunswick Female Academy throughout 1810, including a Latin class. Like Margaretta Cornell, her intellectual transformation—from rote learning at Miss Hay's to advanced Latin studies at a female academy—reflected a larger

FIGURE 2. "Return from Boarding School," by John Lewis Krimmel, circa 1819. A young woman recently returned from boarding school displays vain, superficial behavior (notice the scattered engravings and school materials at her feet), while her father contemplates the "bill of tuition" and her family looks on with disapproval. The Library Company of Philadelphia.

evolution in the world of women's education. By the early nineteenth century, women enjoyed increased access to a growing number of academies and schools, as educators emphasized "the high importance of female education." Long before Mary Lyon established Mount Holyoke in 1837, and for half a century before colleges began admitting women, scores of academies were available to young women seeking to obtain what Catherine Frelinghuysen referred to as a "well-grounded education."[13]

No exact figures or statistics exist to determine the number of schools established or the number of young women who attended female academies in early national America. Common estimates citing "thousands" of women seem at once vague and conservative because individual academies maintained enrollments ranging from hundreds to thousands of students. Nearly 3,000 women attended Sarah Pierce's academy in Litchfield, Connecticut, from 1792 to 1833; while between 1815 and 1837, 2,500 women enrolled as students at Catherine Fiske's Female Seminary in Keene, New Hampshire.[14] Attempts to quantify women's educational history remain incomplete. We have at best only fragmented records for most schools and few detailed enrollment records that would enable historians to compile accurate statistics. Some may consider the number of women attending academies as statistically insignificant, but the same may be said about the number of men who attended academies and colleges during this time.[15] Yet scholars generally agree that a sea change occurred in the opening decades of the early republic, resulting in the establishment of many new educational opportunities for both sexes.

The historiography on women's education has focused largely on schools such as Sarah Pierce's Female Academy in Litchfield, Connecticut, and the Young Ladies' Academy of Philadelphia because rich records exist to document the histories of these institutions. Founded in 1787 and incorporated in 1792, the Young Ladies' Academy of Philadelphia gained national prominence for its serious commitment to women's education. Benjamin Rush and other prominent men lent their support to the school, and its progress was tracked in numerous newspapers and pamphlets. As James Neal, an educator at the academy, enthusiastically proclaimed, "I believe it will not be controverted, when I assert, The Young Ladies' Academy of Philadelphia, to be the most perfect and best regulated institution of any in this country, or perhaps, the world."[16] Sarah Pierce might have challenged James Neal's claims. According to Catherine Beecher, who attended Pierce's academy from 1810 to 1816, "the reputation of Miss Pierce's school exceeded that of any other in the country." Young women from several states traveled to Litchfield to study with Pierce. As Mary Chester, a student, noted, "Litchfield Academy is very popular. There are ladies here from Canada, Albany, Vermont, New York, Massachusetts and Pennsylvania."[17]

Despite the scholarly attention they have received, institutions such as the Young Ladies' Academy and the Litchfield Academy should not be regarded as particularly "exceptional" or "unique" because they had dozens of counterparts across the country. Female academies could be found in large cities, small towns, and remote villages from Augusta, Maine, to Lexington, Kentucky. Most enrolled female students exclusively, although some schools, including the Bradford Academy in Massachusetts and the Newark Academy in New Jersey, were co-educational for at least part of their histories. As the *Ladies' Literary Cabinet* confidently reported in 1820, "It is with peculiar pleasure that we notice the multiplication of *Female Schools,* in almost every part of our growing Republic. It promises well for the rising generation."[18]

As female academies multiplied, women had more educational choices and opportunities. Some women might attend an academy for only a single term; for others, their education lasted several years and involved multiple schools. Between 1799 and 1801, Sarah Ripley went to Proctor Pierce's academy in her hometown of Greenfield, Massachusetts, where she studied "Reading, Spelling, Writing, Arithmetic, Grammar, Geography and Speaking." Four years later, Sarah "spent three months quite agreeably" at the recently established Female Academy in Dorchester, where she was one of "36 boarders and 20 day scholars." In 1814, Linda Raymond left her hometown of Rindge, New Hampshire, to attend Lucy Burnap's academy in Woodstock, Vermont. A year later, Linda was one of "between 30 and 40 scholars attending" Catherine Fiske's academy in Keene, New Hampshire, where she studied "history, geography, painting [and] composition." In April 1818, Elizabeth Pierce began attending a school in Northampton, Massachusetts, run by Miss Perkins, "a very accomplished young lady." Although Elizabeth been a student in other settings for several years, she continued her studies "to perfect myself in Grammar and Arithmetic."[19]

Opportunities for women's education were not as abundant in the South, but by 1820, female academies could be found in most southern cities, including Baltimore, Richmond, Knoxville, and Nashville. The Female Seminary in Salem, North Carolina, consistently reported strong enrollment figures. In 1811, nearly eighty students had enrolled, and by 1814, the school was "much crowded" and had a waiting list of candidates seeking admission.[20] The Ann Smith Academy in Lexington, Virginia, provided hundreds of southern women with educational opportunities. Incorporated in 1807, Ann Smith Academy quickly outgrew its original building and expanded to fit the growing demands for female education. According to one observer in 1808, "the number of ladies now amounts to 40. . . . The general expectation is that there will not be less than 60 young ladies next session." In 1809, Elizabeth Lindsay excitedly reported that one of her friends would be attending Ann Smith's "most celebrated" female academy: "Polly will I hope make good use of her time and return home to her delighted friends rich in those mental acquirements which are certainly the most enviable of all earthly attainments or possessions."[21]

At various academies throughout the nation, young women approached the pursuit of education with enthusiasm, rigor, and determination. They had access to an ever-widening set of instruction and subject matter because educators were determined to promote the success of both their institutions and pupils.

"Different Studies That I Have Pursued"

In 1820, Sophia Sawyer enrolled as a student at Joseph Emerson's Female Academy in Byfield, Massachusetts. Prior to arriving in Byfield, Sophia attended the New Ipswich Academy in her home state of New Hampshire. At Byfield, Sophia began with courses in "Natural Philosophy, History and

Composition." In a letter to a friend, she described her plans for the winter term: "My studies are to be Writing, Grammar, Arithmetic, Goldsmiths Manner & Customs of Nations, Ancient Geography with Maps; I shall also draw Chronological, Historical & Biographical Charts." Her instructor, Joseph Emerson, promoted high academic standards: "I have thought it expedient to place the mark of female improvement so high; because it really appears desirable, that every female should, if possible, actually attain it." While regretting that "our female institutions are [still] so imperfect," Joseph Emerson expressed his approval of female academies that "are so excellent, and so rapidly improving; [and] that they are so well patronized."[22]

Although the curriculum at individual schools varied, scholars have demonstrated that most female academies adhered to rigorous courses of study. Despite variations in the content and form of their curricula, these schools reflected the evolving seriousness accorded to women's education in the early national period. Grammar, arithmetic, history, geography, rhetoric, composition, chemistry, and natural philosophy were among the subjects regularly taught at most female academies. The study of languages, including French and Spanish, as well as Latin and Greek, was also part of many school curricula. Most female students could expect to receive an education equivalent to that offered at male academies during this period.[23]

Although male and female students received similar academic training, the inclusion of "ornamental" subjects—including music, dancing, needlework, drawing, and painting—was standard practice at many female academies. Educators believed that certain acquirements could be at once "useful and ornamental"—particularly if they served to enhance women's domestic or social skills. As Margaret Nash points out, needlework and sewing were practical domestic skills that also provided vocational training for women's potential employment as seamstresses. Other ornamental subjects were geared more toward social accomplishment. Dancing and vocal or instrumental music, for example, were talents that added charm and entertainment to social gatherings. As John Ogden asserted in *The Female Guide,* "[Dancing] promotes health and cheerfulness. It is a part of the amusement of social hours." Likewise, the study of music, as Mary Ann Bacon noted in her school composition book, enabled women "to entertain your friends; [and] to confer pleasure upon others." The focus on accomplishment at most female academies, as Catherine Kelly argues, enhanced "book learning" and helped prepare women to enact social roles based on the display and performance of refinement and taste.[24]

Most educators, however, privileged academics over the ornamental. "Ornament, in the education of a female, should occupy but a secondary place," educator Nancy Maria Hyde stressed, and "should never be suffered to supercede [*sic*] the acquirement of more valuable knowledge." Eager to emphasize the rigorous academic nature of their coursework, academies assured potential students that they offered "all the useful and scientific acquirements which are taught in the best female academies, while a limited attention is paid to the ornamental arts of painting and embroidering."[25] Some schools restricted the amount of time students could spend on their ornamental branches of study. "We are allowed to go to sewing school two days in a week," Catherine Frelinghuysen reported to her sister. Catherine's school kept up its regular academic schedule during the sewing classes: "Those who do not go say all the tables in the weight and measures...then return to writing." At the Young Ladies' Academy in Woburn, the "six young ladies a learning to draw and paint," as Polly Raymond noted, "have two afternoons to learn to do it. The rest of the week they attend to other studies."[26]

Thus, although ornamental subjects were offered at most female academies, educators repeatedly insisted that these pursuits "should never be allowed to encroach on the more important cultivation of the intellectual powers." At many academies, these activities truly were designed to ornament, not compromise or replace, the scholarly focus of their curricula. Many students incorporated academic elements into ornamental work by adding representations of historical events, maps, and literary themes to their embroidery or paintings. "I am reviewing my Geography, and drawing a map," Mary Wilson informed her friends. "I think I shall draw a Map of the United States," Linda Raymond wrote to her mother, "that will assist us greatly about remembering the Geography."[27] Employing their ornamental skills in the service of their academic studies, young women created integrated patterns of useful and ornamental knowledge.

Some students were content to focus on ornamental subjects, even though their teachers and classmates privileged academic subjects. As Mary Chester, a student at Sarah Pierce's academy, noted in a letter home, "Miss Pierce frequently laughs about a couple of ladies who came here last summer to get an education: they did nothing at all but paint; staid about three weeks finished their education and return'd home." Many students, however, devoted substantial time and energy to their academic studies. "I left off music as I found it required more of my attention than I could bestow without my other studies suffering by it," Violetta Bancker informed her mother in November 1801. Some female academies chose not to offer ornamental subjects, part of a deliberate attempt to set themselves apart from existing boarding schools. As James Neal of the Young Ladies' Academy of Philadelphia argued, women's education was no longer "for the purpose of displaying superficial attainments"; instead, "it has for its object, the promotion and advancement of literature,—the cultivation of true wisdom,—the expansion of virtue, and the elucidation of the mind." Such academies sought to advance women's education far beyond ornamental studies and to promote rigorous academic standards. "If these, the most laudable of all human purposes, are not thought important," Neal continued, "I know not what can be considered as such."[28]

In their efforts to transform women's education, female academies instituted demanding schedules. Students at female academies typically attended classes Monday through Saturday. In the mornings, students read or studied before attending classes, where they heard lectures or recited lessons. In the afternoons, students studied in their rooms and then typically returned to school for more classes and recitations. Jane Swann Hunter attended to her studies "every day except Monday and Saturday....I have this week finished Campbell...three Latin grammar lessons...and got one Italian grammar lesson." In one week, Lucy Sheldon "studied three geography lessons, drawn out a large picture, and heard the history read twice." Two weeks later, Lucy noted that "the preceding has been spent as usual in studying geography, hearing the history and painting, have written one composition and ciphered one evening." Jane Lewis recorded her summary of a week's lessons in a matter-of-fact tone: "Monday to Saturday nothing particular happened. I attended school and recited my usual lessons in Logic and Modern Europe—and attended to the usual occupations of school, mornings and evenings generally devoted to study."[29]

As they recorded busy days marked by constant employment, young women expressed a quiet sense of pride and accomplishment. "Attended to my studies all day, as usual," Linda Raymond noted in her journal. "In school my time has been wholly taken up in my different studies that I have pursued," Mary Wilson wrote to her friends. Abigail Bradley informed her mother that she had "employment enough to fill all my time....I have recited 64 pages in Geography and 54 in Rhetoric." Immersed in her studies, Margaretta Cornell found that the hours passed quickly: "It seems when dinner is ready, as if I only had been up and hour or two, and tea comes before I am aware."[30]

By providing students with rigorous courses of study, female academies helped transform the institutional landscape of women's education in early national America. The students who attended these schools experienced their own transformations, as they encountered new environments and new forms of knowledge. Their experiences help us to see past the institutional histories of individual academies' successes or failures, and to better appreciate what these new educational opportunities meant to the young women who attended these schools.

"To Roam in Quest of Knowledge"

In 1816, Rebecca Beverley of Virginia arrived in Philadelphia to attend a female academy run by the Miss Lymans, described by Rebecca as "very fine sensible and accomplished women." While at Miss Lyman's school, Rebecca was one of "about 50 scholars here and 30 of them boarders." Rebecca expressed a strong desire to acquire a proper education: "I should be void of feeling for myself and friends, were I to neglect my studies, as I exiled myself from the society of all my friends for my improvement, I am determined to attend most rigidly to it." Rebecca studied "Blair's Rhetoric, Natural history, a little Philosophy, and astronomy," the "History of Modern Europe," as well as French and music. She attended to her studies with a determination that her father may not have expected when he first agreed to send her to Philadelphia: "I dare say you will be surprised to hear I rise regularly at day break and sit up until 11 o'clock."[31]

Rebecca remained in Philadelphia for about a year, until her father cited monetary constraints. Rebecca resigned herself to the end of her studies, thanking her father for having "been as generous as you possibly could been to me this last year, for I have been permitted to learn every branch that I fancied and have had quite enough pocket money." Rebecca Beverley's ability to attend a female academy was predicated on her father's financial support. Young women's access to education was often tied to class status, whether they pursued rigorous academic studies or were sent or to "finishing" schools. Yet for many young women, the opportunity to attend a female academy was not merely a tool of class formation, it was also a critical means by which they fashioned new identities for themselves as educated women. Although her father was not willing or able to pay for her continued studies, Rebecca regarded the year she spent in Philadelphia as priceless: "I know the expenses of our educations will diminish our future prospects but that I should never lament for I would not resign the little knowledge I have acquired this last year for five times that sum that I have expended in acquiring it."[32]

Rebecca Beverley's father expressed only limited support of his daughter's educational efforts, but other families placed a high value on their children's education. "Papa ... will not grudge the expense I warrant when he knows you are so industrious," Maria Cornell informed her daughter after she began her term at the Female Academy in New Brunswick. Many parents encouraged their daughters to attend diligently to their studies. "*Every day is of importance* to you, in fact you are laying up treasure for life," Elisha Boudinot stressed to his daughter Julia while she was attending school in Philadelphia. "My dear child I hope you will improve your time to good advantage this summer," Mary Raymond urged her daughter Linda during her attendance at Catherine Fiske's academy. Young women were grateful for their families' financial, emotional, and intellectual support. "How shall I express my gratitude to you my Dear Mother," Linda Raymond wrote, thankful that her parents agreed "to place me in School for the purpose of improving my mind." "I don't know how I shall ever repay my parents for their goodness in sending me to school," Eliza Odgen noted, "but I think if I improve myself as much as they expect and to their satisfaction they will want me to repay them no better."[33] Parental support enabled women to pursue educational opportunities that took up months, if not years, of their time.

Some students went to academies established in their hometowns, but many young women, including Violetta Bancker, Margaretta Cornell, and Rebecca Beverley, traveled to attend school. These young women either boarded at school or with friends or relatives in the area. Transitioning to a new environment required a period of adjustment, and some students inevitably experienced feelings of homesickness. "A boarding-school, I know, my dear Sister, is not like home," Eliza Southgate mused, while reassuring her sister "that no woman was ever better calculated to govern a school than Mrs. Rawson." Family encouragement could help young women adjust to the experience of being away from home. "You remember that I too had been at boarding school and have experienced all the various feelings of a school-girl and am wise in these matters," Sarah Bache reminded her younger sister Catherine. Sarah was pleased to find that her sister recognized "the advantages you enjoy in being with Mrs. Brown, and that your endeavour is to excel in the studies you undertake." Families urged young women to take full advantage of the opportunities that their time at school provided. "No exertions should be spared, and no time should be lost," John Shippen advised his sister Elizabeth, then attending school in Philadelphia.[34]

After adjusting to life away from home, many young women expressed contentment with their new situations. While at the Litchfield Female Academy, Abigail Bradley assured her mother, "I have not been homesick at all." Jane Bowne found life at the Pleasant Hill Boarding School "comfortable and agreeable and I think I am as happy as I could be any where from home." "I confess I enjoy myself much better than I expected," Polly Raymond wrote to her parents from the Young Ladies' Academy in Woburn. A decade later, Polly's younger sister Linda quickly settled into her studies at the Keene Female Seminary: "Seven weeks have fled rapidly since I have been in this place and I have enjoyed myself perfectly well." While living with her grandparents to attend school, Elizabeth Pierce was "convinced I am better off here, I mean in regard to my studies." And as Eliza Southgate informed her mother during her time at school, "I have a great desire to see my family, but I have a still greater desire to finish my education."[35] There were, of course, some young women who were unhappy to be away from home or who were less than dedicated to their studies. Rachel Van Dyke referred to the students at Miss Hay's boarding school as "a parcel of wild school girls." Abigail Bradley described the variety of young women who boarded with her at the Litchfield Female Academy in more measured tones: "Some of my companions are very agreeable others less so—some steady and some wild—but in general the society is pleasant."[36]

Although some young women lacked the discipline for academic life, most students expressed their commitment to education. Caroline Chester began a new term at the Litchfield Female Academy with "a determination to improve all in my power." Mary Ann Bacon desired "to improve every moment of the time—which is given us to acquire knowledge." Lucy Sheldon vowed "to renew my former studies with greater assiduity than ever, and shall endeavour to improve enough to merit the approbation of my Parents, and instructress." Eliza Ogden "was very glad to have school begin again, for I wish to improve all my time." Although some students may have made such statements to gain the approval of their instructors and parents, young women were often surprised by their deep attachment to their studies. "You mentioned that you did not feel so deeply the affection you had, for your Instructors, before, as since you parted with them," Lavinia Stafford wrote to her former classmate Lydia Clark Abbott. "Like you, I thought, if I could but return to my family and friends, I should never wish to leave them again," Lavinia confessed, "but I feel more anxious than ever again to quit the family circle and again to roam in quest of knowledge."[37]

Women's educational experiences at female academies varied, but many wrote about their experiences as positive, life-changing events. In their "quest for knowledge," women experienced internal transformations that suggest the powerful role of education in their lives. Shortly after beginning her studies at a female academy, Anne Brewer noted, "The school excites new interest every day and I love Mrs. E. more & more. So many *great subjects* offer themselves daily to my consideration. . . . I had no idea when I left home, nor for weeks after, that I could have entered with so much ardour the study of *philosophy;* for this study attracts me more powerfully than history, nor had I any idea, at the first of the time that I should derive so much *benefit,* as I now hope to."[38]

Many young women seized the opportunities for intellectual growth available at female academies. After a year of studies at Mr. Rawson's academy in Providence, Rhode Island, Sarah Crawford Cook "gained more instruction than the one before hope I shall profit by it to the end of my life." Betsey Metcalf also attended school in Providence, noting, "I never felt so well pleased at any period of my life as when at school." As her school term ended, Sarah Connell reflected, "I must leave, with regret, *Andover* amid whose Academic shades I have pas'd so many happy hours." Although attending school often took them away from home and loved ones, students thrived in academic environments that nurtured their intellectual growth. Understanding the transformative powers of education, Anna Giles Morris wrote longingly of her desire to attend school with her friend Ann Haines: "I still think I could conform to the regulations of a school life with pleasure, and be reconciled to the little privations I should there meet like a young stoic."[39]

Their hard work and commitment to academic excellence provided young women with a sense of personal satisfaction. These efforts did not go unnoticed by their teachers, who proudly showcased their students' intellectual accomplishments to surrounding communities.

"Homage to Their Genius"

In 1810, Eliza Pintard Boudinot was a member of the "First Class" at the Newark Academy, New Jersey. "We have talents put into our hands," Eliza wrote in a school composition dated January 6, 1810, "and they ought not to be hidden." As she began her school term, Eliza reflected on the educational opportunities available to the students attending the Newark Academy:

> This year opens with more propitious aspects to our youthful minds, than any former one. Our parents have procured for us a preceptor, whose abilities appear equal to his exertions and whose whole time is employed for our improvement. If our advances in every branch of useful learning should not equal his expectations, what would be the sensations of our parents and friends, and we should have reason deeply to deplore that folly which suffered opportunities to be mis-improved that may never return.[40]

Determined to please her instructor, parents, and friends, Eliza devoted herself to her studies. Over the next 12 weeks, she wrote 36 "quarto pages of composition," recited 240 lessons, and earned 11 certificates "of approbation and applause." At the end of the term in March, she was first in her class for penmanship and had earned top honors in several subjects, including

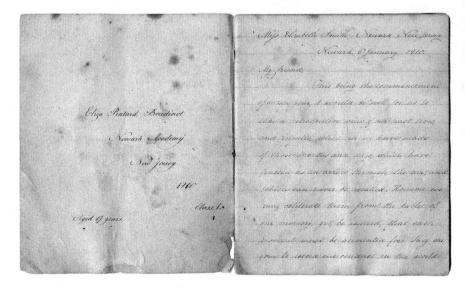

FIGURE 3. Eliza Pintard Boudinot, Letter Book, 1810. Eliza kept this composition notebook while a student at the Newark Academy. In her first entry, dated January 6, 1810, she expressed renewed commitment to her academic studies. Special Collections and University Archives, Rutgers University Libraries.

"particular commendation" for her skills in composition. For the next six months, Eliza, along with several of her classmates, remained at the Newark Academy as "Exempts." As Timothy Alden, their instructor, explained, these "young ladies, who having in a manner finished their education, have been pleased to enter the Newark Academy, with a view to revise some of the more important branches, to which they had previously attended." Eliza's additional studies included Emerson's Evangelical Primer, Painting in Water Colors, and Arithmetic. Eliza's instructor kept careful track of his students' progress, which he published and presented "as a token of his best wishes for their rising reputation, usefulness, and happiness."[41]

The Newark Academy was one of many schools to publicly highlight their students' educational achievements. Academies throughout the nation held various commencement ceremonies, examinations, and exhibitions. At these events, students were examined in various branches of study, including grammar, geography, history, rhetoric, and natural and moral philosophy. Students' ornamental work was often displayed, including "needle work, drawings, writing, &c.," along with "maps of the world" and "elegant manuscript arithmetics." As part of these ceremonies, students delivered original orations, recited poetry, or performed "dramatic dialogues" before audiences that typically consisted of both men and women. Linda Raymond described the examination held October 9, 1814, at Lucy Burnap's academy in Woodstock: "The School was examined by a number of Ladies and Gentlemen in the village. After the examination of our studies, writings, journals, compositions, paintings, needlework's, and maps, there were several observations made, and the School was closed by Singing."[42]

These events provided young women with opportunities to enact public identities as learned women. Lavinia Stafford's account of the 1815 examination held at the Bradford Academy underscores the seriousness with which women approached these symbolic displays of education. "Miss Elizabeth Gage's [composition] on Female Education was delightful," Lavinia reported to her former classmate Lydia. "With a modest but graceful dignity, she came forward, and vindicated the rights of her sex." Elizabeth Gage's address won the crowd over. "It was so good," Lavinia boasted, "that it received this high compliment, from one of the trustees, 'that it could not be bettered' and the applause of a crowded audience."[43]

As Nancy Maria Hyde's description of an 1811 ceremony held in Connecticut illustrates, such ceremonies were often highly ritualized and performative in nature:

> At two in the afternoon our room was prepared for the reception of visitors, and the young ladies assembled to be examined in their several studies. We began with Arithmetic, Grammar and Geography, and History succeeded. Recitation of pieces followed, and many distinguished themselves, in a very honorable manner, by the propriety with which they spoke. Compositions were then read, and received the applause they deserved. Filigree baskets were then exhibited, and maps ornamented with painting. The different exercises appeared to be much approved by the spectators, and our young ladies were encouraged by encomiums.[44]

Commencement exercises, as Nancy Maria Hyde noted, "encouraged by encomiums"—educators used awards, applause, and approval to motivate students to take pride in their intellectual accomplishments. "You are requested to dismiss timidity from your hearts," William Staughton instructed the students at Mrs. Rivardi's Seminary in 1807. "Approach in your classes with respectful confidence, and endeavor to impart to your parents and friends the pleasures they are waiting to receive."[45] Such public encouragement enabled young women to develop confidence in their academic achievements.

At these ceremonies, young women displayed their talents and accomplishments to admiring audiences. "A respectable number of citizens" took interest in these ceremonies.[46] A published account of the December 18, 1794, commencement at the Young Ladies' Academy of Philadelphia attests to the seriousness placed on women's education:

> A numerous and brilliant audience were assembled on the occasion. The lady of the President of the United States; the members of the House of Representatives of the United States; the members of the Assembly of this State; likewise the most eminent of our citizens: the whole composing a bright assemblage of those patriotic personages, who encourage the growth and expansion of literary knowledge. The scene was truly magnificent, and exhibited incontrovertible demonstration that valuable learning will never want patrons, in this land of liberty.... The Dialogues and Orations, were pronounced by several young ladies, with uncommon propriety and elegance; plainly evincing their superior powers in elocution.[47]

Together, the students, educators, and audience constituted a gathering of citizens who came together to regulate and legitimate the importance of women's education. The presence of congressmen and state assemblymen in the audience surely accorded the commencement added political and national importance. This attention placed female students and the subject of women's education squarely within the public sphere. Like other forms of social and educational interaction—including literary clubs, voluntary associations, and learned societies—these ceremonies created modes of communication that were central to the process of community and nation building. Such events provided men and women with opportunities for intellectual, social, and political exchanges that helped create a shared conception of enlightened citizenship that was central to the young republic's sense of stability and progress.[48]

Those unable to attend these ceremonies could still read about women's intellectual achievements in accounts that appeared in numerous early national pamphlets, newspapers, and periodicals. Susanna Rowson regularly published reports of her school's commencement ceremonies in the *Boston Weekly Magazine.* The *Pennsylvania Gazette,* the *Port Folio,* and various other Philadelphia, New York, and New England publications featured accounts of the Young Ladies' Academy of Philadelphia's commencement ceremonies. Some academies, including the Young Ladies' Academy and the Newark Academy, published their school catalogues, printing the names of all students who attended their institutions, along with the merits and honors they received. As Charles Stearns, educator, explained, "The insertion of their names does homage to their genius, improvements, and virtue; and may give them a degree of celebrity, which one day or another may be of use to them." Although some young women may have felt uncomfortable with this "degree of celebrity," others welcomed the public praise. At a commencement ceremony held in Providence, Rhode Island, as Betsey Metcalf recalled, the members of the examining committee "were highly pleased with the behavior and forms of education and voted to have it published in the public papers which raised the ambition of the scholars to such a pitch that we almost thought we knew everything."[49]

To encourage academic excellence, academies frequently awarded premiums and merits to their top students. Timothy Alden developed an elaborate system to keep track of his students' progress at the Newark Academy. At the end of each term, top students such as Eliza Pintard Boudinot received certificates of merit and written commendations in the school *Quarterly Catalogue*.[50] The Litchfield Female Academy also gave awards in several categories, based on "credit marks" that students accumulated throughout the term. Final decisions were made during the school's examinations by a "number of ladies and gentlemen" from town. According to John Brace, educator, students exhibited an impressive array of talent: "Miss Bradley was distinguished for the elegance of her composition—her journal showed that her genius was of the first order—but Miss Leonard far exceeded her in her workmanship and to her the prize was unanimously adjudged." Determining which students should be awarded prizes was often a difficult decision, according to the trustees at the Young Ladies' Academy of Philadelphia, because "so ably did the several pupils contend with each other in the different branches of science upon which they were examined."[51]

While competing for prizes, many women applied themselves to their studies with focused determination. As Rebecca Beverley noted, "This is a grand time here the prizes are to be given out in a few days, all in suspense anxiously waiting to see who will get them." The next quarter, Rebecca had the "pleasure of informing" her father that she had earned three prizes: "one for attention to all my studies, one for improvement in French, and the other for improvement in Arithmetick." Although Rebecca recognized that some individuals might regard the practice as "childish," teachers and students viewed these ceremonies with seriousness. The awards, Rebecca informed her father, were "considered meritorious and honourable by the Miss Lymans that we prize them very highly." Another young woman proudly informed her friend, "I was so fortunate as to obtain five premiums, and a crown" at her school's recent examination. She planned to carefully preserve her crown, "as it may in future life stimulate me to conduct myself with more propriety, that I may not lose the favorable reputation obtained in my early years."[52]

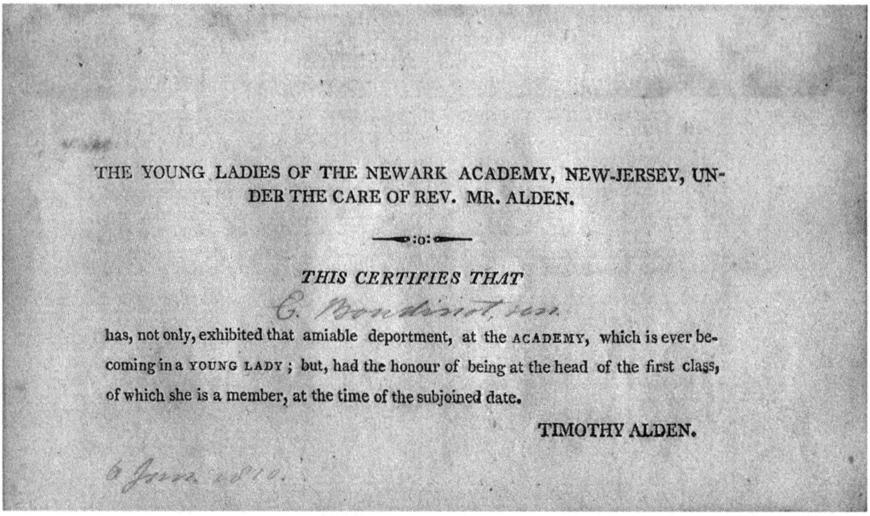

THE YOUNG LADIES OF THE NEWARK ACADEMY, NEW-JERSEY, UN-
DER THE CARE OF REV. MR. ALDEN.

THIS CERTIFIES THAT

C. Boudinot, jun.

has, not only, exhibited that amiable deportment, at the ACADEMY, which is ever becoming in a YOUNG LADY ; but, had the honour of being at the head of the first class,
of which she is a member, at the time of the subjoined date.

TIMOTHY ALDEN.

FIGURE 4. Eliza Pintard Boudinot, Certificate of Merit, 1810. Eliza received several certificates for academic excellence while a student at the Newark Academy. This 1810 certificate commends her for "being at the head of the first class." Special Collections and University Archives, Rutgers University Libraries.

Competitions, exhibitions, and ceremonies provided public proof that women's educational capacities were equal to, if not superior to, men's intellectual attainments. Indeed, commentators frequently compared women's performances to men's college commencement ceremonies. A ceremony held at Susanna Rowson's academy in 1804 "engaged the attention of the public quite as much as the commencement at the college in the neighboring town of Cambridge." John Brace proudly noted that the Litchfield examination "was conducted in real college style." An attendee at the 1818 examination of the Female Academy in Lexington, Kentucky "never witnessed in collegiate examination classes acquit themselves in a better manner." And according to a "spectator" at 1820 Waterford Female Academy, "In all these studies they acquitted themselves in a manner that has seldom, if ever, been surpassed in any of our Colleges."[53]

Public performances and displays provided convincing proof of women's intellectual capacities. With so much public praise, young women gained confidence in their identities as learned women. But did these ceremonies satisfy those critics who remained skeptical of women's education? Despite their significant intellectual accomplishments and despite the public support they received, educated women understood that "many have a prejudice against learning in women."[54]

"I Do Not Wish to Appear Pedantic"

While a student at the Litchfield Female Academy, Mary Ann Bacon wrote a composition in which she confidently asserted women's intellectual capabilities: "[why] was the rational mind given us was it not to be stored with useful Knowledge which alone can render life pleasing and above all fit us for the blessed society which all hope to enjoy?" By attending properly to her studies, a young woman could, as Mary Ann reflected in another school essay, achieve ideal characteristics: "[She] cultivated her mind and stored it with useful knowledge—she confers happiness on all her acquaintances and she—has the sweet satisfaction of knowing her conduct—is approved of by her Parents and what ever may be her situation in life she can find—pleasure in her own reflections."[55]

Mary Ann Bacon expressed confidence in women's educational pursuits, focusing on the many benefits that educated women would bring to early national society. As they acquired education, women were optimistic about their identities as learned women and hoped that "we may now speak and write with propriety without the imputation of pedantry." Yet women recognized that their educational efforts could be subject to criticism. In particular, educated women understood that even the mere *suggestion* of pedantry could be used to discredit their intellectual accomplishments. During a visit to her city's circulating library for books "which I thought would improve me," Rachel Van Dyke faced the pressure of having her intellectual pursuits scrutinized by male observers and confessed that she "was afraid of appearing pedantic by asking for such books." Rachel feared that the male visitors of the circulating library would read her interest in scholarly works not as a positive sign of her serious attention to learning but, rather, as a negative symptom of her excessive preoccupation with knowledge. Rachel was an enthusiastic advocate of women's education, yet she remained sensitive to "the sneers which are thrown upon such *presumption* in a female—such *vain ambition*."[56] She worried that others would dismiss her ardent interest in education as vanity or ambition—negative traits for any woman to possess.

Although women's private journals and letters expressed their enthusiastic embrace of education, in public they often demonstrated more sensitivity to and awareness of the criticisms that the prescriptive literature often aimed at educated women. Rachel Van Dyke's journal is filled with references to her rigorous daily lessons and conveys her ardent love of learning; yet in the library that day, she still felt judged and scorned by male observers. Fear of "appearing pedantic" often caused women to self-censure their public representations of themselves, especially if they were unsure of male response.

Writing to her cousin Charles Bancker, Maria Taylor wondered what subject matter would be appropriate for their correspondence, "as I do not wish to appear pedantic and . . . enter upon some literary subject." Equally hesitant to fill her page with "trifling" subjects of "dress, fashions, &c.," Maria struggled to articulate herself as an educated woman. As Eliza Southgate admitted to her male cousin Moses Porter, "I have ever felt a disagreeable restraint when conversing before you." Although Eliza freely wrote to Moses about a variety of subjects, including the importance of female education, she feared that he would view her writings as "egotism" and dismiss her with a biting critique: "But she is *female*, say you, with a *manly contempt*."[57]

Although educators, parents, and friends supported their educational endeavors, young women feared criticism from those uncomfortable with their pursuit of intellectual equality. In an oration delivered while a student, Sarah Teackle focused on a commonly feared reaction to women's pursuit of education:

> But say Columbia, do thy sons, who claim
> A Birthright liberty, dispense the same
> In equal scales?—when then does custom
> In chains of Ignorance, the female mind
> Why is to them the bright ethereal ray
> Of Science veiled, why does each pedant say
> Shield me propitious powers not clog my life
> With that *supreme of plagues*—a Learned Wife.[58]

Women embraced the pursuit of education, eager to claim "equal scales" of knowledge. Yet, in their quest for intellectual equality, educated women understood the importance of avoiding vain or pedantic behavior. "When learning is pursued from proper motives and on proper principles," Maria Cornell noted to her daughter, "it is a delightful employ." Nevertheless, Maria warned Margaretta to avoid improper pursuits of education: "I hope your acquirements may never be dedicated to the shrine of Vanity."[59] Maria was an ardent proponent of her daughter's education and provided constant encouragement while Margaretta attended school in New Brunswick. Yet she also understood that educated women walked a fine line—too much interest in education could easily be discredited as signs of vanity or pedantry.

In their public displays of education—whether at the library or the podium—women sought to make sense of competing ideas about female intellect and to carve out identities for themselves as educated women. Tensions about women's uses of education are poignantly revealed in their orations and other public enactments of education, and reveal how early national women responded to debates about women's education and their corresponding social roles. Sensitive to criticisms about overeducated women, students self-consciously addressed these concerns by drawing attention to themselves as intellectual women. Molly Wallace, student, acknowledged that some critics doubted "whether we ought *ever* to appear in so public a manner."[60] Yet women continued to participate in ceremonies in growing numbers, undeterred by those who criticized the propriety of female oration.

In 1794, Ann Harker delivered the "Salutatory Oration" at the Young Ladies' Academy of Philadelphia. Throughout her oration, Ann made bold statements that directly challenged critics of women's education: "They deny us the means of information, and then blame us for the want of that very knowledge they have put out of our power to acquire." In language that echoed key Enlightenment principles, she declared, "In this age of reason, then, we are not to be surprised, if women have taken advantage of that small degree of liberty which they still possess, and converted their talents to the public utility." Yet at the conclusion of her oration, Ann abruptly switched tones, assuring her audience that, "I would not wish you rashly to conclude that I mean to advocate the indiscriminate pursuits of the same studies by different sexes." Ann Harker's comments reveal a persistent tension between women's capacity for acquiring knowledge and the potential effects of educating women. Young women enthusiastically viewed education as a source of self-empowerment, but at the same time they astutely recognized that their acquisition of education needed to conform to prescribed models of acceptable feminine behavior. As Ann noted, "pedantry and ostentation are odious in men, but they are despicable in women."[61] The oration's abrupt change in tone at the end provides a poignant illustration of the gap between women's intellectual capacities and the approved uses of their education.

Sensitive to this tension, educated women often insisted that they had no interest in pursuing the "thorny path of politics." Of course, female students *were* claiming space as public orators—a practice typically associated with politicians and other male professions. Yet, as Ann Harker's classmate Molly Wallace was careful to note, educated women's ambition extended no further: "That she should harangue at the head of an Army, in the Senate, or before a popular Assembly, is not pretended."[62] Although educated women asserted that they had the intellectual capacity equal to that of men, they simultaneously insisted that they would not seek access to traditionally male spheres of power and prestige. Although eager to carve out identities for themselves that privileged the worthiness of their education, women were cautious about overstepping the boundaries of prescribed gender roles. Mere equality had its limits, at least in public realms controlled by men.

"A Very Excellent Companion"

If women understood that their ambitions could not extend to politics and other male spheres of power, they remained eager to put their education to good uses, asserting that "numerous are the instances, in which the display of our intellectual powers may be attended with pleasure to ourselves and advantages to others."[63] Despite criticisms about pedantic behavior, women privileged their intellectual interests and proudly identified as learned women. In an 1811 letter to her sister, Nancy Maria Hyde described her "employments and situation" by highlighting her literary pursuits: "Behold me, then, seated in my chamber, by a comfortable fire, and writing at one end of a table, adorned by a multifarious collection of journals, common-place books, pins, wafers, slates, and letters unanswered. . . . My friend sits writing with all speed at the opposite side; . . . and both writing with as much apparent zeal, as if the fate of the nation depended upon the motion of our quills."[64]

Women such as Nancy Maria Hyde took their education seriously and found contentment in their intellectual pursuits. At the same time, women recognized that there were clear limits to the uses they might make of their education. The motion of male quills could, quite literally, determine a nation's fate in ways largely unavailable to most women. Yet the acquisition of education inspired women to envision alternate forms of mere equality. In their personal and socials lives, women sought relationships with like-minded men and women who valued and supported their educational interests. It is significant that Nancy framed her own educational pursuits by noting that her like-minded friend sat across from her. Educated women sought the company of "very interesting young friends" who bonded together through "a desire of mutual improvement." Maria Cornell was pleased that her daughter Margaretta found "so agreeable a companion and friend" at school. "May your hearts and hands unite in aiding each other's progress," she wrote to her daughter.[65] And Violetta Bancker's strong interest in education undoubtedly influenced her choice of friends: "I find Eliza so very agreeable, that I do not feel the want of any other society; she has paid great attention to the cultivation of her mind, and has stored it well with many excellent and well chosen works; her conversation is sprightly and shows her learning, without the least pedantry or affectation. . . . she will make a very excellent companion, for some one, who can appreciate her good qualities."[66]

Violetta Bancker's praise of her friend encapsulated the benefits as well as dangers awaiting educated women in early national society. Eliza successfully acquired education without the all-pervading stain of "pedantry or affectation." Eliza was bound to make "a very excellent companion," but as Violetta noted, her worth was dependent on the companionship of those "who can appreciate her good qualities." Those skeptical about the benefits of women's education might read Eliza's learning as pedantry. Sensitive to common criticisms against women's overeducation, Violetta was careful to note that her friend possessed no hint of this negative trait.

As Violetta Bancker's comments about her friend suggest, the education that women received would be put to the test in their various social and personal relationships. "Believe me that not until you leave school, and your present opportunities are passed away," Sarah Bache reflected to her sister, "will you realize to their full extent, their importance and influence on your future life."[67] Female academies offered women nurturing, supportive spaces to enact identities as learned women, but the end of school represented a commencement of new roles and relationships. As Linda Raymond reflected in one of her school notebooks:

For tho' my dear from school you're freed
You've entered on a task indeed
To act as you proceed through life
As daughter mother friend and wife[68]

While in school, Linda continued, a young woman was apt to use her "charming active lively mind" to imagine "gay painted scenes of happiness."[69] What opportunities and challenges awaited those young women eager to create happy, fulfilling lives for themselves as learned women? The remaining chapters of this book offer close examinations of women's experiences in friendship, family life, courtship, marriage, and motherhood to assess how successful they were in crafting social and personal lives merely as the equals of man.

✒ CHAPTER 2

"Various Subjects That Passed between Two Young Ladies of America"

Reconstructing Female Friendship

In 1803, Eunice Callender wrote to her friend Sarah Ripley, pleased that they had begun a correspondence. "By the end of the year we may have letters enough in our possession to make a handsome volume," Eunice mused. "What say you to it don't you think it would be a good plan, to make a book, and entitle [it] 'Letters upon various subjects, that passed between two young Ladies of America'—how do you like the plan?" Eunice had read several works modeled on the epistolary form, so the idea for her book fit nicely with literary conventions of the day. In a playful vein, Eunice ascribed importance to her life experiences and her friendship with Sarah. In particular, Eunice expressed a desire to create a shared identity for her and Sarah as literary women. Although the proposed book never materialized, a surviving packet of Eunice's letters to Sarah offers valuable insights into these women's experiences with friendship, education, and sociability.[1] Over three decades, Eunice and Sarah crafted a close friendship based on common emotional and intellectual interests. Eunice and Sarah maintained a regular correspondence that spanned the long length of their friendship, providing a chronology of their changing life cycles and personal experiences.

At first glance, Eunice Callender and Sarah Ripley's relationship offers a classic example of the female friendships studied by women's historians. Typically begun in youth, these relationships represented a "female world of love and ritual" in which women shared intense emotional bonds. In her now classic essay, Carroll Smith-Rosenberg has suggested that female friendship was perhaps the only means of comfort available to women living in a world marked by the "emotional segregation of women and men."[2] Although the characterization of female friendship as emotionally fulfilling is accurate, the paradigm of separate spheres tells us only part of the story. By emphasizing segregation and distance between men and women's lives, scholars have focused primarily on the emotional needs that such friendships met for women. Many scholars have discounted the possibility that intense bonds could also be forged between men and women; they may also have obscured bonds between women that were not exclusively emotional in nature.[3] Nonetheless, other kinds of bonds, such as intellectual, did exist between women.

Using Eunice Callender and Sarah Ripley's lifelong friendship as a case study, in this chapter I reexamine the various meanings that female friendship held for educated women in the early national period.[4] Women such as Eunice Callender and Sarah Ripley maintained close friendships rooted in bonds of sensibility, emotion, and intellect. For the generations of women who were the first to attend newly established female academies, female friendships provide spaces for them to enact shared intellectual identities as learned women. Friends eagerly exchanged ideas, books, and favorite authors with one another as they created a world in which they could celebrate their intellectual interests without fear of criticism or disapproval. These friendships provided emotional fulfillment at the same time as they validated women's educational endeavors.

Understanding the intellectual components of female friendships allow us to examine how education affected early national women's sense of themselves, as well as their aspirations for various personal and social relationships. Female friendships provided safe, nurturing environments for young women to craft identities that celebrated and validated their intellectual capacities merely as the equals of man.

"An Intellectual Feast"

"I am certain there is no friends in Boston that I think of oftener than I do of you," Eunice wrote to Sarah in May 1803. "I question if there is any of my gay trifling acquaintances that I esteem so highly." For many early national women, female friendships provided not only emotional satisfaction but also intellectual nourishment. Many such friendships began in youth, when women were exploring their places in their world and were eager to find congenial companions with common interests, outlooks, and dispositions.

Eunice Callender and Sarah Ripley's friendship began during a common state of transition for young women—largely done with formal schooling but unmarried and living at home. In 1803, Eunice was seventeen years old and lived with her parents in Boston, and Sarah, a year older, lived with her family in Greenfield, Massachusetts. In Boston, Eunice regularly attended church, plays, parades, processions, meetings of various voluntary associations, and other public events. An avid reader, Eunice remained "deeply interested" in books that were "sentimental, entertaining and instructive." Eunice continually developed her intellectual powers and took advantage of various educational opportunities offered in the city. In 1819, she was "very much pleased" to attend "the Introductory Lecture to a course of Astronomical Lectures by Mr. Emerson (Preceptor of the Byfield Academy)."[5]

In Greenfield, Sarah Ripley also had access to a growing number of social and educational opportunities. Although many early national academies were single-sex institutions, Sarah attended a co-educational academy in Greenfield from 1799 to 1801. Sarah's experiences at school were largely positive and played an instrumental role in her understanding of friendship: "At school I have spent some very agreeable hours," she noted in her diary. "The society of the students, the conversation and precepts of the Instructor, and the various studies in which we are engaged make it a scene of pleasure I do not often experience elsewhere."[6] While attending school, Sarah enjoyed the companionship of a network of friends who regularly studied, read, and socialized together.

Sarah completed her studies in Greenfield in 1801 and also briefly attended the Dorchester Academy during summer 1804. Eunice's younger sister Susan attended this school throughout most of 1803, as did Sarah's friend close Rachel Willard. "[I] wish that you would persuade your Mama to let you accompany her and go to the Academy," Eunice wrote to Sarah in May 1803. Although Eunice did not discuss the possibility of attending the school herself, the following summer Sarah enrolled at the Dorchester Academy. There, Sarah joined her fellow students in forming "a society to be called 'The Band of Sisters.'. . . We are to meet every Saturday and read in some instructive Book and on Sunday in the Bible, we are all to live in perfect harmony and friendship." Sarah spent only three months at Dorchester, but she actively created a social world with her fellow students based on shared intellectual pursuits. In her diary, she carefully transcribed a list of the names, ages, and residences of the students with whom she boarded, suggesting the importance she ascribed to her community of classmates.[7]

Female academies were breeding grounds for close friendship because they provided spaces for young women to cultivate both emotional and intellectual bonds. "There are a very agreeable company of young ladies here," Polly Raymond wrote in 1805 from the Young Ladies' Academy in Woburn. Describing her attendance at a female academy in Woodstock a decade later, Polly's sister Linda used language that echoed Sarah's description of her experiences at the Dorchester Academy: "We have spent this summer as a band of Sisters in the most perfect harmony." Friendships formed at schools were rooted in emotional and intellectual compatibility. "*Your* situation is highly desirable," Mary Moody Emerson wrote to her niece at school. "You can add to the pursuits of literature, the pleasures of friendship." As Richard Godbeer argues, many lifelong male friendships also began at school because the experiences of learning and boarding together often "fostered close and lasting relationships."[8] As they navigated new school environments, male and female students relied on friendships for emotional and intellectual support.

One female student captured the intellectual attraction of school friendships in a poem published in the *Philadelphia Repository and Weekly Register:*

All your external charms, tho' half divine,
Are not to be compar'd to those within:
Your Mind—a Mind with ev'ry virtue fraught—
Claims, therefore, ev'ry praise and ev'ry thought.
There, knowledge, and each graceful Art reside:
There, Wisdom, Science, and their train abide.[9]

This young woman found a "worthy friend" at school—and it was her friend's mind that was the subject of strongest admiration. In a culture that expressed continued ambivalence about the place of educated women in early national society, female friendships offered women opportunities to share the pleasures of learning with like-minded friends. Like many women who developed fulfilling friendships while attending school, Charlotte Hills found it difficult to leave behind her friends at the Bradford Academy: "It was with much reluctance that I bade adieu to my friends there," she wrote to her former classmate Lydia Clark Abbott. "What a source of unspeakable pleasure, is the idea of having true friends!" Charlotte mused. "Painful indeed were my sensations," Sarah Connell reflected on leaving the school she had attended for eighteen months, regretting her departure as "the moment that separated me from friends so tenderly beloved."[10]

After leaving female academies, many women remained drawn to friendships rooted in intellectual affinity. They maintained ties with their former classmates while searching for local friends with similar educational interests. Writing to Sarah, Eunice praised her new friend Harriet Green: "she has a cultivated mind, has read much, . . . can converse (and well) upon every subject." Eunice wished that Sarah could cultivate a friendship with another of her friends because "her considerable wit and genius, will amply compensate you." Educated women valued opportunities to spend time in the company of other learned women. "How I should have admired to have been with you at Concord," Eunice wrote to Sarah, "it must have been truly an intellectual feast to have a conversation with Sarah and Miss B." Young women wrote admiringly of friends with whom they could freely discuss shared intellectual interests. Harriet Margaret Wharton praised her cousin as an ideal companion: "her mind very much improved by reading and an intercourse with the best society. She is the delight and admiration of her family and friends which is to be expected."[11]

Educated women longed for friendships with like-minded women, but were often disappointed in their quests. "Oh how different I find the World from what I had expected before I went in society," Harriet Margaret Wharton mused. "I had flattered myself with hearing sensible instructive conversation on subjects likely to improve;" yet she discovered a different world: "Seldom very seldom do you meet with a congenial mind," Harriet noted with disappointment. Mary Cogswell expressed similar dissatisfaction with her social experiences: "Since I have been here I have scarcely heard an intelligent sensible conversation, or a rational remark in a large party," she complained to a friend. Sarah Vaughan lamented "the chains of ceremony" that required her to "pay that scrupulous attention to dress and fashion," noting that in her local social circle she had only one friend "who is indeed an amiable and interesting character."[12] In the face of such superficial encounters, young women deeply prized friendships founded in mutual intellectual interests.

For many young women, the ability to share intellectual as well as emotional bonds with other women was essential to their identities as educated women. "I *sensibly feel* all that you say as to my having a companion," Eunice wrote to Sarah. "The most beautiful prospects, most charming walks, and the best books how insipid without you have some one to join and participate [in] your pleasure." The ability to share both "charming walks" and "the best books" with trusted friends enabled young women to cultivate a world in which both sense and sensibility reigned. Friends such these were motivated, as one woman wrote, by "a reciprocal desire to do those things that will be agreeable to each other."[13]

Scholars have demonstrated how the emerging culture of sensibility, in which an emphasis on mutuality and affinity prevailed, inspired early national friendship ideals.[14] Affectionate ties of sensibility enabled friends to experience a sense of deep connection with each other. According to one author, friendship promised a world of affinity that was extremely rewarding: "From esteem proceeds friendship, a charming sentiment, which dilates the heart, and transports to sympathy; opens the wide field of mutual confidence, and forms a treasure to which we may at all times resort for advice; a depository for any gloomy ill fated occurrences which may thwart the mind; and doubles the joy we feel at any fortunate event." Engaging in "mutual confidence" with friends allowed individuals to give meaning to their own identities and experiences by validating them in relationship to others. In this respect, individual identity was inherently social in nature and expressed primarily through intimate relationships with like-minded companions. "All within me was moved with emotions of affectionate sensibility towards the heart I hold so dear," a woman named Susan wrote to her friend Jane Bowne. "'Twas then I felt the sanction of an union of Friendship—'twas then my affections were riveted to thee from the knowledge of that congeniality of sentiment subsisting between us."[15]

This sense of shared experience and sentiment was particularly important to young women who self-consciously sought to craft identities as learned women. Although early national writings focused on emotions and sensibility as the key traits of friendship, the bonds of female friendship frequently included the cultivation of intellectual interests. Eunice captured these friendship ideals in an 1803 letter to Sarah: "I often wish I could transport myself under the crooked tree, where I have spent so many pleasant hours with an improving book, or a more improving companion; or more especially under the spreading shade of those two united trees, whereon we carved our names. You did not mention in your last how they flourished, I assure you I shall never forget them or the afternoon we took our last walk, they are ever fresh in my mind and till my memory deserts me, their images will never be effaced."[16] The "two united trees" on which Eunice and Sarah carved their names served as an apt metaphor for their friendship. Emphasizing mutual pleasures—reading under a shady grove or walking together—Eunice and Sarah created a sense of emotional *and* intellectual affinity. The united trees could refer to Eunice and Sarah's growing sense of closeness and attachment; they could also represent the intertwined nature of their emotional and intellectual bonds. "Sally and I walked down to bid farewell to the Bower," Eunice wrote in her diary at the end of one of her visits to Sarah's house in Greenfield. "Sally read to me as we sat beneath *our trees* Thomson's Seasons, never shall I forget this morning."[17]

Sarah and Eunice treasured their visits with each other, when they were able to converse freely, engage in common interests, and create rituals that strengthened their friendship. For much of their relationship, however, they remained separated by geographical distance and family obligations. As Sarah mused in her diary after one of Eunice's visits, "After enjoying the sweet intercourse of confidential friendship for almost two months, we are again separated."[18] During these lengthy absences from each other, Sarah and Eunice relied on letter writing to bridge the distance between them.

"Very Much Interested in Your Heroine"

Writing to Sarah in 1809 about her visit with a mutual friend, Eunice mused, "I wish you could have joined our trio, then indeed we should have had an intellectual feast; till that happy period shall arrive I must be satisfied with *Letters.*" For separated friends, letter writing provided the means to maintain both intellectual and emotional bonds. Letters between absent friends were eagerly anticipated and received. As Eunice noted, "Surely there is nothing to be compared to the exquisite pleasure of receiving a packet from a long absent friend!" Letters themselves were treated as special artifacts and symbols, representing both the sender and the friendship. "As the enjoyment of personal communication is precluded," Jane Bayard wrote to her friend Sally Wister, "my pen, while the light continues, shall be the substitute, and present to my dear Sally, some image (tho' faintly) of her friend." Letters served as substitutes for the physical presence of absent friends—presenting at least "some image," as Jane noted. "I take your letters with me to peruse for though I cannot enjoy your charming company," one woman wrote to Delia Hayes, "you are always present to my view."[19]

Like many friends in early national America, Eunice and Sarah's correspondence contained reminisces about past moments spent together, news of family and friends, and accounts of various social scenes. Friends also used their correspondence to cultivate the "intellectual feasts" that Eunice prized. Educated women engaged in letter writing, one friend wrote to Jane Bowne, "believing it to be a channel through which we may not only derive instruction, but frequently hear of each other's welfare, which is an unspeakable satisfaction." For friends separated by distance, "we have the pleasure of conversing with them by letters," which, as Linda Raymond mused, was "a useful part of education to friends."[20]

Cultivating a sense of shared intellectual development was especially common among young women who forged friendships while attending school together. "I sometimes take a retrospective view of the happy days of our childhood 'our school day friendship,'" Deborah Norris reminisced to her friend Sarah Wister, "and always recall the idea with pleasure." Friends frequently recollected their "school day friendship" with fondness. "The happy hours spent at the School often recur to my remembrance," Jane Bowne's friend Emma wrote. "Our ride and several other occurrences frequently furnish subjects for conversation, which is always agreeable as it calls to mind those whom absence doubly endears."[21] Women prized the emotional bonds such relationships provided; in addition, friendships begun at school reminded women of their shared educational histories.

Friends and former classmates kept track of and encouraged each other's educational pursuits. One of Jane Bowne's friends "was indeed pleased to find the School answered thy expectations." Eliza Payson inquired about her friend Linda Raymond's new school situation: "I hope, my dear, you will soon favor me with a long letter and pray, inform me how you are pleased with your Preceptress, schoolmates, etc." Expressing her wishes for her former classmate's continued intellectual development, Lavinia Stafford wrote to Lydia Clark Abbott, "I hope my dear that you will have a good school this summer and improve your transient hours to better advantage than I have mine." Maria Wilson missed Delia Hayes during her friend's extended visit to Richmond, but was pleased to learn she had "recommenced study." Ann Haines' friend was "pleased to learn that you continue to prosecute your botanical studies."[22] In keeping track of one another's studies, young women used their common interest in education to strengthen the bonds of friendship.

With the support and encouragement of like-minded friends, women expressed and enacted identities that celebrated their educational accomplishments. In effect, women used their letters to create a "narration" of their lives as learned women. Often, women's letters contained self-conscious constructions of the self that individuals shared with trusted friends. Jane Bayard recognized the scripted element of correspondence when she informed her friend Sally Wister, "I could have enjoyed many pages of so pleasing a narrative, I feel my self very much interested in your heroine." Like a good novel, women's written efforts to narrate their life stories were read eagerly by like-minded friends and confidents. "I do not doubt but you could soon write an interesting good Novel, or anything else you undertook," Eunice assured Sarah after reading one of her letters. "Never doubt your ability again," Eunice urged her friend.[23] In referring to themselves as heroines and comparing their life stories to novels, young women implicitly recognized the power of correspondence—letter writing was an act of self-narration.

Thus, when Eunice playfully suggested that she and Sarah could create a book based on their correspondence, she underscored the importance of educated women's efforts at self-expression through letter writing. "Will you not epistle to me," Marcia Hall wrote to her friend Weltha Brown. "If I could go on doing my duty and careless of the 'world's dread laugh,'" Marcia mused, "I should do as much and perhaps more than many persons who have had their names and reputed virtues handed down to posterity." Quoting from "Mrs. Montague's" published letters, Marcia underscored the importance of correspondence in shaping women's identities: "Be careful that you do not burn my letters...for after my death they may be printed and become the admiration of the world." Although their personal correspondence might never be published, educated women implicitly recognized the value of their writings. "It was quite fortunate that the Squire found at *last* my epistle," Eunice wrote after one of her letters to Sarah was temporarily misplaced, "else what a vast loss the literary world might have sustained, all those brilliant effusions of my brain might have been consigned to oblivion."[24] That educated women would even playfully consider the possibility that their lives and letters were worthy of publication reflected their growing pride in their identification as learned women. The published writings of women such as Elizabeth Montagu, whose letters *were* deemed important enough to publish, provided particular sources of inspiration. The lives and letters of such literary women validated everyday women's more personal efforts at self-expression.

Correspondence with trusted friends, along with various sources of inspiration found in the literary public sphere, enabled women to write themselves into being as educated women. Taking up their pens, women wrote the narratives of their own lives, encouraged and emboldened by their friends' interest. "I comply with your wishes my dear friend in endeavoring to recollect occurrences which have taken place in life," Harriet Margaret Wharton wrote as she began a journal intended as a lengthy letter to a friend. Although Harriet suggested, "there is nothing very interesting to relate," she spent the next several months carefully crafting a narrative of herself as a thoughtful, intellectual woman. Harriet repeatedly made note of her reading and studies: "I am now going to begin to translate French from Madame DeGenlis' Adele and Theodore," she wrote in September 1813. "I am determined I will not do as girls are too apt to, give up all improvement because I am no longer in school." Harriet presented herself as an educated woman whose primary sense of self came from engaging in intellectual activities: "Today I am seated at my desk writing with my books around me," she wrote in October 1813.[25] Harriet's journal was written with her friend's readership in mind, so we may presume that her friend approved of, and shared in, Harriet's presentation of herself as an intellectual woman.

Although eager to portray themselves as learned women to like-minded friends, the act of self-narration could, at times, create a sense of ambivalence

or insecurity. Friends strove to present accurate representations of their intellectual lives rather than the more restrained public personas that they might
reserve for social dealings with mere acquaintances or strangers. Yet, at the
same time, women feared revealing this "true" self to one who might not
share or appreciate their ardent interest in education. Fears of false friends
permeated both the prescriptive literature and private writings of the early
national period. As the prescriptive literature warned, "however advanta-
geous it may be to have a sincere friend, it is as dangerous to have a false
one." According to many commentators, friendship was a rare, elusive gem
that had become little more than a shadow of its idealistic self. As one author
argued, "The real signification of the word is well understood, but the substance has long since been exiled from society in general, and reduced to a
'name.'" Such pessimistic warnings suggested that true friendship was but a
"deceitful vision" that lived only in the "imagination." Moreover, in some
writings, a gendered skepticism prevailed: Were women even capable of real
friendship with one another? "There is a prevailing passion amongst Females
of decrying and depreciating each other," one critic noted, "and in general,
the sex is always sure to suffer more from themselves than the men." This
author felt that women were too preoccupied with petty suspicions to form
lasting friendships, asserting that "[t]here is an unhappy jealousy which is
ever predominant amongst the ladies."[26] In contrast to a "female world of
love and ritual," skeptics viewed relationships among women in negative and
suspicious terms.

Sensitive to concerns about false friends, educated women feared condemnation from individuals who did not share their intellectual interests.
Rachel Van Dyke worried about the changing nature of her friendship with
Maria Parker: "We still keep up the appearances of friendship, but I do not
think there is that intimacy subsisting between us which ought to between
true friends." Rachel's concerns stemmed primarily from Maria's lack of
support for her continued studies. Upon finding a Greek book in Maria's
house, Rachel asked if her friend was studying Greek, to which Maria replied:
"No—I have not *genius* enough to study any other language but my own."
Rachel, then enrolled in a Latin class, understood that the remark "was evidently meant for me." Maria's criticisms stung, and Rachel admitted that she
lost affection for her friend: "Maria is not the same girl she used to be or else
I never knew her."[27] Without Maria's support for her educational journey,
Rachel found it difficult to sustain their friendship.

Disheartened by such uncomfortable encounters, women longed for
friendships in which they could celebrate the joys of learning without fear
of criticism or disapproval. And despite its pessimistic predictions about

friendship—and female friendship in particular—early national print culture praised true friendship, with paeans such as one that extolled it as "the language, the harmony, the mutual gratifications, of congenial and sentimental spirits; thy presence [is] the light, the comfort, and glory of humanity." Immersed in a culture that valued this kind of sentimental expression, early national women persistently believed in the promise of true friendship. As Elizabeth Lindsay entreated to her friend, "some is of the opinion that friendship is but a name. Let us my dear Apphia by our attention to her sacred ties prove her being." True friendship was held up as a bulwark against a world that could be cold, calculating, and critical.[28]

Eager to craft true friendships with like-minded women, young women repeatedly assured their friends of their sincerity. This was especially important to educated women, who sought to build friendships based on shared intellectual interests. Eunice was upset when Sarah criticized the tone of one of her letters: "You seem to think me prone to flattery and also to satire. My dear friend it quite distresses me that you who are very penetrating should think me possessed of two such disagreeable qualities." Eunice defended herself against these charges, insisting that the comments she had made praising Sarah's "superior understanding" were rooted in appreciation of her friend's intellect. As to the charge of satire, Eunice insisted that she would never "hurt the feelings of any of my friends to be called the greatest wit in the universe," explaining that any satire she might "indulge" in was "always aimed at vice or folly."[29] In sharing witty comments or criticisms on particular literary works, Eunice did not want to be seen in a negative light for doing so. Instead, she hoped that Sarah would appreciate that such comments were part of her efforts to cultivate a world of shared literary exchanges and sensibilities.

Cultivating common interests and sensibilities played essential roles in friendships between educated women. "When Silvia and myself are admiring persons or things," one woman wrote, "the conclusion of our sentiments are—Jane would like this—Jane dislikes another etc.—that we consider thy opinions quite a standard." Knowing that friends shared common interests provided support for women seeking validation of their efforts at intellectual expression. Friendship "founded on esteem, similarity of tastes, and congeniality of sentiments," as Elizabeth Shippen mused, "is worth everything and highly to be prized." By cultivating friendships with like-minded individuals who shared "similarity of tastes," educated women crafted shared identities as learned women while also hoping to silence critics who doubted whether true friendship could flourish between women.[30]

"To Read Some Book Alike"

Closing one letter to Sarah with poetry she "selected out of a magazine," Eunice illustrated how the sentimental and emotional ties of female friendship were, at times, inextricably linked to intellectual and literary interests. The poem's setting, "*Beneath the oak's whose tops in friendship meet,*" reminded Eunice of the intertwined trees where she and Sarah enjoyed countless hours together:

> Within some bower by Ethelinde form'd,
> With books and music, pass the tedious hour,
> My mind by friendship, pleasing friendship warm'd,
> Defy old time, and Melancholy's power.[31]

The use of sentimental poetry enabled Eunice to express her feelings to Sarah through a literary conduit.[32] This poem celebrated the pleasures of friendship and reading, and featured a setting (intertwined trees) that held particular resonance for Eunice and Sarah. Through transcriptions of poetry and quotations from favorite authors, friends added layers of meanings to their correspondence. Shared literary interests provided a language of intellectual and emotional expression that enabled friends to craft a heightened sense of affinity.

Eunice and Sarah's letters contain frequent references to literary works, as well as transcriptions of poetry and other favorite quotations. "I thank you kindly for sending me the Messenger," Eunice wrote to Sarah in 1813. "The perusal of 'Rokeby' gratified me much. I should be delighted to read the whole, I think what I have read is excellent." Eunice eagerly read the selection from Sir Walter Scott that Sarah enclosed with her letter. "There certainly is something peculiar in 'Scott's Poems,'" Eunice mused, "a *something* that fixes and enchains the attention that delights and interests you more than any other writer."[33] Such exchanges served a variety of purposes. The various referents to educational and literary material prevalent in their correspondence underscore that, for many young women, female friendship was as much about the cultivation of intellectual interests as it was about emotional affection.

Engaging in "mutual" reader's response to particular texts, friends used shared reading practices to help create a sense of identity for themselves as learned women.[34] As Eunice noted, "how much it adds to the pleasure of perusing a favorite book to have some one to compare your observations with." Along with other forms of socializing (conversations, visiting, and letter writing), reading books together provided friends with a deepened sense of connection. For friends living in close proximity to one another, varied opportunities existed for shared reading practices. For women who attended school together, for example, education was a social experience that brought them together—both in classroom settings and informal gatherings—to discuss particular books, authors, and ideas. Everyday practices of sociability provided various opportunities for intellectual exchanges. Sitting around the parlor, friends and family members frequently listened as one person read aloud, and together they discussed the book's contents. During a visit to friends, Ann Haines described the morning activities in her host's parlor: "we there sew and read, one reads aloud while the others are at work." Sharing books provided friends mutual improvement and enjoyment: "the work you are reading will afford much more entertainment than if you each read it alone." Sarah Vaughan admiringly described her niece's social circle as "the enjoyment of friendship and domestic pleasures, they read to each other."[35]

Many friends read to each other, but some took this process a step further. Students attending female academies sometimes formed, as Sarah had at the Worchester Academy, societies devoted to mutual improvement. In 1821, Susan Minturn wrote enthusiastically to her aunt Jane Bowne Haines about a "reading society" that she had formed with friends. As Susan explained, the group met "once a week to read History and Poetry and every other week to write compositions. It is a very delightful way to passing the evening and I hope will have the desired effect of improving." In 1817, Elizabeth Pierce attended a meeting of her local reading society: "the members meet together every Thursday evening, and sew for the Education Society and Mr. Waldo Flint reads to them."[36] Through such activities, women seamlessly integrated shared reading practices into other forms of sociability.

When separated by distance, friends relied on letter writing as a means of continuing patterns of shared reading that marked their time together at school and in other social settings. As Harriet Burnham wrote to her friend Abigail Bradley, "You will recollect that we engaged in our correspondence to inform each other what we had been reading and to make remarks, which pleased [us] and I hope we shall yet carry that into effect." Jane Bowne's friend Eliza reminded her, "we once concluded, to read some books alike and at the same time." For many young women, shared reading practices constituted deliberate efforts at continued intellectual development. "I rejoice that we are again pursuing the same studies!" Eunice wrote enthusiastically to Sarah in 1809. "It will give an additional relish to the banquet, to know that you are participating, and it will serve as a spur (what I want) to me to be more diligent and more accurate in committing to memory." The ability to read books together enhanced the individual enjoyment of reading while also serving as intellectual inspiration. "Permit me to tell you that I highly approve the plan for our mutual benefit," Eunice mused to Sarah.[37]

Whether they took place face to face or through correspondence, shared reading practices transformed the act of reading—which is often thought of as a solitary, individual endeavor—into a collective process that created a communal identity between like-minded friends. Reading books together brought women out of the solitary practice of reading and into a shared space of intellectual exchange. This process could play a very important role in their emerging sense of self. As Mary Kelley suggests in her analysis of nineteenth-century women readers, women who read books together shaped and validated identities as educated women.[38] The opportunity to read with other like-minded friends was a source of both emotional *and* intellectual fulfillment for many women.

Friends eagerly shared their literary worlds with each other. "You wish to know Dear Sally what I am reading," Catherine Van Schaack wrote to her friend in 1811. "I have not yet begun any particular book," she noted, "may I in return ask what books you are perusing, and your opinion of them, and I will endeavor to improve by your remarks." As Catherine's comments suggest, friends discussed favorite books not just to share the pleasures of reading but also for continued instruction. "Is there any particular Author that my Dear Sally would recommend to me?" Catherine wondered. "I am sensible that I want instruction and will be happy to receive it from one whom I esteem so highly." Two weeks later, Catherine provided a list of her recent reading activities, which included "an abridgement of Rollin's Ancient History, Lyttleton's History of England for the second time, the Shipwreck, a sweet little poem, and have now commenced Johnson's Lives of the Poets."[39] These works helped shape her identity and experiences as an educated woman.

Sharing their intellectual interests with trusted friends, women explored what it meant to be an educated woman in early national society. In the process, they looked to various texts, particularly the lives of learned women, as models of inspiration and emulation.

"A Pattern for Me and Every Female"

"I have been gratified lately by reading the life of Mrs. Graham," Eunice wrote to Sarah in 1817. "I was pleased with this Book.... Her active benevolence and charity for all was so great one could not but be charmed."

Although women shared a variety of books with each other, including poetry, literature, and history, they expressed particular interest in the lives and works of "worthy women." As Sarah Wister wrote to female relatives in 1802, "Let me recommend...Hannah More on education, it is a work well deserving the attention of our sex, who are desirous of moral or religious improvement." As she noted, Hannah More served as a valuable role model: "How great an ornament is this excellent woman to the present age—whilst others are wasting invaluable time in frivolous empty pursuits—on dress, at the Theatre and the card table." By recommending books written by and about worthy women, female friends celebrated a world of female accomplishment. As Lucy Vaughan wrote to her friend, "We read the work of Mad. de Stael's you mention with much interest, and are now reading her influence of Literature." Ann Haines recommended Francis Cox's *Female Scripture Biography* to Jane Bowne Haines, praising it as "a very interesting book, gives woman her just due." Writing to her cousin Margaret Shippen, Catherine Eddowes expressed admiration for *The Lives of Illustrious Women* by Mary Hays, a collective female biography. "I have there read of and admired the Roman Matron who by the aid of philosophy and love of glory, has appeared raised above the natural timidity and weakness of our sex, and supported with heroic firmness the greatest of human evils."[40]

Early national women eagerly looked to various "examples of female erudition and talents" to provide inspiration and precedent for their own intellectual ambitions. As Susanna Rowson, educator, remarked, female biography inspired "a noble emulation to equal those who have gone before us; to young females, the memorials of exemplary women are peculiarly interesting." Rowson's ardent support of female biography reflected her desire to provide her students with what historians often refer to as a "usable past"— that is, a record of accomplishment to validate women's aspirations. "Every page of history abounds with accounts that do honour to the sex," Rowson noted. The lives and writings of past worthy women served as role models for early national women embarking on their own intellectual journeys: "it is in our power to rise into consequence, and make ourselves venerated. Others have done so, why may not we?"[41]

Worthy women served as models of inspiration and emulation. As Lusanna Richmond wrote after reading *The Life of Martha Laurens Ramsey*, "she was a pattern for me and every female: may I imitate her virtues, if I cannot her extensive learning."[42] Rachel Van Dyke requested *The Life of Miss Elizabeth Smith* from her town library after friends wrote to her about the book "in a very flattering manner, and they both seem to think that I must have read it." *The American Lady's Preceptor* praised the intellectual acquirements of Elizabeth

Smith, who had largely self-studied geometry, algebra, poetry, history, and philosophy, along with several languages, including Latin and Greek. "With all these acquirements," as her memoir insisted, "she was perfectly feminine in her disposition."[43] Not only did women benefit from the content of such books, the examples of learned women validated their own intellectual interests. In particular, the admiration these worthy women received suggested that it was possible for women to acquire extensive education without being labeled pedantic.

Educated women often identified strongly with worthy women, embedding famous women into a network of accomplished women that spanned time and space. Eunice admired Hannah More as an "excellent writer" and shared her admiration with friends. "I was conversing with Sarah C. the other day upon this topic, she said some great character she forgets who it is, observed that Miss More possesses all of the learning of Lady Jane Grey without her pedantry, and all the religion of Mrs. Rowe without her enthusiasm." In one breath, Eunice's friend Sarah C. evoked three worthy women, all noted for their intellectual accomplishments. Despite Sarah C.'s appreciation of these women, Eunice expressed her puzzlement at her friend's observation: "Now I never thought that Lady Jane Grey was a Pedant, did you?"[44] Eunice preferred to praise the accomplishments of female intellectuals without criticizing them as pedants. Sensitive to the charge of pedantry that every learned woman feared, Eunice defended Lady Jane Grey—although she had been dead for over 250 years—from such criticisms.

In her defense of worthy women, Eunice cultivated understandings of female accomplishment rooted in celebration, not condemnation. As Eunice discovered, responses to particular women's writings could be intense and highly personal, creating a unique sense of connection between reader and author: "I have been reading lately the memoirs of an American Lady (Mrs. Schuyler)…she writes in that easy natural style that speaks to the heart at once and you feel yourself quite at home and quite acquainted with her. I am not afraid to declare that I am certain her writings would please you, there is not a doubt—for do not laugh at me when I tell you that—I have often whilst perusing her thought I was reading your own sentiments."[45] By writing in an "easy natural style that speaks to the heart," Schuyler replicated the expressive communications prized by close friends. As a literary woman, Schuyler also provided an inspiring role model for Eunice and Sarah. In Eunice's mind, Schuyler became a type of literary substitute for Sarah—merging the two, Eunice imagined Sarah as the author of these writings. Eunice's response to this book blended emotional and literary sensibilities, creating a shared identity that encompassed Eunice, Sarah, and the author alike.

The lives and works of worthy women were a frequent topic in Eunice and Sarah's letters. In May 1814, Sarah wrote in her diary, "I have this day been reading the Memoirs of Mrs. Harriet Newell—it has made a deep impression on my mind." She recommended the book to Eunice, who later wrote to Sarah with her response. Aware of Sarah's positive response, Eunice apologized for her own halfhearted reaction: "it may be a want of taste in me, but really I was not so much pleased with it as I expected." Eunice expressed regret for not sharing Sarah's warm regard for Harriet Newell: "I do not feel as enthusiastic as you would have me." Eunice was careful to note that, despite her criticisms of Newell's letters, she was "not for depreciating them by any means."[46]

As Eunice's tepid response suggests, friends prized a sense of affinity when it came to favorite authors and books. When friends did not share the same enthusiasm for particular books—especially books by or about female role models—it could create an uneasy sense of discord. Upon recommending *Rowe's Letters* to Sarah, Eunice anxiously awaited her friend's opinion but cautioned, "you must not say anything against them." Eunice checked herself, admitting that it was "enigmatical" to ask Sarah for her "candid opinion and then restrain you." Eunice hoped Sarah would also enjoy this book but also sensed that her enthusiasm might have made it difficult for Sarah to reply in a way that was wholly candid. When Sarah offered an "odd description" of *Rowe's Letters,* Eunice was uncertain "whether you approve them or not." Eunice was disappointed with Sarah's equivocal response: "I thought to have a long dissertation etc. when you abruptly leave off and say you are *incapable* to decide."[47]

Shared reader's response to particular authors or books was an important aspect of female friendship, especially when those works directly related to women's identification as learned women. Friends naturally expected that they would develop similar reading tastes; any enjoyment gained from a particular work was enriched by the knowledge that a close friend had experienced the same joys. Disagreements about literary subjects, then, could create tension. If unsure of a friend's opinion about a particular book, women sometimes presented their reactions in measured tones in order to avoid discord. "Has thou ever read Interesting Memoirs," one of Jane Bowne's friends inquired. "I think some of the letters are elegant—I have often heard Adelaide speak in their praise but not too highly." Through such equivocation, women avoided appearing too interested in a book that a friend might not have enjoyed as much. Their discomfort with literary discord suggests the ways in which young women were socialized to harmonize, but it also underscores the importance that intellectual affinity played in female friendships.[48]

Friends longed for like-minded individuals with whom they could enthusiastically discuss favorite authors and books without fear of criticism for their
intellectual interests.

Although disagreements over particular works could at times create uneasi-
ness, Eunice and Sarah continued to engage in spirited discussions about
their literary tastes. An ardent fan of Sir Walter Scott, Eunice wondered how
anyone could not enjoy his writings. "Does it not seem strange to you that
good judges, sensible folks should dislike the poem and the author?" Eunice
wondered about his *Lady of the Lake*. "For my part I cannot conceive of
it," Eunice wrote to Sally, "but Mary Roulstone joins with Emily, Mary B.,
and her Father . . . *all all* dislike it, and do not see its beauties." Although
they did not always agree, Eunice and Sarah remained comfortable expressing strong opinions to each other, which in turn shaped their identities as
learned women.[49]

"Truth and Fiction Agreeably Blended"

In addition to creating a common sense of identity as learned women, reader's
response practices provided women with the means to discuss a variety of
ideas and subjects. Whenever Eunice began reading a book that was particularly engaging or inspiring, she was eager to share her insights with Sarah:

> I assure you there has been quite a *revolution* taken place in my
> sentiments—start not my dear girl and think not I am going to be mar-
> ried; I mean I have imbibed a taste for *History!* entirely owing to Rollin.
> I have read a great deal in it particularly the four last volumes which
> are particularly entertaining. I have almost read the last volume, how
> far have you proceeded? I do really almost prefer reading it to Novels, I
> never felt more interested in any book; but some wicked people say that
> I only like to read the history of Egypt etc., because it is in the *Novel
> stile* [*sic*], now what is your opinion? Are you so uncharitable or will
> you allow that my taste is corrected, as my judgement grows mature?[50]

As Eunice noted, reading introduced individuals to new ideas that could
spark a "revolution" in their sense of themselves and the world around them.
Her phrasing provides a powerful reminder of how access to education and
knowledge was a transformative experience for many women. Eunice's
comments also reveal the importance of female friendship in helping young
women to process and make sense of their evolving intellectual identities. While rethinking her own taste in reading material, Eunice anxiously
sought Sarah's opinion. Eunice felt that her efforts at self-improvement were

somehow incomplete until her friend validated them. This intense need for validation reflected not only the importance of crafting a common sense of identity but also demonstrated Eunice's awareness of the era's confusing and competing ideas about educated women. Sensitive to concerns and criticism about women's education, female friends used their correspondence as a place to discuss the larger implications of their intellectual interests.

In comparing history and novel reading, Eunice alluded to common criticisms surrounding women's educational pursuits. The prescriptive and popular literature contained frequent criticisms of novel reading, describing it as an extravagant and sensationalized form of literary consumption. As the preface of one popular compilation of essays directed at women warned, "Are they not calculated to bewilder, rather than to direct? Do we ever find in real life the romantic scenes they paint?...Some of them might be read without harm, though seldom with any benefit." As literary critics and historians have argued, the very characteristics that made novel reading so "dangerous" were tremendously appealing to readers, particularly to young women.[51] Reading played a central role in young women's coming of age. In particular, novel reading enabled women to examine the significance of courtship and marriage in their own lives. Thus, it was quite revealing that Eunice linked her recent revolution in reading habits to thoughts of marriage—another event almost certain to bring revolutionary changes to a woman's life.

Of course, courtship and marriage were central to the plots of many early national novels. Praising Hannah More's *Coelebs in Search of a Wife,* Elizabeth Lindsay wrote to her friend Apphia Rouzee, "I wish you could read it—as I think you are one among those who could even read a novel with interest if it afforded nothing more to amuse the imagination than a sweet picture of family love and domestic happiness, unlike any book of the kind I ever read." More stressed the importance of companionate marriage and domestic harmony, inspiring young women to seek similar relationships in their own lives. Harriet Margaret Wharton copied a passage from *Coelebs* in her journal that reflects the hero's wishes for an ideal wife: "She must be elegant, or I should not love her, sensible or I should not respect her, prudent or I could not confide in her, well informed or she should not educate my children."[52] Although this passage presents a woman's accomplishments in terms of how to best serve her husband, it also supports the idea that a well-educated woman made an ideal companion. Through identification with certain characters or plots, women imagined certain narratives for their lives; in the process, they sought to shape their destinies in ways that supported their intellectual aspirations. Critics recognized this potentially subversive aspect of novel reading and urged women to read books that provided more suitable preparation for traditional gender roles.

Women's correspondence reflected their astute awareness of the debates surrounding novel reading. "I think your observation just respecting Bennet's Letters and I will readily agree to all he says about novels, etc.," Eunice wrote to Sarah. "I am often to conviction but not to amendment," Eunice confessed respecting the criticisms of novel reading contained in John Bennett's *Letters to a Young Lady*. Yet Eunice defended her reading habits when Sarah questioned her continued love of novels: "What makes you think I indulge myself too much," she asked. "I read but very few hardly any lately, and one must have some kind of amusement to while away the time." Such comments illustrate how women positioned their reading habits against prescriptive warnings. As a friend admitted to Jane Bowne, "reading has, of course, been one of my amusements, but I have not sufficient resolution to withstand the temptation of once in a while *perusing a novel* if it falls in my way." Women admitted that they occasionally read *"pernicious books,"* but were careful to defend the practice or to find value in particular novels. Commenting on a novel that Sarah had recently read (despite her comments to Eunice, Sarah was also not immune to the charms of novels), Eunice noted, "I am not surprised you was absorbed with that 'witchedly enticing' volume the Wild Irish Girl, I read it some time since and I cannot but admire the style and sentiment; though I agree with you there is no great variety and the story is not very deep."[53]

Recognizing the continued appeal of novels, some commentators attempted to defend them. As one essayist noted, "I am inclined to think that many excellent precepts, and morals are inculcated in by far the greater part of them." Novels that provided descriptions of "life in accurate colors" were particularly praiseworthy. Such works, this author continued, "are doubly excellent; because, while they inculcate the best morals, they give the readers an accurate knowledge of life and manners; of which it is highly proper young people should have a correct idea." Eunice agreed that certain novels could serve as a form of instruction, especially if they were properly written. "I wish that you would peruse Thaddeus of Warsaw," Eunice wrote to Sarah, "and give me your opinion upon it, there you find truth and fiction agreeably blended, you would find it instructive amusing and very interesting, it being founded on fact."[54]

As Eunice suggested, novels that had a basis in truth were popular in the early national period, and such works probably encouraged her growing interest in history. Indeed, history and novels often competed for women's reading attention. Harriet Manigault and her sisters devoted their mornings

to reading history, but as she noted in her diary, "Our evening book is generally some *novel,* as we read such serious books in the morning." Anna Maria
Cornell engaged in similar reading patterns. "I have laid aside my history and
am reading Coelebs which I am very much pleased with," she wrote to her
sister. "It is well written and I think too good to be a novel." Eunice expressed
her desire to read Hume's *History of England,* "for I find that novels has not
taken away my relish for any other good reading." Some women viewed history and novel reading as compatible rather than competitive. "We are now
reading Fox's historical work and find it very interesting," Lucy Vaughan
wrote to a friend. "It causes us of course to refer to other works and throw
light on those periods of History Scott has of late rendered so interesting."[55]
Women enjoyed both novels and history, refusing to let prescriptive warnings
limit their reading habits.

Social commentators, however, continued to offer their prescriptions.
Although they sharply criticized novel reading, prescriptive writers generally approved of women's interest in history. To reinforce history as a subject
particularly suited for women, David Hume's observations on women and
history were reprinted in a variety of early republican periodicals and newspapers. As Hume wrote, "There is nothing I would recommend more ear-
nestly to my female readers than the study of history, as an occupation, of all
others, the best suited both to their sex and education; much more instructive
than their ordinary books of amusement." Introducing women to historical
narrative, Hume suggested, gave them a greater appreciation of "important
truths" that shaped human history. Among these truths, Hume hoped that
women realized "*That* our sex, as well as their's are far from being such perfect creatures as they are apt to imagine; and *That* love is not the only passion
that governs the male world, but is often overcome by avarice, ambition,
vanity, and a thousand other passions."[56] Hume argued that history presented
a more balanced view of human nature than novels, which instead presented
romanticized flights of fancy and idealized feats of heroism.

Hume argued that history contributed to women's cultivation of "quiet
and repose" in a way that novels did not, but reading history could have its
own subversive elements.[57] While reading Rollin's *Ancient History,* Eunice
began to transform her ideas about power and authority. As she noted to
Sarah, "[Y]ou cannot read History through without being often severely
shocked at the enormities committed by their Kings; and how seldom do you
meet with a noble or generous action! Fathers dethroned by their sons, and
children murdered by their Parents; yet it makes those few noble actions shine
brighter by being contrasted with the vices that surround them."[58] Although
Hume suggested that women read history to learn about the "passion

that governs the male world," he may not have predicted that women would use that understanding to develop what was, in essence, a gendered critique of patriarchy. By reading history, Eunice discovered that the male world contained more vice than virtue, criticizing male leaders who failed to demonstrate "noble and generous action."

To make better sense of her emerging thoughts, Eunice eagerly shared them with Sarah. Having a trusted friend to discuss ideas with was essential to many women's intellectual journeys. Accordingly, Eunice was anxious to hear Sarah's observations on history: "Here I have been writing about History (which to be sure is an uncommon thing for me) and intruding my observations, when undoubtedly you have made much better ones in the course of your reading; do send some of your observations on a distinct piece of paper, as I shall be *delighted* with any of the observations and remarks of which I *know* you must have made on reading them."[59] By seeking one another's opinions and thoughts about their reading choices, friends validated their educational efforts and sharpened their thinking about a variety of subjects, including novels, history, and politics. In the process, female friends constructed identities for themselves as well-read, articulate women eager to partake in a world of intellectual and literary expression. Female friendships enabled women to develop and sustain their educational interests well beyond their youthful days at school.

"Firm and United to the Last"

Initially, the similarities in their lives facilitated the intense friendships enjoyed by women such as Eunice Callender and Sarah Ripley; these friendships often began when women were young, unmarried, living at home, and possessed with enough leisure time to devote to writing, reading, and socializing. In 1808, Eunice's aunt remarked that such closeness would necessarily fade over time. The conversation struck a chord in Eunice, and she related it in detail to Sarah:

> continued Aunt E. "it is fifteen years since I have seen [her] and the acquaintance seems wholly broken up for she was engrossed with a multitude of other cares, and it was the most natural thing in the world; when people changed their situation etc. that they bestowed their affections elsewhere." But upon seeing me smile with an air of incredibility, . . . Mrs. Pritchard joined her and said nothing was more natural; but still I am incredulous. I have heard of certain people continuing their most fervent affections for each other till the latest hour of their existence, and such I trust will ours be firm and united to the last.[60]

Eunice remained "incredulous" to the idea that her friendship with Sarah constituted anything less than a lifelong commitment. She was confident that other cares and concerns—undoubtedly references to marriage and children—would not interfere with their friendship. If Eunice and Sarah could overcome the obstacle of physical distance through letter writing, Eunice was convinced that time and changing life cycles would not break the bonds of friendship.

Eunice's aunt may have spoken from experience about the transient nature of youthful friendships, but many friends were determined to sustain their relationships over time. In 1813, Eunice returned to her aunt's conversation, writing that her then decade-old correspondence with Sarah represented "a convincing proof to the contrary of what Aunt E. and Mrs. P. advanced in regard to the ability of youthful friendships; you ask what is my opinion now after four years have elapsed—the same as it ever was, if I was ever inclined to *doubt* surely your welcome epistle has banished all such disagreeable intruders." By 1813, Eunice was twenty-seven and remained unmarried, but Sarah had "changed her situation." In 1812, Sarah married Charles Stearns, a merchant, and moved to Shelburne. "At first I could hardly realize my Greenfield correspondent when transplanted to...Shelburne," Eunice admitted. "But now I am ready to love Shelburne for... [the] retirement in which you live seems favorable to our correspondence." Sarah's marriage made Eunice "more sensible than ever" about the importance of their friendship.[61]

As time progressed, as Eunice reflected in an 1817 letter, these two friends experienced life-cycle changes. "You have entered the conjugal state and have become the Mother of three sweet infants and are doubtless as happy as the day is long, while I am equally as happy...although almost wholly secluded from the world." Eunice remained single, devoting her time to the care of her aging and often ill mother. "To contribute to my Parents' comfort as much as is in my power," Eunice insisted, "is both my duty and my greatest pleasure." Their increasing duties at home offered both Eunice and Sarah fewer opportunities to engage in the lengthy, out-of-town visits that they previously enjoyed. "How I should rejoice to accept your challenge of a romantic ramble in the fields," Eunice mused to Sarah, "but I must submit to my destiny and remain within the narrow bounds of this City, though my spirit soars far beyond and meets with you in many of bower of sweets."[62] Over time, the substance of Eunice and Sarah's friendship had become their youthful friendship remembered, and letter writing rather than visiting had become the primary means of maintaining their sense of closeness.

Yet in the years following Sarah's marriage in 1812 and the birth of her four children, their correspondence became increasingly erratic and subject to lapses. "Dare I tell you how I miss your *valued* letters what a deprivation do I suffer," Eunice lamented to Sarah. "Here in this world of deceit, false friends, and petty trials, I could resort to them with confidence and felt assured if any one took any interest in *me* it was my *friend,* it was a balm to me." Friends separated by distance often worried, as Rebecca Root wrote to Weltha Brown, whether "time and absence has in some measured weakened that affection I imagined you felt for me." Friends called on each other for understanding and empathy as they struggled to balance the obligations of friendship with the increased duties of domesticity. After her marriage, Elizabeth Lindsay Gordon assured her friend Apphia Rouzee, "[I] beg of you if ever hereafter I neglect answering your letters that you will attribute it to the cares which a mistress of a family and a mother of young children must always *have* and not to any want of affection on my part." The demands of mothering and housekeeping, as another woman insisted, could not "eras[e] the recollection of our friends from the mind."[63] Eager to sustain friendships cultivated in their youth, women reassured each other of their continued affection, even if they were unable to write as frequent or as lengthy letters as they once did.

As they matured, Eunice and Sarah accepted the temporal lapses in their correspondence as inevitable. "I missed your letters," Eunice wrote in 1830, "I did not however my friend impute it to any neglect on your part, I concluded you must have sufficient reasons for your silence." Eunice and Sarah continued to correspond with each other, despite occasional silences, over three decades. "*Our friendship* is indeed of long standing," Eunice mused in an 1830 letter, "like the trees which bear our names, its roots is deeply and firmly fixed." Eunice referenced the trees on which she and Sarah had carved their names almost thirty years earlier (and that Eunice first wrote about in an 1803 letter). No matter who else entered their lives—a husband or other close female friends—the bonds between Eunice and Sarah remained as "deeply and firmly fixed" as the entangled roots of their intertwined trees.[64]

Despite the demands of marriage, childrearing, and domesticity that had kept them busy throughout three decades, Sarah and Eunice's friendship had an enduring quality to it. "There is none who can surpass *you,* in giving an interest—a *magic* to letters which make them so dear, so valuable to me," Eunice wrote to Sarah in 1830. As Deborah Norris wrote of her lifelong friendship with Sally Wister, "The long acquaintance that I have had with you makes you inexpressively dear to me, I shall never cultivate any new friendship comparable with that heart felt one I entertain for you—it is no common attachment, but a harmony, a cement of soul that binds the union." Women treasured such friendships for both the emotional *and* intellectual substance they provided. "That union of affection which is supported by mental assistance in the task of duty," as Harriet Margaret Wharton mused, "instead of growing weaker must be more strongly cemented by added years." "From my earliest remembrance *Sally Sarah* was the first friend in my affections," Eunice reflected. "*You* could always understand me, you penetrated into my feelings and knew my mind better oft times than I did myself.—And what friendship that I have since then commenced rivals you in my heart?"[65] Eunice valued the emotional contours of her friendship with Sarah, but she equally treasured the ability to discuss her thoughts on novels, history, and other literary interests. Their long correspondence enabled Eunice and Sarah to cultivate and sustain identities that spanned their lifetimes as learned women.

"So Many Subjects in Which We Take a Mutual Interest"

Well beyond their youthful days, Eunice Callender and Sarah Ripley Stearns relied on their friendship for continued support, validation, and encouragement. "How many things press on me when I take up my pen to write you," Eunice began an 1827 letter to Sarah. "There are so many subjects in which we take a mutual interest that I hardly know which to select first." Forty-four years old in 1830, Eunice maintained her keen interest in a variety of intellectual pursuits. She described to Sarah a "History Class" she had recently attended. "We have been reading almost all Scott's practical works which you know can be read over and over again with delight." In October of that year, Eunice recounted her visit to a female school in Boston. "I was very much pleased with the appearance of the School, the young ladies all appeared very happy."[66] Eunice continued to share her intellectual interests with Sarah, confident that her friend would appreciate her lifelong love of learning.

Female friendships provided women with powerful bonds of intimacy and expression. In seeking to explain the intensity of such friendships, historians have tended to emphasize emotional bonds. Yet such friendships also served the intellectual needs of early national women who were eager to discuss various subjects with like-minded friends. Female friendships helped educated women sustain an enduring sense of identity as learned women. By understanding the importance that shared intellectual interests held for educated women, we can better appreciate their hopes and ambitions. In various heterosocial relationships, educated women sought to maintain the intellectual selves they had so carefully created at school and with like-minded women. Emboldened by female friendships that nurtured their intellectual selves, young women would continue to explore what it meant to live merely as the equals of man.

 CHAPTER 3

"The Social Family Circle"

Family Matters

In 1796, sixteen-year-old Elizabeth Shippen and her younger sister, Margaret, left their family home in Chester County, Pennsylvania, to attend "Grammar" and "dancing" school in nearby Philadelphia. Although their brother John would miss his sisters' presence at home, he took "pleasing consolation" that an extended visit to Philadelphia offered "advantages of improvement in an important degree, and at a very important period of Life." Philadelphia was home to some of the most prestigious institutions in the nation for women's education and would provide the Shippen sisters, as John noted, "the golden opportunity...of becoming sensible, amiable, and accomplished women." Along with access to formal education, a visit to the city offered young women such as Elizabeth and Margaret Shippen "other essential opportunities...of improving your mind and manner." Chief among these opportunities was a rich world of social interaction, in which "the best company resort in the sociable way." Their participation in various social engagements provided the Shippen sisters with another important form of instruction. In society, John continued:

You hear subjects discussed that will give you much valuable information. You see the best of good breeding, untainted by a reserve, a preciseness, and affectation of manners. And, at the same time, you have frequent opportunities of discovering what is proper behavior and good manners in circles, where etiquette, form and fashion, are from convenience and necessity, obliged to prevail. All these insensibly steal upon the mind; and your mind is just ripe for deriving benefits from them, by care, by attention, and by a desire of improvement.[1]

John urged his sisters to consider social activities as a source of both entertainment and education. To learn to conduct oneself in a "sociable way" was a valuable lesson indeed. Education and sociability were the essential, linked building blocks of a young woman's coming of age and character development. Accordingly, Elizabeth and Margaret's education focused on a combination of both "useful" (grammar) and "ornamental" (dancing) subjects, as well as the appropriate display of education in a variety of social settings. As James Neal, educator, of the Young Ladies' Academy of Philadelphia noted, proper attention to education enabled women to be "more perfect ornaments of society, fully calculated to render happy beyond expression, those who participate with you." Educated women gained numerous advantages that were "inseparably connected with refinement of manners, and a cultivated mind."[2]

With their refined manners and cultivated minds, young women such as Elizabeth and Margaret Shippen were well trained to assume their roles in early national society. Families such as the Shippens inhabited a social world where polite ideals of sociability and sensibility reigned. "I . . . often picture to my mind the social family circle," Elizabeth noted, where family and close friends gathered together, "enjoying each other's society, and listening with a pleased attentive ear to Papa's improving conversation, and instructive account of his travels &c." The family engaged in social practices based on the intellectual and pleasurable sharing of thoughts, ideas, and emotions. Family members and close friends delighted in "the pleasures of that easy and social intercourse, which is no where more happily experienced than in domestic circles." Happily assembled around the "fire-side and tea-table," the Shippen family entertained one another with social converse, often by discussing politics and current events, or perhaps by reading aloud from a newspaper or book.[3]

Defined by historians as the "cradle of the middle class," the family unit has received attention from scholars concerned with gender and class formation in nineteenth-century America.[4] A study of family and domestic life can also yield insights into the lives and aspirations of educated women. By placing Elizabeth and Margaret Shippen at the center of this family story, I seek in this chapter to move beyond a study of the family as a socioeconomic unit to consider the intersections among women's educational pursuits, their family life, and their search for mere equality. Surrounded by supportive family and friends, women enacted identities for themselves as "sensible, amiable, and accomplished" members of early national society. The practices and rituals of family-based sociability offered educated women a glimpse of what it might mean to live as the mere equals of man.

"Education That Makes the Man, or the Woman"

Elizabeth and Margaret Shippen were the daughters of Joseph Shippen III and Jane Galloway Shippen. The Shippens had family and kinship ties throughout Philadelphia and the surrounding Pennsylvania countryside. Five generations of Shippens had lived in America since the seventeenth century, building extensive family, political, and commercial networks. Shippen men held a variety of political offices in colonial Pennsylvania. Elizabeth Shippen's grandfather Edward Shippen served as chief justice of Pennsylvania and as a trustee of the College of New Jersey (Princeton University). Edward Shippen founded the town of Shippensburg, where Elizabeth's older brother John later settled. Elizabeth's father, Joseph, graduated from the College of New Jersey in 1753 and served as a member of the Pennsylvania colonial government from 1770 to 1775. During the American Revolution, Joseph lost his political office and spent the war years as a merchant outside of Philadelphia. The family suffered financial setbacks during the war, yet continued to acquire land throughout Pennsylvania.[5]

In 1783, Joseph moved his family to Lancaster in the hopes of improving their financial situation. By 1789, the family settled in Chester County on a farm Joseph named Plumley, "in memory of his mother, Sarah Plumley Shippen." The farm was located 23 miles from Philadelphia, which allowed the Shippens to visit regularly with members of their extended family. Plumley was a fine home, but Joseph never regained the material prosperity enjoyed by previous generations of Shippens. After the American Revolution, according to Randolph Shipley Klein, historian, Joseph was unable to "assume the family role and responsibility" held by his father and grandfather.[6] Although Joseph became a judge in the Lancaster county court, he did not maintain a steady economic affluence and worried about his children's financial futures. Joseph counted on rents from his land holdings in Shippensburg for income. The family patriarch became dependent on his son John, who managed these properties, for cash. As Elizabeth wrote to John in 1799, "Papa desires me to acquaint you further, that after you have made the yearly settlement and received the monies due on acct. of the sale of Lands and the rents at Shippensburg, he shall want his share of those monies, as soon as it is convenient for you to bring them or to send them by a safe opportunity, having depended on a supply of cash from that part of his Estate to answer his necessary purposes."[7] Joseph Shippen relied on such gentle dispatches written in his daughter's hand to convey his economic needs to his son. This exchange indicates how for the Shippens the American Revolution disrupted both patriarchal authority and the family fortunes. Elizabeth and her siblings thus came of age during a transitional time for her family in particular and for American families in general. Throughout the colonial period, the family had functioned as a "little commonwealth," serving as a model for various social, economic, and political systems based on deference, hierarchy, and patriarchy. This colonial family model was grounded in a worldview that emphasized women's "innate" subordinate status to fathers, husbands, and other male authority figures.[8] The American Revolution partially challenged this political and social order, calling into question the organization of both government and the family. As new political and family models emerged in response to these various changes, a more egalitarian emphasis on union, harmony, and affection replaced—at least in theory—patriarchal authority.[9]

Influenced by Enlightenment thinkers such as John Locke, who conceived of children as "blank slates," the era recast the family unit from a little commonwealth to a more child-centered model.[10] Early national child-rearing guides increasingly emphasized affectionate bonds between parents and children, softening puritanical notions of children as inherently sinful. "The state of childhood is, in itself, so attractive," as John Burton wrote in 1794, "that they, who can behold it, without pleasing emotions, must be destitute of sensibility. We are naturally affected at the sight of infantine beauty, innocence, and simplicity." Various writings privileged tender familial bonds, stressing parents' "natural affection" for their children and "those finer feelings of love and tenderness."[11]

Along with nurturing affectionate bonds between parents and children, early national families increasingly regarded education as a critical component of childhood. As Samuel Whiting, author of *Elegant Lessons,* explained, "The foundation of knowledge and virtue is laid in our childhood; and without an early care and attention, we are almost lost in our very cradles: for the principles we imbibe in our youth, we carry commonly to our graves. It is education that makes the man, or the woman." Authors encouraged parents attend to the social and intellectual development of their sons and daughters to make them good men and women. "As their years advanced, they were admitted into the best companies and conversations," Whiting advised, "and had such books put into their hands as might acquaint them with rules of prudence and piety in an easy and familiar way."[12] Whiting's preoccupation with the "best companies and conversations" mirrored John Shippen's advice to his sisters about the importance of "improving your mind and manner." As did many early national families, the Shippens imparted valuable lessons to their children about education, sociability, and family life.

These cultural and class-based changes in family values reflected larger political, economic, and demographic transformations. Increasingly, families regarded the proper education of sons and daughters as a necessary means to achieve or maintain their socioeconomic standing. Although Joseph Shippen's children inherited the status associated with the family name, they would have to find their own ways to achieve material success in post-Revolutionary America. There was no guarantee that future generations would achieve the levels of affluence enjoyed by colonial Shippens. With the family's socioeconomic status uncertain, any individual pursuit of education inevitably served familial as well as personal ambitions. Writing to his brother Joseph in 1806, Henry Shippen, Joseph Shippen III's youngest son, acknowledged the role his family played in his educational decisions: "Your writing to me about going to College is the cause of my going. When Papa read the letter, he said he expected I would go to Carlisle this spring but would not think of Princeton at all. 'Twas quite out of the question." It is unclear why Joseph Shippen refused to consider Princeton for Henry, as he had graduated from there in 1753 and Henry's grandfather Edward Shippen had served on its Board of Trustees for twenty years.[13] Despite the objection to Princeton, the family expected that Henry would attend college. Early national families increasingly viewed college education as a means for men to secure professional careers in emerging market economies.[14]

As Henry's comments suggest, individual educational plans were family matters, subject to family council and approval. After a tutor left his position in the Shippen home in 1798, the family worried about the educational prospects for Joseph and Henry, ages fifteen and ten, respectively, at the time. As Elizabeth informed John, "I wish an eligible plan could soon be fixed upon for the Boys, particularly for Joseph, as the backwardness of his education render it necessary that something should be done speedily." Elizabeth took an active role in procuring "an eligible plan" for her younger brothers. She wrote to her mother in early 1799 from Philadelphia, providing information about Joseph and Henry's options: "Dr. Hall is highly recommended by Dr. Rush as a teacher, and Dr. R. thinks it is the most eligible place to send Boys to, that he knows of, and that he designs to send another of his sons to him. The charge is £60 per annum for teaching, boarding, &c."[15] Henry and Joseph spent the next several years attending various academies, and both eventually attended Dickinson College in Carlisle, Pennsylvania. In a letter home, Henry reflected on his long educational journey:

> After having long strolled from place to place, and wandered from school to school, I feel very happy in being at last permanently situated at a College where I am to finish my education. And although Dickinson College is none of the best, yet it is best at which it was in my power to take a degree. I had not formed any high idea of the excellence of this seminary, and consequently I am not disappointed. . . . I feel satisfied with it; knowing that a good education does not depend as much on the College as on the attention and application of the student.[16]

Although Henry and Joseph benefited from access to new educational opportunities, each step in their educational journeys was subject to council from various members of the Shippen family and also dependent on Josephy Shippen III's ability to provide financial support. The Shippen family's ardent interest in Henry and Joseph's educational pursuits reflected the preoccupation of the era with career success for young men. It is worth noting that despite his financial setbacks, Joseph also supported the educational aspirations of his two youngest daughters, whom he sent to be educated in Philadelphia. Although often strapped for cash, Joseph recognized the value of education in assuring his family's continued status.

Yet, if a son's education was designed primarily to provide economic prosperity to the family, a daughter's education was directed toward the social family circle. "If thou has a daughter," as one essayist remarked, "remember that she is formed for social life." The proper training and education of women were part of a new cultural landscape, reflecting the emerging values of the "republic of taste." Proper education, as Catherine Kelly argues, "was intended to cultivate the values and behavior that marked the virtuous citizen."[17] Properly educated women embodied the traits of intellect, sociability, and sensibility that were vital to early national visions of gentility, refinement, and status. Elizabeth and her siblings made sense of their individual pursuits of education within this familial model. While in Philadelphia attending school, Elizabeth wrote home to her mother, "For though I am very happy in being with my good Aunt and Cousin and particularly as it was for my improvement that I came, yet I shall not regret leaving the City to enjoy the company of my dear parents and brothers."[18] Elizabeth understood that her pursuit of education ultimately served the social family circle. Indeed, both her extended visit to Philadelphia and her brother's attendance at Dickinson College were part of the same family project. The Shippens looked to education and sociability as key vehicles by which the family would reinvent itself in an era marked by both fresh opportunities and constraints.

Compared to their brothers, however, Elizabeth and Margaret enjoyed only limited opportunities for educational pursuits. Because no colleges admitted women at the time, the sisters' educational journeys came to an end well before that of their brothers.[19] The Shippen sisters could not expect to attend colleges, prepare for law practices, or find professional employment in growing commercial economies. Law and custom circumscribed the outward expressions of women's intellectual accomplishments. Society— especially the social family circle—remained the chief outlet for educated women's energies. Thus, when Samuel Whiting wrote, "it is education that makes the man, or the woman," he aptly revealed the fundamental paradox of mere equality.[20] Although men and women possessed equal intellectual capacity, there were clear gendered differences regarding the prescribed uses of education. Men acquired education to pursue a variety of professional and economic opportunities, whereas educated women trained primarily for their roles as sensible, amiable, and accomplished members of the social family circle.

Families who supported their daughters' educations may have had class-based motivations for doing so, yet for many young women, access to education had individual effects, inspiring them to enact new social identities that celebrated their intellectual capacities. Within their family circles, educated women experimented with what it meant to live merely as the equals of man.

"Encouraging You in Writing"

While visiting her brother John, Elizabeth wrote home to her sister Margaret, "I went to take a walk in a beautiful grove which is near the town. My companion was Cowper's task, a great favorite of mine, but I should have enjoyed both that and the walk with a much greater relish, had I been accompanied by my Sister Peggy."[21] In a single passage, Elizabeth linked several elements that were central to Shippen family values: the importance of letter writing for keeping in touch with absent family members, the culture of sensibility's romantic idealization of nature's sublime beauty, and family members' pursuit of shared literary and educational interests (with a book serving as a substitute for her sister's companionship).

Like other young women coming of age during this period, Elizabeth Shippen developed a sense of self that was firmly rooted in the ideals of sensibility, sociability, and intellect. Elizabeth valued the opportunities for intellectual and social exchange available in her social family circle, relying on her parents and siblings for support and validation of her educational efforts. Undoubtedly, she would have agreed with the sentiments expressed by another early national woman about the bonds of sisterhood:

> Sister by nature, such we have been in truth
> Near of an age—with hearts connected
> Hand in hand—together we have trod thus far
> The path of life—together fled our years
> From scenes of sport—of toys—and tolls—Through all
> The laboured hours of school, and toils.
> Amidst the court of book, expanse of thought,
> And growth of mind—mingled our tasks, and joys.
> Our hours of home retreat, and sober bliss,
> We passed as one—Our hearts were concord.[22]

Anna Marie Cornell, the author of these verses, conveyed her familial, emotional, and intellectual bonds with her sister Margaretta. Siblings who together experienced "growth of mind" helped shape their "home retreat" into a place that celebrated the presence of educated women. In a poem addressed to her brother, Elizabeth Wister also praised her family home: "Where friendly hearth and blazing fire/Shall mutual cheerfulness inspire."[23] That these women used the medium of original verse to communicate with their siblings indicates their desire for continued literary expression, even after their school days had ended. For many young women, their family circle provided a safe, nurturing space for them to enact identities as learned women.

Family members nurtured and supported women's intellectual development in various ways. Rachel Van Dyke's older brother Augustus assisted in her efforts to learn Chemistry. "It is my own fault that I have not done it before—for he is very willing to teach me," she noted after reciting a lesson to him. In addition to such direct oversight, parents and siblings lent and discussed books with one another, engaging in patterns of mutual reader's response similar to those common in female friendships. "I was very much pleased with 'Wakefield's Family Tour,' which you was so kind to lend me," Elizabeth Pierce wrote to her father. Eliza Teackle expressed gratitude to her brother-in-law for "the book he was so good to send me, and feel well convinced that it contains a great deal of useful instruction." Violetta Bancker reminded her brother Charles of his promise "to write out for me a catalogue of books, such as would be useful to me."[24] The willingness of fathers and brothers to share and procure books for their daughters and sisters helped create a supportive environment for educated women within their family circles.

Like other early national families, the Shippens regarded education as an essential family value. As we have seen, family members weighed in with their opinions on tutors and schools, and kept track of one another's educational journeys. At one point, John Shippen helped procure a tutor for his younger brothers, who in turn also provided instruction to a visiting niece. "I am highly pleased to hear that our niece Polly is under the tuition of Mr. Thomson," John wrote to Elizabeth, expressing his hope that the tutor "will be found a useful member of our family."[25] The Shippens actively cultivated a family circle marked by mutual instruction and improvement.

Supportive family circles enabled women to continue academic pursuits, even after they returned home from attending school. Elizabeth asked her brother John to point out "any incorrectness" that appeared in her letters, an indication of her continued desire for intellectual improvement. John assured Elizabeth that "you shall always find a candid cheerfulness on my part to discharge of so agreeable a duty towards you." Although eager to offer his assistance, John modestly wondered if he was capable of the kind of instruction Elizabeth was seeking: "With respect to your remarks on my capableness of affording you instruction I am obliged to say that had I in my younger days paid that attention to my studies and the improvements of my mind which I might and ought to have done and which I enjoyed such great opportunities of doing I might have felt a confidence of fully deserving the compliment you have paid me."[26] John did not present himself as superior in intellect or understanding. Instead, he urged his sister Elizabeth to confide in him as an equal: "You know my dear Betsey you command my friendship my advice my opinion my candor my confidence—fear not then my dear sister to be unreserved with me on every subject that concerns your happiness."[27]

With John's encouragement, Elizabeth gained confidence. Inspired by her brother's support, Elizabeth in turn became a mentor to her younger sister Margaret. Elizabeth offered constructive criticism about her sister's writing, indicating the siblings' continued interest providing advice and instruction to each other:

> In answer to your letter of yesterday I must say that, although it contains a few mistakes in orthography, and is in some parts a little incorrect, yet it is extremely well expressed; Nor do I tell you this last merely for the sake of encouraging you in writing, tho' the idea of its having this desirable effect, makes me feel greater pleasure in telling you this truth... being encouraged by it to continue the useful practice you have lately commenced of writing letters, the great advantage of which will more and more forceably strike your mind the longer you continue it.[28]

Letter writing provided siblings with opportunities to engage in various modes of intellectual expression. As Sally Wister mused to her sister Elizabeth, "We have frequently *felt* the satisfaction arising from literary intercourse during the hours of absence, as a substitute for those free communications we used to hold at the conclusion of the day—when our visitors had left us, and we had lain our work and books aside."[29] When separated, the Shippen siblings also relied on patterns of "literary intercourse" to take the place of lively and instructive conversations typically held within the family circle.

Correspondence allowed family members to discuss a variety of intellectual subjects and philosophical musings. Away from the family home to study law, Horace Binney assured his sister Susan that his weekly letters would contain "a mixed mass of Marriages, Births, Deaths, Politics, Religion, Law, Lots and Funded Debt." Family letters expressed affection for loved ones but also contained witty refrains, literary references, or recommendations of favorite books. The Shippen siblings took this process a step further, at times inserting "mini compositions" within letters otherwise devoted to general news about family members' health and well-being. In one letter to Margaret, Elizabeth included a lengthy essay devoted to friendship: "What my dear is more delightful than true Friendship? What affords greater relief to the mind than opening the heart with unreserved confidence to a dear and faithful Friend? It calms and tranquilizes the mind, which is agitated, with painful or pleasing emotions, or both at once; for I believe they are often felt together." These stylized conversations served multiple aims. They allowed the Shippen siblings to practice expressing themselves on a variety of topics to sympathetic audiences. As Elizabeth noted to Margaret, "it is very clever to exercise yourself in writing on a particular subject."[30] As individual letters were often shared with other family members, these particular portions may have been read aloud, serving as springboards for continued conversations in the family circle. Letters were at once instructional and entertaining, replicating the intellectual and emotional exchanges that took place during face-to-face gatherings.

Eager to emulate her older sister, Margaret asked Elizabeth to recommend specific topics for their letters. Elizabeth's suggestions for subjects revealed the values she held most dear:

As to what you mention respecting my giving you some subject to write upon, I confess I feel somewhat at a loss, as I don't know what subject to propose. I think however it ought to be of a familiar easy nature, which would not require much reflection, and I am not certain what you would consider as such. But I can mention two or three, namely, the pleasures of a country life, and the advantages to be derived from retirement, the advantages and pleasures of reading History and other well chosen books; on the study of Astronomy, how greatly it must improve the human mind.[31]

Just as her brother John did when she asked him for instruction, Elizabeth evoked a note of humility. Yet she quickly embraced the role of mentor to Margaret, eager to provide instruction and guidance. Elizabeth's recommended topics—including history and astronomy—indicate the importance of education to her sense of identity, and her desire to impart similar lessons to her younger sister.

Through such conversations—which took place both in letters and in the family circle—Elizabeth and Margaret cultivated a shared identity as learned women. They celebrated the joys of intellectual expression, while reinforcing values at the heart of the Shippen family ideal. Not surprisingly, Elizabeth chose sociability as the subject for another composition:

I do not envy the Hermit in his cell, who has no friends to share with him in anything, for he must either be entirely destitute of social feelings, or must lead a life of penance indeed! I envy neither the solitary Hermit, as I said, nor beings of a class exactly the opposite, those who are constantly in the round of dissipation, for as the former has no society to enjoy, so the latter has too much to be capable of enjoying it with any satisfaction. A happy medium between these two extremes is much the happiest state, and the state I think we possess at the dear place Plumley, which I love more and more every time I leave it, and it now often presents itself to my mind as the most delightful spot in the world.[32]

Elizabeth considered her family home "the most delightful spot in the world," because it provided space and support for her to unapologetically enact an identity as a sensible, amiable, and accomplished member of polite society. With the support of her parents and siblings, Elizabeth enthusiastically cultivated the traits of intellect, sensibility, and sociability that were central to her sense of self. The family circle represented an ideal social space—neither solitary nor dissipated, but rather a "happy medium"—where educated women could put their training in both mind and manner to good use.

"Amusement Blended with Instruction"

Musing to his sister Margaret, Henry wrote, "Brother Joseph and I often sit by the fire and think, what are you doing at Plumley, one time we suppose you are sitting round the fire talking, or reading, another time we suppose you are drinking tea or perhaps something else and so my thoughts run on."[33] Families such as the Shippens cultivated patterns of enlightened sociability that provided supportive environments for young women eager to improve in both mind and manner. As Maria Cornell urged her daughter while visiting an uncle's home, "In such society you must be a ninny (as the saying is) not to derive benefit and the advantage of so good a library must be an additional source of improvement."[34] Within their social family circles, educated women inhabited a world full of promise and potential, in which they envisioned lives as the mere equals of their supportive male family members. In her description of the Wirt family home, Margaret Bayard Smith encapsulated the ideals of family sociability that promoted and celebrated women's intellectual accomplishments:

> We were ushered into a very large and elegant drawing room, in the middle was a round table, cover'd with books, engravings, work-boxes &c &c lit by a splendid lamp. Round the table was seated the young ladies and 2 young gentlemen. A rousing hickory fire blazed in the chimney and diffused warmth and cheerfulness through the room. On one side of the fire Mrs. Wirt, with a small table and candles by her, sat reading. I have never seen such a union of comfort and elegance, I might say splendor.[35]

The Wirts embodied the characteristics of the social family circle idealized by early national Americans. Central to this vision was the warm, easy sharing of books and ideas. As Margaret Bayard Smith stressed, "the best part of the entertainment was intellectual." The Wirt daughters "brought me their albums to look over, full of beautiful paintings, and original poetry—they were quite a treat." The evening was marked by lively conversation, interspersed with singing and musical instruments. "The domestic habits, style of living, and the character of this family," Margaret mused, "come nearer to my beau-ideal, than that of any other I know."[36]

Educated women received praise for skillfully enacting a style of living rooted in the easy sharing of intellectual pleasures. Harriet Margaret Wharton described one acquaintance as her family's "brightest ornament," commending her "graceful animated manners and a cultivated mind." Henrietta Teackle was particularly pleased with a new friend, whose "good sense renders her the most agreeable companion." Mary Cogswell was charmed by her hostess in Albany: "[she] is a most agreeable woman, her conversation is always interesting and improving and often lively and entertaining." Eliza Southgate described her aunt as "both a useful and instructing companion."[37] Although educated women expressed admiration and respect for each other, they also counted on support from male relatives and friends. "How instructive and desirable is the converse of a man whose natural endowments has received the sweet culture of education," Elizabeth Wister mused. "A friendly intercourse with men of sense," she continued, offered "amusement blended with instruction." Jane Bayard Kirkpatrick found "it was really a treat to have the company of a man so intelligent—pleasant and communicative." Eliza Southgate enjoyed the company of one male visitor: "we had a fine 'dish of entertainment' served up with great taste, fine sentiments dressed with elegant language and seasoned with wit."[38]

Within their social circles, educated women looked for—and found— family and friends who valued their intellectual accomplishments. Samuel Bayard, brother to Jane Bayard Kirkpatrick and Margaret Bayard Smith, grew up in a household that valued women's intellectual expressions. Comfortable in the company of his well-educated sisters, he developed close friendships with other intellectual women. Samuel praised the family home of Sally and Elizabeth Wister, "beneath whose hospitable roof we have so often of late enjoy'd the pure pleasures of unceremonious friendly conversation." The Wister home, as Samuel mused, was "the residence of reason, wit and hilarity." Within such family circles, men and women participated in "unrestrained communication of sentiment—grounded on friendship and clouded by no apprehensions of censure or criticism." The ability to freely discuss a variety of subjects without "censure or criticism" may have been particularly appealing to educated women, enabling them to envision a social world marked by expressions of mere equality. Family friends delighted that "we are in some degree actuated by a similarity of taste—a congeniality of feeling—that we are qualified to cultivate the plant of friendship." As Samuel Bayard mused in another letter to Sally Wister, he was pleased to have the "opportunity of establishing an intimacy with persons so suited to his intellectual taste, and so well qualified to improve the manners and delight the heart." For many families and friends, common "intellectual taste" provided a particular source of pleasure. As William Wister noted to his cousin Susan Foulke, "The imparting of our ideas is our greatest pleasure and our greatest happiness."[39]

The emphasis on shared pleasures reflected the influence of the culture of sensibility, which encouraged men and women to empathize and identify deeply with like-minded individuals. "Indeed," as Elizabeth Shippen wrote, "every pleasure in life is rendered more pleasing when joined by our friends in partaking of them."[40] Patterns of emotional and intellectual affinity cultivated in the social family circle served as a framework for men and women's interactions in the world at large. "We were born to be citizens of the world," one author noted, and sensibility and sociability contributed to "harmony and union, without which our lives would be unhappy in the extreme." The presence of educated women was vital to these early national visions of social harmony: "Society requires that females should be well *educated,* and extend their influence as far as possible over the other sex." Family sociability thus prepared women to assume influential roles in early national society. As another essayist asserted, "Cultivation of the female mind is of great importance, not with respect to private happiness only, but with respect to society at large."[41]

"The Harmony of Social Life"

While attending school in Philadelphia, then the capital city of the nation, Elizabeth Shippen had access to a vibrant political scene. In letters home, she discussed political affairs, especially as Congress debated the terms of John Jay's treaty between the United States and Great Britain. Elizabeth hoped to witness some of the debates personally, but she was unable to gain admittance to Congress Hall, "which was no small disappointment." Elizabeth cast her growing interest in political matters with a reassuring disclaimer to her parents: "Do not think I am too great a politician every person has been interested in this affair." Elizabeth's extended visits to Philadelphia introduced her to an array of political, social, and intellectual gatherings. During another visit to the city, she mingled with some of the noted citizens of Philadelphia. "I spent a very agreeable evening at Uncle Shippens last night," Elizabeth wrote to her mother. "The same company . . . are to spend the evening here, and also Dr. Rush's family, and some other Ladies and Gentlemen." Immersed in a world of political, social, and intellectual exchanges, Elizabeth expressed a desire to extend her visit: "Every person tells me, I must stay to go to General Washington's birth night, which will be celebrated by a Ball at the Theatre." Elizabeth embraced opportunities to participate in these varied scenes of interest: "I have spent my time very agreeably since I have been in Philadelphia," she informed her father."[42]

Whether in her social family circle at Plumley or at a grand ball honoring George Washington in Philadelphia, Elizabeth Shippen's experiences of sociability were decidedly heterosocial and representative of a larger social vision expressed by a number of social and political thinkers. Central to this vision was a celebration of women's roles as intelligent and accomplished members of society. As the author of an 1801 essay titled "On the Influence of Female Society" emphasized, "the company of ladies has a very powerful influence on the sentiments and conducts of men." Although some people believed that it was "proper" for "persons of the same age, of the same sex, of similar dispositions and pursuits, to associate together," "J. M. P." insisted that "the true propriety and *harmony* of social life depend upon the connection of people of *different* dispositions and characters, judiciously blending together." Ultimately, the "harmony of social life" could be found in interactions that included both sexes. As "J. M. P." noted, "that union is the happiest and most proper, when wants are mutually supplied." Both men and women benefited from their gatherings together: "The fair sex should naturally hope to gain from our conversation, knowledge, wisdom and sedateness: they should give us in exchange, humanity, politeness, cheerfulness, taste and sentiment."[43]

Like other social thinkers of the era, "J. M. P." expressed a vision of mere equality—men and women freely coming together to create a world marked by social, emotional, and intellectual affinity. "J. M. P." did not suggest that men and women were the same, nor did he advocate for true equality between the sexes. The existence of differences—sexual but also other forms—was a given. Yet difference was not presented in terms of conflict or hierarchy but, rather, as a source of harmony and affinity. *True* equality might seek to erase or discard difference; *mere* equality rested in complementary relationships between the sexes.

The "harmony of social life," as articulated by "J. M. P." and other authors, was rooted within and sustained by heterosocial interaction. Although political and economic forces could create sources of tension, unrest, and discord, society enabled family members and close friends—young or old, male or female, single or married—to gather together harmoniously. Society was governed by the rules of harmony and affinity, and women provided a stabilizing, calming influence. Indeed, the idealization of women's influence in society may have been especially important given the many tensions, disputes, and violence that marked the partisan world of early national politics. A harmonious society was seen as the glue that held the republic together, even—or especially—as political divisions brought the threat of disunity and faction to the young nation.[44]

This prescriptive vision certainly resonated with the social experiences of early national families such as the Shippens. A sense of egalitarianism underscored both prescriptive writings as well as personal experiences with sociability. Whether the event was an intimate tête-à-tête, a walk along the river with friends, or a formal celebratory ball, the practices and rituals of early national sociability provided men and women with varied opportunities to interact together. From parlor games to tea parties, from formal balls to country walks, men and women inhabited common spaces and developed mutual interests. These shared experiences have called into question whether the boundaries of "separate spheres" were as sharply defined as historians once imagined. Evidence from various geographical regions and across the socioeconomic board offers new ways of mapping the social and intellectual landscape of early national America. Charlene Boyer Lewis's study of southern antebellum leisure culture, Catherine Kelly's work on middle-class women in New England, Karen Hanson's account of New England "working people," and Claire Lyon's narrative of the Philadelphian "rabble" all reveal fluid mixes of men and women in a variety of social settings.[45] Although single-sex patterns of sociability and fraternization also existed, heterosocial interaction was an expected, common part of life. Historians' dichotomous associations of separate spheres or sharp delineations between "public" and "private" spaces would have had only limited meaning to most early national men and women, who instead viewed their interactions with others primarily as "social."[46]

As both a shared experience and an interpretative category, the "social" is crucial to our understandings of how early national men and women made sense of themselves and the world around them. Social interactions between men and women took place in settings that historians might have previously defined as strictly private (a parlor, tea table, or similar domestic space) or public (a museum, theater or public square). Nevertheless, although tea parties and intimate talks may have taken place in family parlors, they often consisted of men and women discussing politics and other current events. Generally, it was the interaction between people, not the physical space itself, that defined an event or setting as social. The social blurred binary distinctions in that seemingly private relationships were infused with multiple meanings, depending on the setting and the company present. On July 4, 1798, Elizabeth Shippen took part in a "fishing party, consisting of fifteen young Ladies and Gentlemen." The occasion was the "Anniversary of American Independence"; the celebration itself was informal and heterosocial. A decade later, Sarah Connell "went up to Union Hall, and assisted in ornamenting it with flowers" for the Fourth of July festivities of her town. She later attended a procession "composed of a large number of respectable Republicans," accompanied by music and oration. During their Christmas dinner, the Griffith family and their guests gave a series of literary and political toasts to "Walter Scott—Walsh—Miss Edgeworth," along with one to "The President of the United States of America."[47] Within such settings, individuals would have struggled to draw sharp lines between private and public, between personal and political, between entertainment and instruction.

Although the social was characterized by fluid heterosocial interactions that blurred distinctions between private and public, clear boundaries of class and race defined its borders. In articulating his vision of early national sociability to his sisters, John Shippen tellingly referred to "the best company" and "good breeding."[48] Early national Americans used class, status, and rank to form "select" social circles. These class- and race-based groupings may have actually enabled more fluid interactions between men and women, creating a world of class cohesion. Select social settings sought to create an ideal society where harmony reigned and conflict was minimal. The company of educated women was essential to the harmony of social life "to harmonize our jarring passions, and attune them to virtue."[49]

A brief examination of salon culture reveals the complex ways in which the social family circle functioned in elite society during this era. Salon culture offered intellectual women ample space to shine merely as the equals of man, but it also represented a carefully orchestrated vision of sociability rooted in distinctions of race, class, and wealth. The Manigault-Izard salon of Philadelphia, according to one male visitor, "was the resort of all the intellectual and refined society of our City. . . . Men of wit and science knew where they could always find congenial society of both sexes."[50] Salon culture enabled "intellectual and refined" men and women to engage a variety of literary and political discussions. Salons reflected socioeconomic as well as personal aims as elite families sought to maintain class cohesion, political stability, *and* personal enjoyment. Yet it is important to emphasize that the setting and practices of salon culture sought to mirror the ideals of family sociability. Elite salon families privileged the ideals evoked by quiet evenings at home. As Margaret Manigault mused, "We are sociable—but we all agreed that it was pleasanter to stay at home, and read, and work." Margaret's daughter Harriet shared her mother's preferences: "We always pass our time so pleasantly at home, that any party must be very delightful in order to compensate." Three generations of Manigault-Izard family women agreed that there was no place like home. "I think their own agreeable, rational home will have the preference," Alice Izard wrote to her daughter Margaret Manigault, "yet the contrast, within due bounds, is agreeable, and they will relish the pleasures of their Mother's conversation, and of sensible books the more; from feeling how vain, and foolish, and extravagant the joys of dissipation are."[51]

The stated preference for quiet family-based forms of sociability reveal early national ideas about how to best model social and political interaction. Writing to Marianne Williams, one woman idealized the family circle: "I often imagine I see your little family circle enjoying social harmony with all the unreserved gaiety of pure and affectionate hearts—tell me my dear friend if this picture is realized." By contrast, individuals frequently lamented the dissipation and superficiality that characterized large parties and balls. "My enjoyment has been principally confined to our own family and a few others where we are intimate," Mary Cogswell wrote, "for I never pretend or expect to take the least comfort in large parties or ceremonious visiting." Sarah Connell expressed similar sentiments, insisting, "I am not fond of a large promiscuous acquaintance, though no one enjoys more than myself, the society of a few select friends." Early national Americans reiterated their preference for select social circles, where they could enjoy emotional and intellectual exchanges with like-minded family and friends. "The bustle and gaiety of our little town has measurably subsided," Henrietta Teackle wrote to her sister, "with heart felt pleasure I return to reason and domestic life."[52] Such idealizations reflected individual and cultural desires for harmony and affinity, cultivated in social settings that promoted both "reason" and "pleasure."

For young women, early national patterns of sociability offered a variety of opportunities to enact roles as sensible, amiable, and accomplished members of society. Yet in other ways, the ideals promoted by the social family circle constrained the ways in which educated women might hope to live merely as the equals of man. In particular, the strong cultural emphasis on harmony socialized women to maintain peace and contentment within the family circle at all costs.

"The Peaceful Pleasures of Domestic Happiness"

Writing to Margaret Shippen, Catherine Eddowes, a cousin and close family friend, articulated her vision of intellectual and domestic harmony: "I have now a little leisure for reading, for thinking of my friends, and for walking out, and this I believe is all that is necessary to my happiness." Catherine and her family rarely attended large parties, "content to enjoy the peaceful pleasures of domestic happiness and the society of a few agreeable friends." She was confident that the Shippens held similar tastes: "in idea I join your family circle and am delighted while I contemplate you cheerful, composed and happy." Catherine had accurately described Shippen family values. As Henry Shippen mused to his sister Margaret, "There is more real satisfaction in domestic enjoyment—and in a happy cordial connection with a few families."[53] Along with other early national families, the Shippens privileged scenes of domestic enjoyment cultivated in the family home and shared with close friends. Within the social family circle, men and women cultivated common bonds of intellect, sensibility, and sociability sustained by egalitarian and harmonious interactions.

Yet as the nineteenth century progressed, economic and cultural transitions recast the family circle from a social to private space. Early national Americans viewed domestic enjoyment and family sociability as "social," a fluid continuum of gatherings shared between men and women in a variety of settings. In response to market economies, political unrest, and other cultural forces, antebellum Americans increasingly sought to "feminize" and "privatize" the family circle.[54] A realignment of gender roles accompanied this shift, resulting in an ideological reconfiguration of the family circle. The ideology of separate spheres sought to relocate the source of "domestic enjoyment" from the social to the private. The early national experience of the social family circle contracted to fit the more narrowly defined private sphere of the antebellum period.

The limits of mere equality as a concept for articulating gender roles and relations contributed to this realignment. Within their family circles, educated women could expect to experience a degree of mere equality with their male siblings and supportive friends. Cultivating common bonds of intellect, sensibility, and sociability, early national women and men crafted relationships and social spaces based upon the pleasurable and instructive exchange of ideas. Family and friends valued women's intellectual expressions and contributions to the social circle. As one author enthusiastically noted, "The most delightful moments of our existence are derived from the society of an amiable and intelligent woman!"[55] Yet this focus on the harmony of social life obscured the realities of early national gender roles. As we have seen, the Shippen brothers attended college, preparing for new careers and professional lives that would take them away from the family circle. In 1797, John Shippen moved to Shippensberg, where he managed the family land holdings in that area. Elizabeth expressed confidence in John's abilities and prospects: "Methinks I behold in my Brother John, a promoter of the happiness of his fellow townsmen, by introducing among them the benign spirit of Unanimity and Concord—by inspiring them with just sentiments, and by exciting in them a laudable emulation, in the place of selfish contention."[56] Elizabeth's admiration of John's character reflected values central to the Shippen family, with harmony and happiness chief among them. Yet as John's world expanded, Elizabeth's remained static, underscoring differences regarding prescribed uses of education for men and women.

Despite a growing gender gap, Elizabeth remained devoted to her older brother, looking forward to his letters and visits to Plumley. In 1799, she traveled to Shippensberg, eager to meet her brother's fiancée. Writing home to Margaret, Elizabeth expressed her approval: "I spend my time here, as you will readily believe, very agreeably, and am very frequently in the company of our charming friend Abby." Writing about her growing friendship with her future sister-in-law, Elizabeth noted, "It is just as I would wish, delicate, friendly, unreserved, unaffected, candid, and sincere.... For my part, I can truly say that the more I know her the more I love and esteem her." The traits that Elizabeth found so agreeable in Abby were equally admired by her fiancé. Elizabeth enthusiastically noted that her brother "entertains the most exalted opinion of his amiable Friend, and very justly too for she is highly deserving of the sentiments he feels for her: He is happy in possessing the esteem and affection of one of the finest women in the world." That John and Elizabeth would feel a similar sense of "esteem and affection" for his fiancée is not surprising, given the Shippen family's prizing of both sense and sensibility. In both friendship and romantic love, individuals longed for a sense of mutuality sustained by common interests, thoughts, and emotions. Harriet Margaret Wharton expressed similar approval of her brother's wife, praising her "uncommon sense, and prudence," which her brother—"a Man of superior mind"—clearly appreciated.[57]

Elizabeth was in attendance at John and Abigail's wedding in summer 1799: "I would not have missed coming up for a great deal, particularly as I observe the great satisfaction my being here affords to my dear Brother and his intended Bride." Yet Elizabeth was the only member of the family to attend John and Abigail's wedding, "on account of the expense that would necessarily attend the jaunt." Although grateful for Elizabeth's presence, John expressed disappointment that the rest of his family was not present at his wedding: "Indeed on an occasion so solemn so important and so interesting the presence of my worthy Father and Mother and all my Brothers and Sisters would have been highly grateful to my feelings. But this or any thing like it I was not at this distance to expect."[58] In addition to highlighting Joseph Shippen's continued financial constraints, John and Abigail's wedding marked a growing tension in the Shippen family circle. As the siblings matured and began to set up their own households, their social family circle became increasingly difficult to maintain.

More tragic events complicated the geographical and financial constraints that the Shippens faced. Shortly after John and Abigail's wedding, Elizabeth died during her visit to the newlywed's home in Shippensberg. Elizabeth's unexpected death devastated the family. As one family friend wrote in consolation, "The vague manner in which the news of her sickness first reached us, led us to hope that it was totally unfounded—we were unprepared for the shock which followed." Months after Elizabeth's death, John attempted to express his grief to Margaret: "You are doubly dear to me as a sister, in a manner, which I decline to recite, and it fills my eyes with tears, and would tend too much anew to excite your griefs." Her family deeply felt Elizabeth's loss. As John wrote to Margaret, "I loved that dear girl, I love her memory, I *shall* love her, I shall never lose sight of her." Elizabeth embodied the qualities of intellect, sociability, and sensibility that were central to the Shippen family ideal. As John eulogized, "Wherever she went she did honor to herself and credit to her Parents, and gave happiness to all around her, in many places, she unconsciously gave instruction. I am sure my dear sister Peggy will imitate her amiable example,—nay, I have every reason to believe, they traveled in their journies [sic] together, and that sister Peggy will continue to travel the same paths which she trod in virtue and improvement."[59]

John praised his sister Elizabeth, giving particular emphasis to her qualities as an accomplished, intelligent woman. Through those qualities, Elizabeth gave both "happiness" and "instruction" to those around her. She "set us an example which we ought to be proud of imitating," one friend wrote to Margaret. "Her good sense, her lovely modesty, and innocence, that delicate sensibility, and purity of thought, all which discovered themselves so easily in her graceful yet unaffected manners."[60] Although Elizabeth's intellectual powers received merit, she was also remembered for typical feminine virtues, qualities perhaps best appreciated within the social family circle.

Young women such as Elizabeth Shippen clearly enjoyed the acquisition of education for its own pleasures but were socialized to put their talents to use on behalf of others, not in pursuit of more selfish ambitions. As a dutiful daughter and affectionate sister, Elizabeth directed her energies toward her social family circle, her ambitions presumably extending no further. Eager to express herself on a variety of subjects, Elizabeth Shippen's various compositions on friendship and sociability were penned within family letters, rather than for the literary public sphere. Although family members and close friends celebrated women's intellectual accomplishments, mere equality offered women only limited opportunities to exercise their literary talents.

Indeed, educated women who published their writings sometimes struggled to articulate their desire for intellectual expression outside the family circle. This tension is illustrated in the poetry and prose writing of Elizabeth Wister, who wrote the following verse to her younger brother William:

> A soft vermil light—pierced the shadow of night
> And the Halo of Genius displayed
> I sought to enlighten—to polish and brighten—
> My theme by the radiance it made—
> But vainly I tried—the Muses deride
> Effusions so vapid & dull
> I seldom have time to wander in rhyme
> Or Garlands poetic to cull—[61]

As Elizabeth Wister explained to her brother, "I can not write to my own taste—and have too good an opinion of thine to believe thou wilt derive from thince any pleasure, I aspire not to fame—all its avenues are thorny—its ascents steep—and its Mountain air too refined too pure for me to inhale." In her poem, Elizabeth Wister presented a more ambivalent expression of her identity as a learned woman than the modest disclaimer she penned for her brother. She admitted a desire for "genius," but derided the qualities of her own "effusions," and confessed that she found it difficult to "have time to wander in rhyme." And although Elizabeth Wister published several of her poems in the *Port Folio,* she carefully denied any aspiration for "fame."[62]

Mere equality provided little space for feminine genius to flourish outside the walls of the family circle. Many educated women accepted these constraints, devoting their intellectual and emotional energies toward their families, rather than in pursuit of more individual ambitions.

"I Must Endeavour to Be Contented"

After Elizabeth Shippen's death in 1799, it was up to Margaret to travel in her sister's footsteps of "virtue and improvement." The Shippen brothers all married, established careers for themselves, and settled in various areas across Pennsylvania. Only Margaret remained unmarried, caring for her father after her mother's death in 1801. Joseph Shippen III and Margaret eventually moved back to Lancaster. Both the emotional and geographical center of the family dissolved in the wake of these transitions. "I do not doubt but that you will feel a great deal on bidding farewell for ever to Plumley," Joseph reflected to Margaret, "the place where we have spent the greatest part of our lives, where all our family once lived together and the center from whence they are now dispersed on different sides."[63] In many ways, the promise of mere equality that the family cultivated at Plumley was lost as well. As the years progressed, Margaret took on not only the care of her father but also the primary role of family correspondent. Her brother John found it difficult to write or visit, "situated as I have been for some time past with a very great variety of business and engagements." Her brothers sporadically kept in touch, but Henry also admitted to being an imperfect correspondent: "You know that I am but a poor correspondent at best, and seldom write except for some particular purpose—But I hope Betsy and Frances have sufficiently supplied my deficiency in this respect."[64]

With the Shippen brothers distracted by business and career concerns, the responsibility of caring for the social family circle increasingly fell to its female members. Henry's wife served as a surrogate for his family correspondence, and Margaret took on the role of the family "center." These emotional duties left her with little free time to visit with friends or pursue her own interests. "You say you are determined *never* to leave your Father again," her friend and cousin Catherine inquired, "but my dear is not this *never* a bold word?" Ultimately, Catherine understood that Margaret was "so good a daughter that I suppose I am to take it in the full extent of its meaning." It was Margaret's responsibility to maintain the family circle for her father and male siblings.[65] Her path of "virtue and improvement" led not to personal autonomy but to familial cares.

In nineteenth-century America, the emotional work of maintaining family ties became increasingly gendered. Women's expressions of mere equality within their family circles were constrained by these gendered constructs of home and work. Many daughters and sisters quietly accepted the limits of mere equality, even if they longed for more expansive roles within early national society. As Harriet Margaret Wharton reflected, "I find both duty and inclination lead me to devote my Evenings to my dear Mother." Harriet devoted herself to needs of her family, suppressing her own desires: "I must endeavour to be contented," she sighed. As a dutiful daughter and sister, Margaret Shippen also directed her energies towards her family. A poem transcribed in her commonplace book praised Margaret for remaining "intent upon her destin'd course: / Graceful and useful in all she does." Yet that destined course was within her family circle, "far from the world's gay busy throng."[66]

Within their own natal families, women enacted identities as learned women that were often simultaneously expansive and constrained, reflecting paradoxical understandings of mere equality. In courtship and marriage, educated women had opportunities to create their own social family circles. Would romantic love enable women to live merely as the equals of man?

❧ CHAPTER 4

"The Union of Reason and Love"

Courtship Ideals and Practices

Writing to his fiancée, Linda Raymond, in 1818, Benjamin Ward shared his hopes for their relationship: "I anticipate in you, a companion, whose friendship is not founded on the combustible materials of enflamed passions; but in whom is *'The union of reason and love;'* in whose society I shall ever receive a pleasure, and who would abhor to awaken in the bosom of your friend a sensation destructive of his peace and comfort." Like many early national couples, Benjamin and Linda's expectations for marital happiness centered on a companionate ideal that privileged an affectionate union between loving partners.[1] As Benjamin's comments suggest, the couple placed central importance not only on romantic attraction but also on shared intellectual foundations. The "union of reason and love"— and not any effort to distinguish these two elements—formed the basis for an egalitarian marriage rooted in both emotional and intellectual affinity. Simply put, courtship was a matter of both the heart and the head.

Courting couples frequently relied on the egalitarian language of friendship to stress the importance of compatibility in love and marriage. Friendship and love existed along the same emotional continuum; both stressed mutuality, affinity, and shared interests. Yet there was an important distinction between friends and courting couples—friendship bonds could be permanent and lifelong, whereas courtship was necessarily a temporary and transitional stage. Courting couples inevitably sought an end to their courtship period and a new beginning in marriage. For many courting couples, thoughts of the future produced optimistic visions of companionate marriage as well as deep introspections about the importance of choosing the right partner. "The more I consider how much depends on our choice of a bosom friend," Benjamin noted, "the more I am convinced of the import and consequence attending it."[2]

In their "choice of a bosom friend," Benjamin Ward and Linda Raymond sought a partner with whom they could share intellectual as well as emotional bonds. As an educated woman, Linda may have found a union of reason and love particularly appealing. She came of age in an era and a family that valued educated women's contributions. Linda attended at least two female academies, and her parents also financed the educational efforts of one of their neighbors, who later established a female academy.[3] Linda saw how education could enable a young woman to reinvent herself. Did she hope to translate ideas about the empowering aspects of education into a marriage founded in the principles of mere equality?

Yet was a truly egalitarian marriage possible in early national society? Scholars such as Elizabeth Dillon and Ruth Bloch maintain that, despite the companionate ideal, early national marriages "were still predicated on male dominance and gender difference."[4] Despite these tensions, Benjamin and Linda remained committed to the companionate ideal and found inspirational models—as well as important cautionary tales—in a variety of sources. In particular, the couple engaged in practices of mutual reader's response in which they carefully crafted a "customized" version of mere equality inspired by the various models of friendship and love they encountered in print. Benjamin Ward and Linda Raymond's private interpretations of print culture enable us to explore how men and women responded to and reshaped various prescriptive and literary models for behavior and conduct. In the midst of multiple, often competing representations of friendship, courtship, and love, Benjamin and Linda remained determined to craft a union of reason and love. In the process, they explored both the possibilities and boundaries of mere equality.

"Mutual Exchanges with the One"

In November 1817, Benjamin Ward wrote to Linda Raymond, hoping "to be considered worthy" of her "friendship" and "estimation." Although "as yet unacquainted with your character," Linda assured Benjamin that his request "met with a friendly reception." Thus began a courtship that lasted for nearly six years—from November 1817 until their marriage in September 1823.

During this time, Benjamin and Linda exchanged letters on a regular basis, writing to each other approximately once a month. Throughout most of their long engagement, Linda and Benjamin lived in different towns and saw each other only during his occasional visits to her home. Benjamin, who was twenty-four at the time their courtship began, lived and worked as a law clerk first in Shrewsbury and then in Petersham, Massachusetts. Five years younger than Benjamin, Linda lived with her parents and worked as a teacher in her hometown of Rindge, New Hampshire.[5]

Courting couples who lived in the same towns relied on everyday patterns of sociability to strengthen their relationship. Courting men often became part of young women's social family circles, which enabled couples to spend time together in the company of family and friends, as well as providing opportunities to enjoy quiet walks together or intimate tête-à-têtes. Sarah Connell's courtship with Samuel Ayer developed through his frequent visits to her house and their frequent "walk[s] down to the river" together. Eliza Southgate met her future husband during an extended visit to the Ballston Springs with friends, where "for 4 weeks I saw him every day and probably had a better opportunity of knowing him than if I had seen him as a common acquaintance in town for years."[6]

Many courtships were conducted primarily in person, disrupted by only occasional absences due to work or travel. "How hard it is to separated from those we love even for a few weeks," John Douglas lamented during a brief separation from his fiancée. Yet from the outset, Benjamin Ward and Linda Raymond anticipated a lengthy engagement marked by long periods of physical separation while Benjamin worked to establish himself profession-ally. "Years of separation, Adnil, still to pass!" Benjamin lamented in January 1818. "Perhaps those years if spent in improvement may be most advanta-geous for our future happiness.... Perhaps the endearments may multiple and the ties of affection still strengthen as time passes." Benjamin hoped that "distance is no intervention between sincere and truly affectionate hearts." Linda agreed, assuring him that "absence rather serves to strengthen than diminish the prepossession which has been previously formed."[7]

Because their relationship was marked by long absences from each other, the couple relied on letter writing to maintain and strengthen the bonds between them. "How greatly is the sweet intercourse of friendship improved by an often and sincere correspondence," Linda mused, "and thus my friend we may enjoy all the pleasures of such a connexion let the distance that sepa-rates us be ever so great." "Must not the gratification be infinitely greater," Benjamin agreed, "when, with the same confidence and assurance we have mutual exchanges with *the one,* who in our affections is nearer and dearer to all others?"[8] Letters helped long-distance couples create a world of sentimental expression that substituted for everyday encounters of intimacy. Couples used their correspondence to plan, hope, and dream about their future life together, in essence creating a shared "narrative" or "script" of their relationship. Letters often contained remembrances of favorite moments spent together, scenes of imagined togetherness, and musings about their upcoming marriage.

To help deal with their physical separation, Benjamin and Linda frequently "imagined" the other's presence in their daily lives. As Linda wrote, "Permit me to say had *you* been of the party it would have added greatly to the happiness of Linda."[9] The use of the imaginative enabled the couple to create a sense of shared experience that seemed to transcend time and space. Upon viewing a summer's sunset, Benjamin mentally placed Linda at his side: "Imagination added to my pleasure, for I was actually fancying you happy in the same view. . . . Excited by the real and imaginary, I tho't myself at the side of my friend, fondly pressing her hand; and as we stood enjoying so much from admiration and sympathy, I was ready to exclaim, to the heavens before us, how beautifully sublime!" Letters that evoked this sense of togetherness "brought you in my imagination so near me," as one man wrote to his fiancée, "that for a few minutes I almost forgot, what an extent of land and water lay between us."[10] These imaginative musings evoked the sense of deep affinity and shared experience that was at the heart of the companionate ideal, with letters serving as literary substitutes for actual togetherness.

Perhaps because Benjamin and Linda spent so much time crafting imagined scenes of togetherness, their face-to-face meetings took on elements of heightened expectation. In their visits together, as Benjamin remarked, "all was real." Yet the "real" was bookended by written expressions of anticipation beforehand, as well as by retellings of visits in subsequent letters. Benjamin and Linda reflected on their visits in letters as a means of reliving the joys of togetherness while simultaneously dealing with the freshly awakened pains of separation. As Benjamin wrote after one of his visits, "Our late interview and the circumstances attending it, seemed like the illusions of a very pleasant dream."[11] In the process, the "real" (face-to-face visits) and the "imaginative" (writing and musing about their encounters) became inextricably connected. Letters provided a continual narration of their courtship, serving as sites of both remembrance and expectation.

With so much of their relationship "scripted" through letters, it was often difficult to determine where the imaginative left off and the real began. The relationship existed as much—if not more—in print as it did in person. Benjamin and Linda's writings paralleled the experiences of other nineteenth-century romantic couples, who "often read and wrote love let-ters as if they were in a conversation that might be overheard." Letter writing enabled courting couples to share expressions of love, and as Ephraim Abbot noted in an 1811 letter to his fiancée, to "convey…the overflowings of a warm heart…which is known only to kindred souls." George Munford employed similar language in his love letters, idealizing "free, unrestrained communication between kindred spirits."[12]

Yet communications through writing could be tricky because individu-als doubted their ability to express themselves properly. "I am constrained again to send you a letter," George Munford wrote in another letter his fiancée. "Oh that I could talk with you as we were wont, instead of this writing." John Douglas looked forward to his next visit with Eleanor Hall: "I have a good deal to tell you and prefer the word of mouth plan to any other." Although correspondents urged their loved ones to "write…without reserve," for many courting couples, letter writing was marked by a persistent tension between candor and restraint. After one visit to Linda's home, Ben-jamin noted that "'language is poor' and inadequate an idea of my sensa-tions when reflecting on the scene that had lately closed."[13] Writing words on paper changed the nature of emotional expressions from private speech to printed discourse. Letters helped ease the pain of physical separation, but individuals trusted their face-to-face encounters more than their written correspondence.

Individuals worried that their letters might inadvertently, as Benjamin feared, be "exposed to the world!" Although their letters were privately addressed and meant for each other's eyes alone, the very act of putting words on paper carried the danger of exposure to others. Benjamin recognized that his letters were "not mere sounds uttered in private, but words permanently recorded." Worried about the conveyance of their letters, Linda remained "anxious with regard to their safety—People you know have a curiosity to know and see all that's in their power."[14] Fearful that their letters might fall into someone else's hands, courting couples were ambivalent about fully revealing themselves in print. Individuals sought to share intimate expres-sions, but struggled with the limits of written communication.

Concerns about letters accidentally being read by others may explain why couples rarely used sexually explicit language in their letters. On only rare occasions did Benjamin evoke expressions of physical desire and intimacy. After one visit to Linda's home, he wrote, "My heart still throbs with that ardency of affection as when we last were happy in each other's arms." In another letter, Benjamin fondly imagined a physical encounter in language laced with sexual innuendo: "I press with numerous kisses her lovely lips inspiring rapture at every touch." Yet worried that such ardent expressions "exceed the bounds of prudence," Benjamin rarely used sexually charged language in his letters. There are *no* examples of sexually explicit language in Linda's letters, suggesting that she did not feel comfortable expressing such desire on paper.[15]

Socialized to be modest and diffident, young women may have experienced more ambivalence than men when it came to self-expression through courtship letters. Benjamin complained that Linda's letters were too "brief," and there was truth to his criticism in that his letters generally tended to be more lengthy and effusive than hers. Although Linda wrote shorter letters than Benjamin, she insisted that she would "cheerfully give my opinion upon any subject you wish." Linda worried that her letters were not "interesting or amusing," but she also feared, as she admitted in another letter, "unforeseen accidents [that] might bring them to public view to the great mortification and chagrin of the writer."[16] Linda's diffidence reflected the power of prescription, which stressed the importance of female modesty and prudence. John Burton, author of *Lectures on Female Education and Manners,* advised women "to act with the utmost caution and vigilance" in their communications, especially with men. "If you love him," Dr. John Gregory's popular advice to women urged, "let me advise you never to discover to him the full extent of your love." Such advice discouraged young women from engaging in the effusive communications privileged in courtship letters. Yet their fiancés urged women to write without reserve, to "forget for a moment those feelings which co-operate to check" more expressive sentiments.[17]

Some women seemed hesitant to write freely about their courtship experiences, even in confines of their own diaries. "Since I wrote last Charlotte got hold of it and read it through," Harriet Manigault reflected after her sister found her diary, "and oh how glad I then was that I had been so discreet." Such reticence may have reflected Harriet's guarded personality. "I might choose to write a great deal upon that subject," she later wrote in reference to her fiance's frequent visits, "but I don't *choose* to, and as it appears that I am not always to consult my own will," she quipped, "I shall avail myself of that liberty while I can." Sarah Connell felt more at liberty to write without reserve. Describing a walk with her fiancé Samuel Ayer, Sarah mused in her diary, "How much do I enjoy a walk of a fine evening with a companion in whom I feel interested, and whose sentiments are congenial to my own!...In listening to their sentiments, and telling them all our own with unbounded confidence!" Sarah recognized that "many would call this enthusiasm," although for her, such sentimentality was essential to the courtship experience.[18]

Courting women's expressions of "unbounded confidence" varied, reflecting individual interplay between prescriptive advice and personal experience. In letters to her fiancé, Christine Williams strove to communicate freely, but not without a certain guardedness. "I will endeavour to banish all improper or unnecessary reserve when you wish to converse on any subject that you think important," she wrote. "I am sensible of the propriety of doing so." Christine recognized that restraint in communication could create confusion: "I find that in treating of the ambiguity of your expressions; my own were not sufficiently clear to escape misconstruction." As she found her voice, Christine took her fiancé to task, criticizing him for interpreting her recent silence as "owing to my being in a pet. . . . Indeed if you know me well," she charged, "you would not suspect me of insinuating what I would not say openly."[19] Courtship letters remained subject to misreading or misinterpretation, even when individuals attempted to communicate unreservedly.

If the content of courtship letters was shaped by various concerns over privacy, candor, and self-expression, the conveyance of correspondence was another source of possible tension. Letters that failed to arrive on time could engender doubt as individuals wondered what caused "so great a lapse" in a loved one's correspondence. Linda was "astonished" to learn that a letter she wrote a month earlier had not yet reached Benjamin. Such instances of lapsed or miscommunication were common, particularly due to the idiosyncratic nature of early national mail delivery.[20] More troubling were letters that failed to arrive because they had not been written. "What can be the reason I do not hear from you," Thomas Biddle wrote to his fiancée Christine Williams. "It makes me extremely uneasy." Letters helped sustain courtship during periods of physical separation; any disruption to the expected pace of correspondence could potentially signal a change in one's affections or commitment. In winter 1821, Benjamin neglected to write for three months, distracted by illness and out-of-town visits. Expressing her concern at his lengthy silence, Linda remarked, "Did you know the anxiety I feel when there is a longer space than usual between your letters; particularly when your health is in its present situation, I am sure you would not suffer a neglect in *writing*." Benjamin regarded Linda's reply as "an affectionate reproach that I cannot but feel most sensibly."[21] A year later, however, Linda failed to write to Benjamin for three months, "a longer time than has ever elapsed between my letters," as she conceded. Linda offered no lengthy apology for *her* silence, merely acknowledging "the receipt of three letters" written by Benjamin during that time. Linda's epistolary silence, as Benjamin later admitted, made him "quite anxious."[22] The anxiety these temporary disruptions created was repaired only when their correspondence resumed its typical patterns of frequency.

Discussions about the delivery, frequency, and content of letters reflected larger concerns about love and commitment. Letters were representations of relationships and were thus carefully scrutinized for signs of both sincerity and deception. For truly egalitarian relationships to flourish, couples needed constant reassurance that each partner was equally committed to the union of reason and love.

"Fancied a World of Bliss"

Letter writing was a key means by which courting couples sustained bonds of affection, yet the process was fraught with concerns about expression, delivery, and communication. This ambivalence mirrored the courtship state itself, in which individuals often experienced both optimism and anxiety. The repeated assurances of trust, candor, and sincerity that appeared in courtship correspondence can best be understood with these tensions in mind. As a poem Benjamin shared with Linda early in their courtship suggests, the search for true love often created a state of emotional vulnerability:

> The fond desires, to share the bliss we feel
> With the friend lov'd most, and our hearts reveal,
> In sweet anticipation of imparting pleasure,
> And gaining in return the inestimable treasure,
> Reciprocated love; and feeling realized—
> Not be common friends and basely criticized—
> By false ones—[23]

The companionate ideal celebrated true love in emotionally charged language, but this enthusiasm was checked by tense fears about false friendship. On the surface, true and false affection presented an obvious study of contrasts. As the author of "Real and Pretended Love Contrasted" suggested, true love was "the source of the tenderest enjoyment, and the most pleasing emotions; the other, of misery and discord, of upbraiding and complaint." Too often, what individuals thought was true love ended in heartbreak and disappointment: "Wide as is the difference between real and pretended Love, yet how often are they mistaken the one for the other! For, however base or selfish the *real* motive is, still Love is the constant bait made use of to gain the unsuspecting." In a sense, the companionate ideal made men and women more susceptible to the dangers of deceit and duplicity. Men and women risked being "baited" by false friends all too willing to take advantage of their ardent search for true love. As one article noted, "Much evil and unhappiness is occasioned by discovering too late how woefully we have been deceived by false representations."[24]

Duplicity in courtship and love could be painful and embarrassing. Linda described the cause of one acquaintance's "stupid active life" to Benjamin: "he has been disappointed in Love—A young lady to whom he was partial, has married another person." Mary Guion reflected on a failed courtship by wondering, "why should I grieve for the loss of pretended Friendship from a person who perhaps knew it only by name.... Oh! what a villain!"[25] Although both men and women experienced heartbreak and despair due to emotional betrayal, women also had to fear the physical consequences of sexual seduction. Early national literature abounded with tales of "seduced and abandoned" women who fell prey to the false promises of rakes and scoundrels. Prescriptive writers repeatedly warned that a young woman must guard herself against a "base deceiver" who "seeks his guilty gratification in the destruction of virtue and innocence." As Charles Peirce, educator, warned, friendship was the ready tool of the seducer: "Thousands of women... have been ruined by men, who approached them under the specious name of friendship."[26]

Linda Raymond apparently took warnings about seduction to heart. Before her courtship with Benjamin began, she wrote a poem titled, "Verses Addressed to a Young Lady on Her Leaving School." The poem contains several warnings about men's duplicity. "In friendship with the other sex," Linda warned, "Be cautious they are apt to vex." Throughout several stanzas, Linda reiterated young women's need for caution in courtship:

> To lovers act with modest spirit
> Trust them according to their merit....
> Yet don't too easily believe
> For man my Anna will deceive[27]

Linda's youthful poem contained a guarded distrust of men and stressed the need for caution in relationships with the opposite sex. In conducting her courtship with Benjamin, Linda remained mindful of these lessons. In one letter to Benjamin, she included a cautionary tale about one of her close friends:

> A young lady perfect amiable in her manners and conversation (a particular friend of mine) formed an acquaintance with a young student who is now at the Theological Institute at Andover, received his professions of Friendship and love without suspecting in the least the sincerity of his attachment—But now he is guilty of the crime—Ingratitude—However, she is perfectly cheerful, and presume she thinks herself happy in discovering before it was too late to retract the (disposition of her pretended friend) favourable opinion she formed of him.[28]

Her friend's only solace was that she discovered her "pretended" friend's duplicity before it was too late—presumably, before she had entered into a formal engagement with him or before she became a victim of seduction. The emotional stakes of courtship affected both men and women, but women faced the added risks of sexual seduction and illegitimate pregnancy.

Mindful of various disappointments and heartaches around them, Benjamin and Linda engaged in various discussions about the importance of true friendship and love. Early in their courtship, the couple sought to create clear models for conduct and behavior. As Benjamin wrote in November 1818, "I anticipate in *you, Linda, a friend on whom the most unbounded confidence may ever be placed without the least danger of infidelity!*" Uncompromising in his emotional standards, Benjamin set high expectations for their relationship: "If you tell me, 'that is too much to anticipate of any one'—Then with bleeding sorrow I shall exclaim, Leave me, to float among the stream of time a solitary visit convinced that the boasted name of Friendship is but a phantom, performing a life of 'single blessedness' to the false shew of Matrimony and Love." Benjamin claimed that he would rather live a solitary existence than enter into a marriage lacking fidelity, confidence, and mutuality. His strong demands for fidelity may have seemed overwhelming, but Linda wholeheartedly shared Benjamin's convictions, asserting that "unbounded confidence without infidelity etc." was not "too much to expect" from one's "partner for life." Indeed, she continued, "it is not enough." Linda agreed that she would rather "exclude myself entirely from society and its charms than bestow my heart on one whose every wish was not for the happiness of his friend, and for his fellow creatures."[29] Benjamin and Linda insisted that they were equally committed to the same ideals—and agreed that these ideals required mutual efforts. As Benjamin noted, couples who failed to uphold this mutuality of effort often faced disappointment in married life: "Look into the domiciles of many who are young and have families, and how much do they appear to have enhanced their enjoyments by matrimony? Do we find any who probably fancied a world of bliss before them on tying the nuptial knot, discover . . . disappointment? What do their internal dwellings prove?—the very contrast of their probable expectations!"[30]

The companionate marriage promised a "world of bliss," but couples who entered into marriage with unrealistic expectations perhaps inevitability experienced disappointment. It may seem odd that Linda and Benjamin repeatedly wrote about betrayal and heartbreak in their love letters to each other. But by offering examples of other couples' mistakes, Benjamin and Linda hoped to apply the lessons found in various cautionary tales to their own relationship. Against real-life examples of false friendship, the couple increasingly turned to literary sources to help craft a union of reason and love.

"A Union of Sentiments Cultivated upon Every Subject"

"It is said by an enthusiastic writer that 'letters have souls,'" Linda mused to Benjamin. "If not they have wonderful power and are the source of happiness to Friends." For courting couples in particular, letters were powerful modes of expression. As Linda's reference to an "enthusiastic writer" suggests, individuals often relied on published authors as sources of both emulation and inspiration for their own communications. Throughout their courtship, Benjamin and Linda actively created a world of shared literary expression and mutual reader's response.[31]

Shared literary pursuits enabled couples to craft a sense of intellectual and emotional affinity—or the perfect union of reason and love. As their courtship progressed, Benjamin proposed that they share with each other "the notice of any book...that pleases you." Linda enthusiastically agreed, eager to use their letters for "communicating our own thoughts and those of Authors." In their letters, the couple began "transcribing for the perusal of your friend whatever you find which you thought would be interesting."[32] Through transcriptions of poetry and prose, the words of favorite authors served as conduits for their own communications. In one letter, Linda relied on poetry to describe her ideal companion:

> I've often wish'd to have a friend,
> With whom my choicest hours to spend,
> To whom I safely might impart
> Each wish and weakness of my heart
> Who might in every sorrow cheer
> And mingle with my griefs a Tear
> For whom alone I wish to be
> And who would only live for me[33]

Linda clearly chose this poem with Benjamin in mind, but the use of poetry meant that she did not have to state her wishes directly. Transcriptions provided a language of sentiment, which was useful at times when individuals had trouble or hesitancy expressing their own emotions on paper. Print culture offered various models of behavior and mutually understood "scripts" that helped couples to create narratives of their own relationships. Throughout their courtship, Benjamin and Linda shared a variety of writings with each other, including poetry, novels, periodicals, and history—but clearly favored early romantic authors such as Lord Byron, Sir Walter Scott, and Johann Zimmerman. Mutual appreciation of romantic texts provided Benjamin and Linda with a shared sensibility that strengthened both the emotional and intellectual bonds between them. As Benjamin noted, "There is a pleasure in having made the same observation upon the same subject."[34]

Linda and Benjamin found an ideal model in Johann George Zimmerman's *Solitude Considered with Respect to Its Influence upon the Mind and Heart*. A German romantic writer, Zimmerman extolled the virtues of "enlightened friendship" that existed between like-minded individuals. Inspired by Zimmerman, Linda included a "lengthy quotation" of his writings in a letter to Benjamin:

> A tender faithful and refined friendship . . . is founded on unlimited confidence and affection and reciprocal interchange of sentiments and opinions. . . . The happy pair casting a retrospective glance on the time pass'd, mutually exclaim, O! the delights we have already experienced— If the tear of affliction steal down the cheek of the one, the other with affection wipes it away. The sorrows of the one are felt with equal sensibility by the other—And what sorrow will not on intercourse of hearts so affectionately united, entirely subdue.[35]

Benjamin responded enthusiastically to Linda's selection: "My lovely L— you have pictured to identify the enchanting scenes of *happy life* that my own Fancy often brought to view, and that Hope would persuade me to anticipate." It is not surprising that Zimmerman was a source of mutual delight for Benjamin and Linda. Early romantic writers stressed a heightened degree of affinity rooted in the "reciprocal interchange of sentiments and opinions"— that is, the cultivation of shared emotional and intellectual interests.[36]

Although Zimmerman relied on the language of friendship to describe such affinity, his model translated well to courtship. Romantic writers privileged the individualistic notion that one's "true" or "inner" self was a unique, private, and specialized core of identity. To fully realize one's true self, it was necessary—and desired—to achieve a deep sense of connection with others.[37] An individual's identity was validated in relationship to another individual with whom he or she experienced a heightened degree of affinity. Courting couples sought to create this intense sense of mutuality. As Benjamin mused, the couple longed "to sympathize in each other's feelings and hold the sweet communion of souls." Ephraim Abbot shared similar sentiments with his fiancée: "I have long felt that you are a part of myself. . . . My heart seems to be you, and you seem to be my heart."[38]

This sense of shared identity was at the heart of the companionate ideal, yet it departed sharply from dominant prescriptions that stressed inherent differences between men and women. As several historians have shown, prescriptions for early nineteenth-century gender roles were crafted from the related ideologies of separate spheres and sexual difference. The prescriptive literature repeatedly asserted that men and women were dissimilar beings with contrasting natures, dispositions, and characters. As one author insisted, differences between men and women, "though forming in themselves an evident contrast, serve to illustrate each other." The "evident contrast" between the sexes in turn formed the basis for men and women's division into separate spheres of work and activity. Writers urged women to "consider it not only a duty, but a pleasure, to be occupied in domestic manners." Any deviation from these prescribed roles "would be contrary to the liveliness of their disposition, and for such they were not designed."[39]

Under a separate spheres framework, some historians have suggested that true intimacy and emotional fulfillment between men and women was difficult, if not impossible, to achieve. Yet many courting couples rejected such prescriptive models and instead favored the egalitarianism promised by romantic writers such as Zimmerman. Against prescriptions of gender difference and separate spheres, men and women privileged concepts of shared identity in order to craft alternative models of gender relations. Although immersed in a culture that viewed strictly defined gender roles as normative, courting couples such as Benjamin Ward and Linda Raymond focused not on their differences as man and woman but, rather, on their interconnectedness as romantic and intellectual partners. Courtship and marriage were conceptualized as relatively equal partnerships into which men and women freely joined together. This emotional standard favored a vision of mere equality, in contrast to patriarchal ideologies that enabled male mastery and dominance in domestic matters.[40]

As they created a union of reason and love, Benjamin and Linda were drawn to writers that promoted the ideals of mere equality while ignoring prescriptions that stressed difference and discord. In particular, Benjamin and Linda seemed immune to prescriptive warnings about the supposed conflict between female learning and desirability—what one writer referred to as the "fear of *female pedantry*." Even some supporters of women's education cautioned women not to pursue subjects "useless in the particular spheres in which nature has desired them to move." The literary public sphere was filled with the notion that women too interested in intellectual pursuits inevitability threatened the status quo, especially their desirability to men. "If you happen to have any learning," Dr. Gregory cautioned, "keep it a profound secret, especially from the men, who generally look with a jealous and malignant eye on a woman of great parts, and a cultivated understanding."[41]

Far from feeling threatened by educated women, men such as Benjamin Ward actively supported the intellectual interests of their fiancées. Linda did not feel the need to keep her learning a secret but, rather, freely shared her educational acquisitions with Benjamin. "I have read Virgil and am much pleased with it," she wrote in July 1818, and in the same letter she informed Benjamin that she was reading "the History of America." Benjamin urged her to communicate "any sentiment worthy of preservation" and especially recommended shared reading practices as a means to "enlarge the satisfaction and pleasure generally received from the perusal of books." Ephraim Abbot also encouraged his fiancée to recommend books to him: "I admire your good judgement, be assured I shall always esteem your recommendations sufficient for the perusal of any work." Such men viewed shared intellectual interests as essential to the courtship experience. Awaiting her fiancé's return from a business trip, Harriet Manigault noted in her diary, "I long to read the Iliad and Odyssey, but am under a promise not to read them to *myself.*" Shared intellectual expressions provided couples with additional sources of affinity. As Charles Bancker entreated to his fiancée, "let your pen obey the dictates of your own ingenious mind, in its expressions I should delight.... Hand in hand we will pursue objects of higher import."[42]

Early national Americans developed new appreciations of educated women that, in turn, shaped understandings of and expectations for courtship and romantic love. Remarking on the "slated beaux" for her niece, Catherine Judd singled out one man as worthy of her attention: "you would not be ashamed, he has stored his mind with all the history extant." In a curious reversal of stereotypes, Catherine cautioned, "he is too great a novel reader—but I think him very amiable." Maria Cornell worried that her cousin's suitor fell "far short of the man I would select for my dear Trude." The man in question lacked "that energy of character" and "mind" that Maria felt was essential for "true happiness." Before giving his blessing to his daughter's wedding, John Teackle sought to ensure that the gentleman "in all points of view is her equal." "When I think of your education, disposition, character, and situation," a family friend wrote to Susan Binney, "*you* my dear ought certainly to be well assured you find *real worth* in the person." In particular, this friend insisted that Susan's future husband needed to possess "integrity, sound judgment, real generosity, and rational attachment to you.... Observe I say *rational* attachment," she emphasized.[43] Friends and family recognized that educated women sought partners who would appreciate their identities as learned women. Shared intellectual interests provided expressions of mere equality within courtship and marriage.

Through rational attachment, promoted through the union of reason and love, some educated women began to imagine lives merely as the equals of man. Unlike prescriptive models that warned about the ill effects of women's education, there was no perceived conflict between knowledge and desire; love and learning were inextricably connected. Indeed, in his imaginative visions of Linda, Benjamin often pictured her engaged in intellectual pursuits: "Imagination, my friend, often flits at the close of day to your place of abode, beholds you sitting by your father's fireside ... occupied in agreeable conversation with those around you, or in thoughtful mood ruminating on subjects worthy your choice and attention, but I often see you through the same medium with a book in your hand reading, not merely for amusement, or as is the case with some 'bookish folks,' to pass the dull hours away, but reading for information."[44] Linda's various intellectual interests increased her worth as an ideal partner. Benjamin imagined her as a serious, thoughtful woman who added to the "interest and pleasure" of those in her social circle. Far from being deterred by Linda's educational accomplishments, Benjamin envisioned courtship as a space for men and women to cultivate shared intellectual pursuits. Linda agreed, writing that their "intellectual powers should be expanded" as the couple developed "a union of sentiments cultivated upon every subject."[45]

Yet in their constant search for a "union of sentiments," Benjamin and Linda also had to confront the possibility that they might disagree about particular subjects. What model of conflict resolution was compatible with mere equality? Once again, the couple looked to the literary public sphere for inspiration and guidance.

"My Lady Ashton"

In March 1820, Linda wrote to Benjamin about a rumor her father had heard that Benjamin was "bestowing [his] attentions on a Lady in Vermont and had continued correspondence with her." Linda quickly dismissed the rumor as "falsehood." Benjamin thanked Linda for her "confidence," yet questioned her apparent nonchalance regarding the rumor: "From the wonderful calmness, and perhaps I might say indifference with which you treat the subject I might infer that you have never lost much sleep on account of any serious effects it has wrought on your own mind."[46] Although Linda appeared to dismiss the rumor with "wonderful calmness," Benjamin clearly saw himself as the victim of "fiendlike slander." Apparently, a "detestable accuser" had spoken out against Benjamin's character. His cousins assured him that "your reputation is not hurt nor can it be, by this *false accusation*" and urged him to let the "detested subject" drop.[47]

Two months after this terse exchange, Benjamin shared with Linda his response to Walter Scott's novel, *The Bride of Lammermoor.* "I have been well acquainted with a parallel to Lady Ashton," he wrote in reference to one of the most unfavorable characters in the book. "I revolt with horror at such a character." Linda responded to Benjamin's comments with reserved understanding: "I think I can judge who that Lady Ashton is in the circle of your acquaintance. I have never heard how far she succeeded in her infamous attempts and suggestions at slander upon your character." Benjamin confirmed Linda's speculations, noting that he indeed had been referring to "*my Lady Ashton*": "I must take pains to avoid her ladyship but shall conduct myself much as though no such person was in existence."[48]

Scott's novel ends tragically, with true love thwarted by the extreme interfering of Lady Ashton. Benjamin and Linda may have read the novel as a cautionary tale—a reminder not to let "fiendlike slander" shake their faith in each other. Their discussions of the novel enabled the couple to diffuse tensions sparked by rumor and innuendo. By using characters from a novel to make sense of real-life circumstances, Benjamin and Linda engaged in literary shorthand on a subject that was perhaps too difficult or painful to discuss directly. To call someone a "Lady Ashton" created a useful symbol of behavior that was possible precisely because they were both familiar with the novel from which this character was drawn. Texts thus took on particular meanings as courting couples appropriated characters, stories, and poems relevant to their individual experiences.[49] Through the practices of mutual reader's response, books could serve simultaneously as tokens of affection, as shared intellectual interests, and as models for appropriate conduct.

Shared reader's response enabled Benjamin and Linda to work through tense moments in their own relationship, as well as to find areas of agreement on potentially controversial subjects. After reading a history of England, Benjamin shared with Linda a passage about "a distinguished relation of your late protégé Mary Ann Wollstonecraft her Aunt (I believe) and for whom she was named." The exact identity of Linda's "protégé" is unknown, yet she had an obvious connection to Mary Wollstonecraft, author of the famous eighteenth-century feminist polemic, *A Vindication of the Rights of Woman*. Linda replied that Wollstonecraft was indeed "the Aunt of little Mary" and noted that she had "seen the Book read it half through but did not derive profit or pleasure sufficient to induce me to see the conclusion."[50] Benjamin and Linda's brief discussion of Wollstonecraft illustrates another powerful element of shared reading practices. Literary references provided a type of shorthand that allowed individuals to indirectly discuss sensitive issues that might cause tension or disagreement. Reader's response to particular texts took on layers of meanings that were unique to individual relationships. Without directly debating the rights of woman, Benjamin and Linda quickly and quietly diffused a potential source of conflict.

The couple's critique of Wollstonecraft was neither unexpected nor unusual. By 1820, Wollstonecraft had been the target of substantial criticism, particularly after William Godwin published a biography of Wollstonecraft shortly after her death in 1797. When details of Wollstonecraft's unconventional lifestyle (including her extramarital affairs and having conceived two children out of wedlock) were brought to the public's attention, the censure against her personal life also extended to a denunciation of her political ideas. Critics vilified Wollstonecraft as an "unnatural" woman who threatened the social order. As one essay noted, Wollstonecraft "invited women to become amazons, and states*men* and directors, and harlots, upon philosophical principles." One could not subscribe to the feminist sensibilities of *A Vindication of the Rights of Woman* without also risking charges of immorality and scandal. As Eliza Southgate wrote to her cousin Moses Porter, "I am aware of the censure that will ever await the female that attempts the vindication of her sex. . . . It does not follow (O what a pen!) that every female who vindicates the capacity of her sex is a disciple of Mary Wolstoncraft [*sic*]." Although Eliza "admire[d] many of her sentiments," she equivocated, assuring her male cousin that Wollstonecraft's strong arguments "will not bear analyzing."[51] With such prejudice firmly in place, Linda was careful to distance herself from Wollstonecraft, despite an apparent connection with her niece.

Although Benjamin clearly supported Linda's intellectual pursuits, he may have stopped short of agreeing with the explicitly feminist ideas expressed by Wollstonecraft. Although committed to a romantic ideal that privileged egalitarian relationships between men and women, Benjamin and Linda could not find support for their own relationship in such a controversial source. Mere equality was more malleable than an explicit call for women's rights. Romantic writers such as Zimmerman thus provided more acceptable models for women seeking to live merely as the equals of man. Through the use of more gender-neutral language and the celebration of "tender, faithful and refined friendship," romanticism enabled men and women to craft expressive models of relational harmony that did not have to address directly questions of gender inequity and male power.

Courting couples looked to the literary public sphere for models of egalitarian friendship and affinity, shunning areas of discord that would put the concept of mere equality to the test. In the transition from courtship to marriage, Benjamin and Linda would attempt to put these ideals into practice.

"Are We to Set Forward?"

During the tension created by rumors of his misconduct, Benjamin offered Linda the opportunity to end their engagement: "Should you at any time, Adnil, be dissatisfied with your friend, either as to character, or in any other respect, think yourself at liberty to withhold future intimacy with him. Be assured that what he has often said, he repeats, that he never can desire a union with one whose love and confidence he cannot possess." Benjamin was "testing" Linda, seeking validation of his worthiness as a romantic partner. He expected Linda to remain constant in her affections, despite whatever reasonable doubts she may have experienced on hearing rumors of his possible betrayal. Linda dutifully reassured Benjamin, urging him to "never again indulge in those anticipated evils which I pray may never be so painful to you in reality, as they have been in anticipation."[52]

Yet evidence from their correspondence suggests that Benjamin's imaginative musings often carried more weight than the constancy of Linda's affections. During the six years of their engagement, Benjamin and Linda's relationship was marked by eager anticipation of marriage but also by Benjamin's repeated expressions of doubt. "Are we to set forward, *hand in hand* in the journey of life?" he worried in 1819. "Are we suitable companions for such a joint, but all important undertaking?" Even as Linda continued to reassure Benjamin, she expressed frustration with his bouts of uncertainty: "My friend you must certainly be unhappy to think that you are devoting your time, attentions, and affections to one where the attachment is not mutual." Linda's rejoinders prompted Benjamin to apologize for his "gloomy apprehensions," and he conceded that she never gave him "the least reason to doubt the sincerity of your affection."[53]

Benjamin's repeated doubts may have had less to do with Linda's affection and more, instead, to do with his fears about his professional success and worthiness as a husband. The couple's lengthy engagement was prompted by his desire to achieve a measure of professional status and economic independence that would enable him to provide adequately for a family. Ephraim Abbot, who shared a similarly long engagement with his fiancée, reflected on his situation in language that may have resonated deeply with Benjamin and Linda: "I hope we shall soon be one in name, in family, in affection and desires. I have much reason to thank and love you for waiting on me so long, and for continuing to love me when I have many times ... been so unworthy of your love and so unlikely to make you a suitable companion. ... More than five years have elapsed since I have felt, that affection for you, that a husband ought to feel for the best of women, and since I have hoped our affection was reciprocal."[54] As Ephraim acknowledged, long engagements required patience on the part of women, a willingness to wait on their fiancés. As Sarah Ripley Stearns reflected on her marriage, lengthy engagements presented challenges even to the most committed couples: "Our intimate acquaintance has continued for more than five years. During that space of time we have both met with many trials and disappointments and passed through various changing scenes." Through years of waiting, it was perhaps inevitable that couples would experience moments of doubt and uncertainty. "Our constancy has been tried," Sarah admitted, pleased to be finally "calmly settled in the still, peaceful scenes of domestic tranquility."[55]

By fall 1821, Benjamin and Linda had been engaged for four years. The time had come for the couple to assess Benjamin's career prospects and to set a date for their wedding. During this critical juncture in their relationship, Benjamin traveled to South Carolina for the winter (where his cousin lived), in the hopes of improving his health. Benjamin viewed the decision as "necessary but unpleasant," aware that the distance he traveled would prevent him from visiting Linda for months. From South Carolina, Benjamin sent Linda long letters detailing his travels, yet the trip did not seem to lift his spirits. Disillusioned by his prolonged state of financial dependence and further discouraged by his recent state of ill health, Benjamin presented to Linda an image of uncertainty, regret, and anxiety. Once again, he offered Linda the chance to break their engagement: "if you should desire to be released of all further trouble from your invalid acquaintance, you are at liberty—I never would bind one involuntarily to myself." Linda reassured Benjamin that he was "far dearer than all other acquaintances and will ever continue as long as he has a heart to love Adnil." Yet she also expressed renewed frustration that Benjamin repeatedly questioned her commitment: "I hope he will never consider himself as 'involuntarily bound' to promote happiness of one who is unworthy of his confidence, or has failed to secure his love and respect."[56]

In seeking to remind Benjamin of her constancy, Linda also informed him that her loyalty was not due to a lack of other suitors: "Had I been so disposed I have had frequent opportunities—two within six months; I received two written communications on the subject of marriage. . . . To them both, it was unknown that I had formed an attachment for *you* my Friend, which will never cease but with life." In addition to proving her loyalty to Benjamin, Linda's disclosure of these marriage offers may have served as a subtle (or perhaps not so subtle?) warning to him that others still considered her an attractive marital partner. Benjamin responded to this information with guarded gratitude: "Notwithstanding your opportunities for an honorable dissolution, and repeated solicitations from others to form a new connexion, your preference still seems to remain invariably in favor of one whose circumstances in many respects would seem most strongly to dissuade you from such preference."[57] Although he wondered whether Linda might later come to regret her choice, Benjamin was grateful for her continued loyalty.

If Benjamin's insecurity reflected professional struggles that increasingly defined nineteenth-century masculinity, Linda's constancy underscored both the opportunities and constraints that early national women experienced as they regarded their marital prospects. In many ways, Linda was a model fiancée—she was willing to wait for Benjamin to establish himself professionally, she believed his innocence against rumors of his misconduct, and she passed the tests of affection to which he routinely subjected her. Linda received offers from other interested men and could have broken her engagement if she had desired. As a schoolteacher with supportive parents, Linda had resources that would have enabled her to provide for herself financially had she remained single. Yet, despite Benjamin's repeated bouts of insecurity, she remained constant in her affections and looked forward to their marriage. She had opportunities to make her own choices, and ultimately she chose Benjamin, hoping to live merely as the equal of this man.

After Benjamin's return from South Carolina in May 1822, the couple addressed their most pressing concern: deciding where Benjamin would initially set up his law practice, which would, in turn, determine where the couple would make their home. "I shall deem that a very important day in my life," Benjamin wrote, "when I shall be established in business and blessed with the society of my affectionate Adnil." Before Benjamin's departure for South Carolina, Linda's father shared his opinions on Benjamin's career prospects. "He seems anxious you should come to Rindge," Linda wrote. "He thinks he could assist you in many ways were you here which it would not be in his power were you situated in another place." Joel Raymond's desire to assist Benjamin in his professional career was hardly his only motive for encouraging him to settle in the Raymonds' hometown. Linda's father hoped that Benjamin would assist in "collecting his demands and in many other ways." Benjamin opposed this plan, expressing serious concerns to Linda "respecting a professional man taking a stand in R[indge]." Although acknowledging the "strong inducements" of her father's plan, Benjamin admitted "a degree of repugnance to the tho't of it."[58]

Joel Raymond was equally determined, and he used Linda as the conduit to share his thoughts about the couple's future. "You seem to be 'anxious' respecting my Father's wishes," Linda wrote to Benjamin. "It is *now* his earnest desire that you should commence business in Rindge and yet he does not wish to control you." Operating under the premise of fatherly influence rather than older models of patriarchal control, Joel Raymond hoped to draw on Benjamin's sense of duty and obligation. In an effort to sway Benjamin, Linda's father appealed directly to Benjamin's anxieties. As Linda related, "My Father says, should you commence business in this place and do not find your expectations answered as it respects Law and your Profession you can easily select another and remove, But if you now go to another and do not succeed according to your wishes and he could not render you that assistance he would wish were it in his power, than to return to Rindge would be a mortification to us all."[59]

Linda's father seemed willing to manipulate the fear of failure that was common among men in Benjamin's position. As a young lawyer struggling to establish himself professionally, Benjamin undoubtedly was very aware that his initial efforts would have lasting implications for his future career prospects. By presenting his plan in terms that seemed to best serve Benjamin's professional needs, Linda's father made a convincing argument. When Benjamin received this letter, he struggled to defend his preferences against Joel Raymond's strong opinions. Benjamin admitted that the "same course of reasoning had passed silently through my mind which you say your father adopts upon the expediency of complying with his wishes." He had considered the "mortifying possibility" of failing to achieve career success. Such a possibility was of great concern, knowing he would soon have to provide for a wife and children. After considering the powerful inducements of her father's plan—but before receiving Linda's letter—Benjamin nonetheless had decided, on his own, in favor of "a settlement in Athol [Massachusetts]." "Before the receipt of your letter," he admitted, "I had pretty much concluded that that was the place which, on the whole, presented the most powerful inducements."[60]

Despite his strong preferences, Benjamin did not want to disappoint Linda's father or by extension Linda herself, who seemingly approved of her father's plan. The matter was apparently settled in person, during Benjamin's next visit to Linda's home. In a letter to Linda written after his visit, Benjamin made no direct reference to his decision but, rather, expressed renewed doubts about their courtship. "I almost lament the hour which witnessed the commencement of that friendship," Benjamin admitted, revealing a certain tension between his personal life and his professional career. "If I now was wholly independent, my ambition to rise would be unabated; but my fears of insignificance, or defeat, would be far less terrible."[61] Without Linda (or her father) to worry about pleasing, Benjamin would not have had to weigh personal factors against professional ambitions. Without Linda as his romantic partner, his fear of failure would have been diminished because professional failure would have affected only *him*. Benjamin reluctantly resigned himself to the idea of forgoing his professional ambitions for the sake of marital happiness. In accordance with Joel Raymond's wishes, Benjamin agreed to set up his law practice in Rindge.

Although this was undoubtedly one of the most important decisions affecting their future life together, Benjamin and Linda discussed it with a level of formality and tentativeness that belied cultural standards of true friendship and romantic love. The couple strove to maintain a sense of accord and harmony, despite having different preferences for their place of residence and work. Indeed, it was only after the decision had been made that Linda expressed any ambivalence. "I think of your coming to R[indge] sometimes with anxiety," she admitted. "I have thought and sometimes said heretofore that I never should wish a friend of mine particularly a professional man to settle in Rindge." Yet, significantly, Linda never mentioned such concerns to Benjamin while the decision was still under consideration and, instead, appeared to fully support her father's plans. Her reticence most likely reflected her desire to stay near her family. As she admitted, "it would be hard indeed for me, to leave them and go to a distance."[62]

Linda and Benjamin's decision-making process about the important issues of his work and their residence reveal some of the tensions and limits of mere equality. Under the companionate ideal, Linda could have reasonably expected that her preferences for their future residence would be accorded equal weight and consideration. Yet Linda did not feel completely comfortable expressing her opinions to Benjamin. Instead, she manipulated models of paternal influence, arguing her father's points, not her own. Although Linda did not simply acquiesce to Benjamin's decisions, she also failed to exert herself as a true equal partner. Her hesitancy may have reflected the prescriptive literature's continued insistence on male dominance, which urged women to "avoid, both before and after marriage, all thoughts of managing your husband."[63] Linda did attempt to manage her future husband; however, she did so not by asserting direct control but by subtle maneuvers toward the outcome she desired. Thus, her expressions of mere equality remained tentative, cloaked in stereotypically feminine attributes of passivity and acquiescence. She found it safer to state her father's wishes than to directly assert her own equality. The couple thus settled important issues about their future not with truthful, candid communications between equal partners but by deferring to parental pressures.

Linda attempted to pacify the situation by suggesting that their decision to settle in Rindge was open to future negotiation: "By coming to R. we will not suppose that we must confine ourselves to this place whether you meet with encouragement or not." By implying that the move to Rindge was temporary, Linda consoled Benjamin with the idea that "a more eligible situation may present itself" in the future. With Benjamin's professional decisions settled, the couple was ready to finalize their wedding plans. Benjamin moved to Rindge and set up law practice in fall 1822. Benjamin rejoiced that "my home, where ever it may be, will be the home of my love, of my most faithful friend, as a companion for life." Living in the same town, Benjamin and Linda finally conducted their courtship in person, not on paper. "The inconveniences of personal intercourse," as Benjamin noted, "will soon give place for opportunities of daily meeting with each other, not only as friends but as inseparable companions."[64]

"When Kindred Spirits Are Thus United"

After a courtship that spanned nearly six years, Benjamin Ward and Linda Raymond married on September 16, 1823. Linda's childhood friend Sophia Sawyer wrote to congratulate Linda on "her union with the man of her choice; and feeling that she is now enjoying all the happiness which such a connection is calculated to afford." Sophia emphasized the ideals of shared identity that Linda and Benjamin sought to achieve in marriage: "I no longer feel, when addressing you, that I am writing to you alone; . . . you are united— one in name, one in all the enjoyments, employments, and suffering of life."[65] This vision of companionate marriage echoed the sentiments expressed in various writings, in which life's joys and sorrows were shared equally, as Zimmerman mused, by "hearts so affectionately united."

As a married couple, Benjamin and Linda continued to rely on shared literary experiences to craft a union of reason and love. The couple maintained a commonplace book together, which they filled with transcriptions from authors such as Pope, Shakespeare, Cowper, and Wordsworth.[66] They signed one entry by merging their initials, suggesting their continued efforts to cultivate shared identity (see figure 6). And the fact that Benjamin and Linda carefully preserved their courtship letters suggests their value not only as romantic keepsakes but also as evidence of their efforts to cultivate shared literary expressions.

The couple's many uses of literary culture suggest connections—between reason and love, between private and public, and between knowledge and desire—that offer promising frameworks for better understanding the aspirations of educated women who sought to live as the mere equals of their romantic partners. Confronted with various prescriptive models, courting

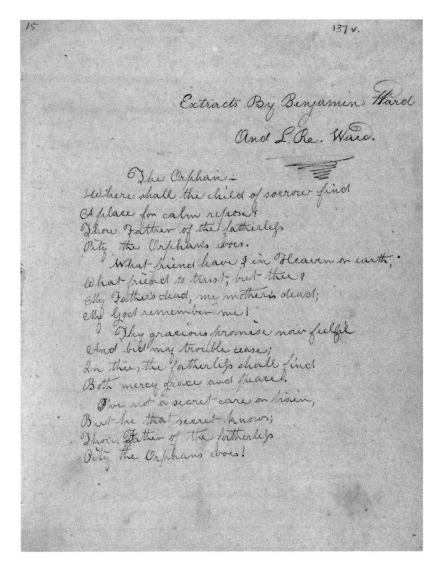

FIGURE 5. After their marriage in 1823, Benjamin Ward and Linda Raymond Ward kept a common-place together, which they filled with various transcriptions of poetry and prose. Schlesinger Library, Radcliffe Institute, Harvard University.

couples appropriated literary references that reinforced the ideals of emotional and intellectual affinity that they sought in love and marriage. This emphasis on a union of reason and love contrasted with prescriptive writings that stressed sexual difference and separate spheres. More understanding is needed about how early national men and women reacted and responded to prescriptive rhetoric—how much of it they accepted, and how much they rejected or

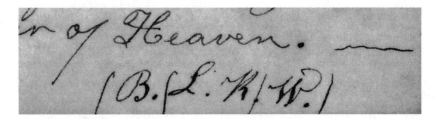

FIGURE 6. Benjamin Ward and Linda Raymond Ward signed one entry in their commonplace book by merging their initials, reflecting their persistent efforts to create a sense of shared identity. Schlesinger Library, Radcliffe Institute, Harvard University.

refashioned. The "enlightened friendship" offered by romantic writers such as Zimmerman may have held more influence over courting couples than a prescriptive writer who parodied learned ladies or one who insisted that there "a line of character between the sexes, which neither can pass without becoming contemptible."[67]

Courting couples such as Benjamin Ward and Linda Raymond did not focus merely on their differences as men and women but, rather, on their interconnectedness as romantic and intellectual partners. They sought the union of reason and love—or what we might think of as the ultimate blending of sense and sensibility. The egalitarianism inherent in Enlightenment ideas of a union between loving partners was a powerful expression of individual choice while Romanticism privileged the unique experiences of individualism and true friendship. The union of reason and love sought to fuse these two strands of cultural thought—combining an emotionally charged romance with the calming influence of rational friendship. One source referred to this model as "rational love," defined as *passion founded on esteem.* Echoing Benjamin and Linda's vision, this author privileged romantic relationships characterized by "sincere regard for the object of our affections joined with a love the most pure, rational, and dignified."[68]

As Benjamin Ward and Linda Raymond's relationship reveals, even "rational love" remained full of both promise and peril. Couples retained strong faith in the companionate ideal, even as they wondered if they would be able to realize their imaginative visions of wedded bliss. "When kindred spirits are thus united," Linda mused, "I think it entirely their own fault if their anticipations of happiness are not realized."[69] Significantly, in Linda's idealization of marriage, the burden of happiness fell to both "kindred spirits"—men and women were equally responsible for maintaining domestic happiness. This subtle shift underscored women's expectations for partners willing to embrace at least some notions of mere equality. Even though many

courting women's expressions of mere equality remained cloaked in tentativeness, their willingness to experiment with new forms of gender roles and
relations remains significant.

As a transitional stage, courtship represented a period of possibility, expectation, and exploration. During courtship, men and women made bold
promises rooted in both intellectual and emotional affinity. Perhaps such
lofty expectations were indeed too high for many married couples. Marriage,
then, might serve as the true test of whether or not educated women could
apply the lessons of mere equality to their own lives and aspirations.

♨ CHAPTER 5

"The Sweet Tranquility of Domestic Endearment"

Companionate Marriage

In May 1812, John Griscom, educator, wrote to Jane Bowne Haines, his former student, offering congratulations on her recent marriage to Reuben Haines. Marriage, he noted, "brings to its final accomplishment the period of education" and "opens to the young and glowing mind, a scene, rising in *alternate* prospect, under the sober colouring of care and solicitude, and shining with all the brilliancy of hope and expectation." The transition from student and daughter to wife and mother would serve as perhaps the best test of a woman's education. John Griscom held fond hopes for his former pupil, certain that the "exemplary attention" that Jane applied to the various "duties of a scholar" would serve her well in marriage. Jane's attention to education qualified her "to meet the various calls of domestic duty with that intelligent firmness and that enlightened zeal which enable an 'affectionate wife' to produce around her a sunshine of enjoyment."[1] A well-educated woman was an ideal marital partner.

Inspired by new ideals that stressed both romantic and intellectual compatibility, many couples held high expectations of married life. As scholars have noted, the emerging companionate ideal refigured emotional expectations for romantic love and marriage in early national America.[2] Softening older, patriarchal notions of male authority and wifely submission, the companionate ideal emphasized affectionate, egalitarian unions. Marriage was characterized as "the friendship subsisting between two persons, who are dearer to each other than all that the world can fancy." Companionate marriage promised a world of equality and affinity shared between loving partners. "Of all the pleasures that tend to sweeten and to endear human life," one author mused, "none can be more worthy the regards of rational beings, than those which flow from the reciprocal returns of conjugal love."[3]

Scholars have explored the emotional standards that shaped the companionate ideal, but intellectual compatibility was also essential to many men and women's understandings of love and marriage. As Daniel Parker wrote to his fiancée in 1817, "Your refined sensibility, your sweetness of disposition,... and your brilliantly cultivated mind, constitute the fatal charms which have constantly burst upon me." Early national men and women idealized marriage as a "union of reason and love"—an egalitarian relationship that appealed to both the heart and the mind. "To support the equality of domestic friendship," one author insisted, "a feeling heart, and an intelligent mind are requisite endowments." The companionate ideal promised the joys of romantic love, coupled with the comforts of rational friendship. "When two minds are thus engaged by the ties of reciprocal affection," they experienced "participated pleasure, which heightens prosperity and joy itself."[4]

Seeking both emotional and intellectual affinity, educated women imagined companionate marriage as an expression of mere equality. Legally, the doctrine of coverture offered women no such notion of equality because a wife's legal identity became subsumed under that of her husband's. Most married women accepted these legal constraints; legislative acts to protect married women's right to property would not be passed until the 1840s. Instead, the companionate ideal represented an emotional and intellectual reconfiguration of marriage, based on egalitarian principles. Although those principles did not translate into true legal, political, or economic equality, they transformed individual women's expectations for and experiences within marriage.[5]

Focusing primarily on the marriage of Reuben Haines and Jane Bowne Haines, I explore in this chapter how the ideals, expectations, and experiences of marriage reflected educated women's search for intellectual and emotional equality. Juxtaposing personal writings and prescriptive representations, I examine how early national men and women interpreted and experienced the companionate ideal. Were educated women able to negotiate a degree of agency and autonomy within their marriages? Did companionate marriage provide opportunities for women to live as the mere equals of their husbands?

"Their Option to be Happy or Miserable"

Writing to his fiancée Jane Bowne in 1811, Reuben Haines warmly described his friends' marriage: "they appear to me to present one of the fairest examples of the interchange of that affection 'which is felt and understood in its true meaning and import by those done, who seek for happiness in the sweet tranquility of *domestic endearment.*'"[6] Inspired by the presence of such real-life examples of tranquility, courting and newly married couples held high hopes for their own chances for marital bliss. Influenced by their Quaker backgrounds, Jane Bowne and Reuben Haines may have been especially attracted to cultural ideals that stressed a sense of equality and harmony in marriage. Quaker theology viewed marriage as a "partnership" between "spiritual equals."[7] Still, by the early national period, cultural and secular understandings of marriage also increasingly privileged egalitarian and affectionate unions.

Envisioning a life based on shared experiences, many early national couples developed heightened expectations for married life. As one husband optimistically declared on the eve of his marriage, "We have each an unbounded confidence in the other—and of course have but little fear of living happily together." Inspired by the companionate ideal, romantic couples envisioned a life of unparalleled companionship and affinity. As Frederick Wolcott mused to his future wife, "We will reciprocate acts of kindness. We will steal a little pleasure from every passing scene, and in every variety of fortune we will have a tender interest in each other's welfare and in the advancement of each other's happiness." This intense sense of mutuality was at the heart of the companionate ideal. His joys became her joys, his cares became her cares, and his sorrows became her sorrows (and vice versa, of course). As Karen Lystra, historian, argues, "the experience of love created a mutual identification between women and men that was so intense that lovers repeatedly claimed to have incorporated part of their partner's inner self into their own inner life."[8]

The companionate ideal promised a world of affinity and mutuality to any willing couple, offering high expectations—and heightened pressure. As one essayist succinctly noted, "It is at their option to be happy or miserable."[9] Both prescriptive and personal writings stressed the joint responsibilities of married life—it was *their* job, together as a couple, to achieve wedded bliss. A friend counseled Susan Binney that marriage depended on "the reciprocal discharge of mutual duty." On hearing of the recent marriage of his friends, one husband remarked to his wife, "May it prove a silken cord of love and affection—It will be their own faults if they are not as happy as this world can make them." Writing about her brother's recent marriage, Hannah Wister hoped "that they will mutually endeavour to do right." John Teackle congratulated his new son-in-law by stressing the sense of mutuality associated with companionate marriage: "Your union being the result of natural affection, formed with deliberation, and cemented with perfect and cheerful justification, nothing (under divine blessing) is wanting to make you both happy."[10] The companionate ideal stressed a sense of shared identity—and shared responsibility—in marriage.

Romantic couples strongly believed that happy marriages were attainable, so long as one chose a life partner with great care. The choice of a mate, as one essayist cautioned, was "a decision that will place you, with the amiable partner of your joys, either on the pinnacle of connubial bliss, or sink...into the depths of hopeless misery." Prescriptive writings stressed the importance of compatibility between spouses: "Suitableness in temper, education, and the means of living, are solid foundations of happiness."[11] In particular, writers emphasized the importance of choosing well-educated and like-minded partners. Educators believed, as John Griscom stressed to Jane Bowne Haines, that a woman's "exemplary attention" to education enabled her to become a model wife. Under the companionate ideal, a well-cultivated mind was an attractive asset. Writers recommended that young women "adorn yourselves with those accomplishments of mind, and acquire those happy dispositions, which are attractive and durable." Women's "only means of charming," another author suggested, "is to improve their minds: good sense gives beauties which are not subject to fade." A good wife "must love to read; she must be able to think, and have opinion of her own."[12] The tenor of this advice suggests that an increasing number of early national men valued intelligence in their wives.

If well-educated women made good wives, improperly educated women were regarded as unattractive partners. Women who engaged primarily in "fashionable idleness" were ill-equipped to make good decisions "in the choice of companions and diversions." Coquettish and vain, improperly educated women lacked both the sense and sensibility essential to the companionate ideal: "A silly uneducated woman cannot long maintain dominion over the heart of a sensible, well informed man." Thus, whereas John Griscom expressed confidence in Jane Bowne's education, John Brace of the Litchfield Female Academy worried about his former student Catherine Van Kleeck, the "last person I should have supposed would have thought herself fit to assume the arduous duties of a wife." Criticizing his former student as "volatile and coquettish," John Brace expressed doubts about her transition to marriage: "I cannot conceive how she will behave as a wife," he sneered in his journal, "when as a girl her feelings and practice were so flighty and thoughtless." On the other hand, women too interested in education risked developing "an over-bearing confidence" that made them unappealing companions. Such "affectation of learning and authorship," Samuel Whiting argued, "draws upon itself the contempt and hatred of both sexes."[13] Early national women were encouraged to strike the right balance between these extremes, avoiding the taint of both coquetry and pedantry. Well-educated women could cultivate shared interests with like-minded partners, but any coquettish or pedantic pursuits were selfish and misdirected.

The emphasis on proper education extended to men as well as women. As one author noted, "an illiterate man, however virtuous cannot be suitable to you. A man without education and refined sentiment may love you, I will confess; but not in a manner that is agreeable to you; for as he will not be able to comprehend the extent of your excellence, he cannot love you as you merit to be loved." Just as the political culture of the early national period stressed the importance of a well-educated citizenry, women also came to expect well-educated husbands. On hearing of the courtship of mutual friends, Harriet Manigault remarked, "I should not be surprised at her accepting of him, for she thinks a *cultivated mind* is one of the first considerations in the choice of a husband, and he is said to possess that." Educated women valued the importance of a "cultivated mind" in both themselves and their partners. Some women joked about remaining single rather than settling for unworthy mates. Another of Harriet's friends "thinks all the clever girls of her acquaintance must be old maids, for the young men are not worthy of them." Prescriptive writings echoed these sentiments, encouraging women to question the intellectual worthiness of any future husband: "Has his education been such as to qualify him to be a pleasing companion to me? Or, if not, can I so far forget my education . . . that he may be so?"[14]

Writers considered men of "weak intellects" to be "insufferable" mates, but they also cautioned women about forming connections with overeducated men. "Beware of a pedant," one essayist cautioned. "He will harass and persecute you with his learning." Some women agreed that overeducated men made poor husbands. Writing to her fiancé Thomas Biddle, Christine Williams noted that her aunt "has a dread of men of genius," fearful that "they are generally too much wrapt up in their own bright thoughts to be alive to the feelings" of others. Christine playfully warned Thomas to "beware how you ever give my kind aunt any reason to suppose you are a genius, or all I can say will never convince her that I have nothing to fear from arrogance and tyranny." Friends and advice writers alike stressed the importance of "being united to men of both sense and sentiment."[15]

Thus, although romantic love played an important role in couples' expectations for wedded bliss, couples also prized intellectual affinity, rooted in men's and women's proper attention to education. Recognizing this shift, some writers encouraged husbands and wives to cultivate shared intellectual interests. "Study some easy science together, and acquire a similarity of tastes, while you enjoy a community of pleasures." Reading favorite books or studying botany together were among the ways that husbands and wives could craft a sense of intellectual compatibility within their marriages—creating what one woman referred to as "a union with mind and affection."[16] As we have seen, this union of reason and love was paramount to Linda Raymond and Benjamin Ward's idealization of marriage.

By emphasizing a union of both the heart and the mind, the companionate ideal stressed a form of mere equality within marriage. This sense of egalitarianism, however, came into tension with prevailing prescriptions governing men and women's marital roles. The husband was responsible for providing a standard of financial security for his wife and children. One man assured his fiancée of his worthiness by noting, "if I be industrious and have health, that I can obtain for us a respectable support."[17] The wife was entrusted with the cares of home and family, including aspects of household management, production, and consumption associated with domestic economy. If a man was expected to serve as the family "breadwinner," a woman's work was viewed increasingly in emotional terms. Upon marriage, a woman's mind and manner were "employed to diffuse cheerfulness over her family." These prescribed gender roles relied on notions of female deference rather than on a true sense of egalitarianism. "To render the married state more happy," one author argued, "the wife ought to make herself as amiable in the eyes of the husband, as it is in her power." Such prescriptions implied that *women*—not couples together, as stressed by the companionate ideal— had primary responsibility for maintaining domestic harmony. "Be assured," one author noted, "a woman's power, as well as her happiness, has no other foundation but her husband's esteem and love." To preserve harmony, wives were expected to defer to their husbands' authority, as some writers pointedly reminded women that "matrimonial service" included "the word *obey*."[18]

Thus, even as the companionate ideal took hold, notions of patriarchal authority in marriage persisted. In an essay titled "On the Choice of a Wife," John Aikin asserted that an ideal wife should act as a *"help-mate,"* the role "for which this sex was created." Aikin's use of the term "help-mate" reflected Puritan ideas about marriage, in which a well-regulated household was valued perhaps more than romantic love. Despite the patriarchal tone of his advice, Aikin's writings also reflected the era's emerging egalitarianism: "I confess myself decidedly of the opinion of those who would rather form the two sexes to a resemblance of character, than contrast them." The characteristics that made for a suitable mate were desirable in both women and men. "Virtue, wisdom, presence of mind, patience, vigour, capacity, application, are not *sexual* qualities," he insisted. "They belong to mankind—to all who have duties to perform and evils to endure."[19] Such competing, often contradictory, descriptions of married life point to a state of flux in which both companionate and patriarchal representations cluttered the literary public sphere—even individual writers often could not seem to make up their minds about what model of marriage to endorse.

These tensions reveal the paradoxical nature of mere equality. The idea that certain characteristics—particularly virtue and intellect—were not gender-specific but, rather, universal qualities, illustrates one way in which early national women were becoming the mere equals of men. Yet prescriptive constructions of separate spheres and women's nature remained rooted in essentialized, supposedly irrefutable, notions of sexual difference. Mere equality attempted to reconfigure gender roles and identity, retaining some notion of difference while also making space for more potentially liberating ideas about shared experience and identity. The growing belief in and support of women's educational capacities, for example, helped to create models of womanhood that focused on women's ability and intellect rather than on prevailing notions of women's inherent weakness and subordination. In a similar fashion, the cultural emphasis on mutuality and affinity privileged by the companionate ideal enabled men and women to craft more egalitarian understandings of love and marriage.

Inspired by the companionate ideal, men and women sought standards of love and marriage based not on distance and disparity but, rather, on mutuality and closeness. Shared intellectual and emotional pursuits, in particular, offered romantic couples the means to enact relationships that celebrated areas of "sameness" between men and women. Thus, although prescriptive writings continued to emphasize notions of female deference, couples often ignored such advice in favor of writings that privileged the egalitarian qualities at the heart of the companionate ideal. By celebrating emotional and intellectual equality, the companionate ideal offered educated women a chance to explore what it meant to live as mere equals within marriage. It was up to newly married couples such as Jane Bowne and Reuben Haines to put these ideals into practice.

"To Change Your Condition"

Courting couples eagerly crafted visions of wedded bliss based on the promise of intellectual and emotional affinity. Yet, at the same time, couples wondered whether they could live out their lofty aspirations. In March 1812, two months before their wedding, Reuben Haines confessed to Jane Bowne that his thoughts were "mingled with emotions of gratitude and regret, of solicitude and hope." His ambivalence reflected both his hopes and fears about his worthiness as a husband, in particular his "hope that one year hence we may mutually experience the correctness of the happy picture which thy glowing pencil has portrayed of thy home, instead of the more sombre one which perhaps a too scrupulous desire not to deceive induced me when in New York to present thee with."[20] Reuben's mixed emotions reflected his concerns about whether the realities of married life could match his idealized expectations. Hope, fear, and ambivalence frequently coexisted in the writings of courting and newly married couples because individuals recognized that "marriage determines, in this world, the happiness or misery of those who engage in it."[21] A legal—and in most cases lifelong—bond, marriage was a decision of tremendous importance. Even couples confident in their compatibility experienced some doubt about their ability to achieve their desired "happy picture."

Prewedding doubts represented measured responses to the heightened expectations of the companionate ideal, but they also reflected the very real changes that accompanied marriage, particularly for women. As John Griscom wrote to Jane, "the ties which [marriage] severs and the sacrifices it sometimes calls for, at its commencement, are painful." Marriage was a serious decision, especially for young women who had to leave the comforts of their natal homes and depend on their husbands for emotional, intellectual, and financial support. The act of leaving "a single life for marriage state," as one brother wrote to his sister, constituted "a change which I hope will be to your advantage." Yet as their wedding days approached, women often expressed reluctance to end the period of their lives marked by what John Griscom referred to as "the immediate guardianship of parental authority and Love." Jane Bowne felt a tinge of remorse when she contemplated her marriage and subsequent move from New York to Philadelphia. "I think I should have been *entirely happy* if thy 'lot had been cast' in our city," she wrote to Reuben during their engagement, "for then I should have been surrounded by every thing my heart could desire." Instead, Jane mused, "when I reflect that a few months hence, I shall leave my native roof and the guardianship of my beloved and indulgent Parents—forever—a sigh and a tear will arise and surely it is not *injustice* to thy worth my friend to indulge them." Jane recognized that her marriage (and subsequent residence in Philadelphia) signaled a permanent severing of her proximity to her parents. "I find that I daily become more sensible of the vast debt I owe to those who have protected me, for now twenty years," she noted, "and I *almost* wonder that I can leave them just as I begin to have it in my power to be useful."[22]

Like Jane Bowne, Sarah Ripley Stearns reflected on the transitions that accompanied marriage with a sense of wistfulness: "I have now quitted the abode of my youth, left the protection of my parents, and give up the name I have always borne to enter upon a new untried scene."[23] For women, marriage represented a change not only in name but also in residence because wives were typically expected to live wherever best suited their husbands' occupations. Linda Raymond was reluctant to leave her hometown of Rindge, New Hampshire, and succeeded in convincing her fiancé Benjamin Ward to set up his law practice there so she would not have to leave her family and friends. Jane Bowne had to accept that her marriage required a move to Philadelphia, where Reuben Haines already had well-established familial and financial ties.

The geographical move accompanying marriage represented a dramatic change for some women, particularly those with close ties to their parents and siblings. Betsey Huntington feared becoming "home sick" on leaving her native city of Norwich to join her new husband in Litchfield, Connecticut. "You can never leave your family and friends without making sacrifices which are common to but few," her fiancé Frederick Wolcott conceded. "And your good sense convinces you that your rank, your condition and happiness in life must depend very much on the person with whom you may become connected." Frederick recognized the "sacrifices" Betsey made in leaving home, but sought to persuade her that the bliss promised by companionate marriage made it all worthwhile: "These are reflections which must arise whenever you leave your friends. They are not of so serious a nature that they ought to determine you never to change your condition. If so, have not *we,* my beloved friend as fair and rational a prospect of finding happiness in the connection we contemplate, as can be expected?—I think we have."[24] Ultimately, men such as Frederick Wolcott and Reuben Haines hoped that their fiancées would reconcile themselves to "change your condition," including the daunting prospect of leaving home and family behind for a new city of residence.

Although eager to embark on a new life with Reuben, Jane struggled to adjust to the sacrifices that marriage called for. Just days following her wedding in May 1812, Jane wrote to her brother's wife, Eliza Bowne, confessing that "nothing but the society of my own family is wanted to complete my happiness." Jane felt torn between her affection for her natal family and her new role as a member of the Haines family. "Tho' my heart gratefully acknowledges their kindness, still it shrinks from their embraces," she admitted to Eliza, "which feel to me as if they were meant to obliterate those I last received from you all." In response to Jane's letter, Eliza explained that "troubles and disappointments" were an inevitable part of any marriage but insisted that, "upon the whole Jane, there is so much *real* happiness to be enjoyed in the married life—that if thee will only *think* so—all trials and troubles will seem light." Eliza sensed how Jane's continued closeness with her family could create tension in her marriage and urged her "not to dwell too much upon past pleasures." As Eliza warned, Jane needed, in some measure, to let go of her former life to achieve true happiness with Reuben. "Think not that I would wish thee to forget *us*," Eliza gently noted, "but I can tell thee—from experience—that it will never do—to think too much upon those subjects."[25] Married life created a new set of priorities for young women; longing for "past pleasures" could only create "troubles and disappointments."

Advice literature encouraged newlyweds to focus their primary energies on their marriage, to "become from that period, a little world of their own: a society consisting of love, mutually connected with love." Cultivating such exclusive bonds certainly appealed to many couples. Newlywed Eliza Southgate Bowne mused to her sister about "the sweet tranquility of my feelings—so different from any thing I ever before felt—such a confidence—my every feeling reciprocated and every wish anticipated."[26] For other couples, strong ties to family and friends precluded such exclusivity. After their wedding, Jane and Reuben traveled to Lancaster and surrounding areas in the Pennsylvania countryside, accompanied by his mother and other family members. This kind of visiting was common for many newlyweds, predating the unaccompanied "honeymoon" travels that developed in the late nineteenth century. Such trips served to bond the newly married couple with larger networks of family and kin, in contrast to later honeymoon trips, which provided a period of romantic seclusion. Jane and Reuben's first months of married life centered not on their own little world but, rather, on family-based patterns of travel and sociability. As Jane noted, these various visits were "rendered agreeable by the great civility of the family and the privilege of an excellent library."[27]

Reflecting on her own life as a newlywed, Jane's cousin Susan described this connection between marriage and sociability: "I feel happy; yes my dear Jane *I am happy* that the most important act in the life of a female is accomplished so much to my satisfaction; . . . thee may imagine me comfortably situated as a matronly Lady—associating the 'Loves & Joys' with all our dear friends who will mingle in the ring." Although urged to cultivate a world of their own, married couples experienced added joy by cultivating social bonds. "A well chosen society of friends and acquaintances, more eminent for virtue and good sense, than for gaiety and splendor, where the conversation of the day may afford comment for the evening, seems the most rational pleasure we can enjoy."[28] Early national patterns and rituals of sociability thus encouraged married couples to share their "rational pleasure" with family and friends.

Finding the right balance between a "little world of their own" and "a well chosen society" could be challenging. Some couples were eager to guard their own world. As Charles Bancker wrote to his wife, "It is not for others to keep pace with our feelings, or participate in our sensations." Jane and Reuben both came from close-knit families, and from the start, their marriage was marked by a persistent tension between intimacy and sociability. Their first test came just months after their wedding. After spending several weeks in New York together, Reuben returned home to Philadelphia while Jane remained with her family. "I returned to my dear mother and friends in Bank Street," Reuben wrote to Jane, "where I was received with open arms, although it seemed but *half* returning home, without *thee*."[29] A month later, Jane was still in New York. Reuben tried to frame their extended separation in positive terms. "Indeed this little separation may be useful to us both," he wrote to Jane, for "'it is only by being deprived of our blessings that we duly appreciate them.'" Reuben understood that they both felt the tug of former family and social ties: "I have returned to my house, to my friends, to my former habits, and accustomed pursuits; I have left thee in the bosom of thy father's family surrounded by thy friends and very dear relatives, they are desirous of thy society, and doubtless more than ever anxious to please and to serve thee; what wish *can* you have that is not gratified. Had I not experienced every flattering proof of thy affection, I should almost have *feared* to leave thee, least thee should have no reason to wish my return."[30]

This separation illustrated the adjustments that Reuben and Jane faced as a newly married couple. Reuben may have felt uncomfortable with, or even displaced by, the strength of Jane's continued affection toward her family. Jane's decision to remain in New York just months after her wedding suggests a desire on her part to maintain aspects of her former identity. Jane's "exemplary attention" to education was designed to enhance her marital state, but it also provided her with a sense of autonomy that made it more difficult for her to adjust to the changes marriage necessitated.

During the first months of her marriage, Jane struggled to adjust to a new set of expectations and circumstances. Eight months after her wedding, she reflected on her transition to married life: "I wish my beloved mother could have seen how comfortably and quietly her children were situated this afternoon when her dear letter arrived—we were quite alone—seated at a table—Reuben engaged with his writing—and I busily sewing." Jane portrayed a quiet picture of domestic tranquility, yet her initial adjustment to married life proved challenging. Jane's parents had visited her in Philadelphia and witnessed her unease. "I was then so dissatisfied and restless," Jane admitted, "but I had not been used to disappointment and could not *cheerfully* bear even the unavoidable delays attendant on a settlement." Strong-willed and independent-minded, Jane initially bristled at the many changes that married life demanded. "I am now quite at ease," she reassured her mother. "[I] have excellent servants, good health and every thing my heart can desire, excepting the society of my much loved family which privation often crosses my mind most sorrowfully."[31]

Whether a woman felt "dissatisfied and restless," or "quite at ease" in marriage often reflected the distance between expectation and experience. E. W. Ware, a member of Jane's social circle, seemingly managed the transition to marriage with more ease than Jane. "Seven months of a married life has now passed away, without disappointment in any anticipation whatever on my part at least." Ware suggested that her pragmatic notions of marriage occasioned her happiness: "We were not romantic in our views of life, and we owe much of our present contentment to the regulation of our expectations." Although Ware's tempered views accounted for her contentment, she recognized that not all married couples were willing to rethink their idealized visions of married life: "How very different must be my reflections, since my marriage, than those of Ann Collins, whom you mention, as having just been married."[32]

Ware's moderate views fell somewhere in the middle of the emotional spectrum of marital expectations. Ranging from idyllic visions to troubled ruminations, women's attitudes toward and experiences of married life could vary widely. Understanding the emotional universe of married women can be challenging because, as Martha Tomhave Blauvelt has noted, "women's sense of self varied with their life cycle."[33] Expressive writing in diaries and letters enabled educated women to "narrate" important aspects of their lives. Yet young women's deeply expressive writings often concluded with marriage. Sarah Ripley Stearns began a new volume of her journal after her 1812 marriage to Charles Stearns because "so important a change in my Life, merits some alteration in my journal." After her marriage, however, Sarah's entries became less frequent; as she acknowledged, "I do not find so much time to write in my journal as formerly when I lived in my father's house." Harriet Manigault stopped writing in her diary altogether after her marriage, wryly noting, "it is not customary for the story to go on after the heroine is married." Married women often found themselves too busy to write, especially once they became mothers. "I have a large family to attend to," Polly Cutler admitted to her sister Linda Raymond, "and find it more difficult to find time to write."[34]

Although personal writings that would enable us to more fully explore women's marital experiences are less abundant, letters exchanged during periods of temporary separation provide valuable clues about how married couples articulated their understandings of the companionate ideal.

"A Faithful Transcription of Feelings"

As he traveled back to New York to reunite with Jane after their first separation as a married couple, Reuben wrote to a friend, expressing his eagerness for his wife's companionship. "I cherish a fond hope that she feels that her 'best friend' is absent, and my heart *is cheered*...that I am thus far on my way to obliterate that absence, which I hope will not soon be repeated."[35] Despite Reuben's wishes, their marriage was marked by frequent separations because Jane regularly visited her family in New York and he occasionally engaged in business-related travels. Indeed, Reuben and Jane Haines have left behind their rich cache of letters precisely because they both traveled frequently throughout their marriage.

In their letters, married couples evoked the ideals of companionship that might otherwise only be expressed in face-to-face communications. Spouses lamented geographical separations that felt "so *long* and painful." As Gertrude Meredith wrote to her husband while visiting her family, "The sacrifice has been too great for any pleasure I have derived." Gertrude was astonished to learn that other couples were seemingly indifferent to lengthy separations. "When I look around me, and behold men and their wives separated for five or six months, and without appearing to feel regret, I wish that such was my nature." Gertrude, who had been away from home for about six weeks when she made these observations, implied that only a lack of affection could account for a corresponding lack of regret. Charles Bancker wondered how his sister endured her husband's absence "for 12 months on a distant voyage." "It may be a weakness in my nature," Charles reflected to his wife Sarah, insisting, "I could never have submitted to a separation of the time."[36]

When separations did occur, couples relied on letter writing to help bridge the physical distance between them. "You can form no idea of the state of mind until I received your very affectionate letter," Coleman Sellers insisted to his wife. As Rachel Boudinot noted, letter writing helped ease the pain of separation: "nothing makes our absence tolerable but those dear transcripts of your mind." Sarah Bancker wrote to her husband, "confident that my letters will afford you great satisfaction, and render less tedious the moments of our separation." Gertrude Meredith assured her husband that his "affectionate attention in writing me every day will greatly hasten the period" of separation.

William Munford shared similar sentiments, writing to his wife: "If any thing could make me amends for the pains of absence, it would be the tenderness and affection displayed in your letters." Yet, ultimately, the "sweetness" of letter writing, as William noted in another letter, remained "far inferior to the comfort, the unspeakable gratification it would afford me to see you at this moment." Sarah Bancker agreed, writing to her husband Charles, "You will not doubt I sensibly feel the loss of your society, nor partake of any pleasure without regretting the impossibility of your participating with me."[37]

Married couples who subscribed to the companionate ideal invested their letter writing with weight and importance. Correspondence enabled couples to maintain ties of affection during separations, but letter writing could be an imperfect means of communication. Writing from Washington, D.C., Daniel Parker mused to his wife about his chances at political success: "If you had been an ambitious political lady, fond of politicking, talking & entertaining…I might possibly by this time have become a distinguished candidate for some distinguished office." Anne took offense at Daniel's remarks criticizing her "deficiency of electioneering talents." Insisting that "it was a compliance with *your wishes*" that kept her out of the "busy circles" of Washington society, Anne sought to downplay the relationship between her sociability and his political success: "I should have imagined that you depended on your own powers and talents for advancement, and not on the fawning and flattering of your wife." Daniel insisted that Anne had misread his intent: "You have made what I consider the best compliment a lady can receive a subject of abuse upon me. Look at my letter again and I am sure you will see that I was congratulating myself on a prospect of quiet domestic enjoyment."[38]

The Parkers' inability to read the nuances of sarcasm and wit in each other's writings created discord. Letters were powerful modes of communication. Properly written, they evoked ideals of togetherness and harmony that were central to companionate marriage. Subject to misinterpretation, letters could create emotional distance that only compounded the sense of disruption that geographical distance created. Yet even couples such as Daniel and Anne Parker, who repeatedly struggled to communicate effectively in print, recognized the symbolic importance of letter writing: "Although your letters are not calculated to inspire me with either good humour, or good spirits," Anne mused to Daniel, "yet I feel unhappy and anxious if I do not receive one every day or two."[39]

The desire for heartfelt communications during periods of separation took on added meanings once couples had children. Even before becoming parents, married couples evoked idealized depictions of family life. As Geredith

Meredith mused to her husband shortly after their marriage, "Our book case should offer instruction, our piano forte amusement: but our sweetest bliss and diversion should arise from a dear little Boy and Girl." After couples had children, the companionate ideal evolved into a family-centric space where parents and children cheerfully gathered together. "It is only in domestic life any thing like real happiness is to be found," Daniel Parker wrote to his wife, undeterred by their recent conflicts. The family circle became the emotional and intellectual center of marriage. "Amuse yourself with your child and your books and your work," one woman advised her married daughter. "When [your husband] comes in amuse him with cheerful conversation—and enjoy all the happiness that you can at present."[40]

In 1813, Reuben and Jane's first child, Sarah, was born; in the years that followed, Jane gave birth to nine children (two of whom died in infancy). "We miss thee most exceedingly and shall rejoice to welcome you back," Jane wrote to Reuben during one of his travels, "in the meantime hope to hear often from you." Separations could test the strength of an absent family member's affection for those left behind. Jane judged the frequency and content of Reuben's letters for how well they conveyed a sense of concern and love toward both her and the children. "I was much disappointed my dear R. in not receiving a letter by brother B.," Jane wrote, "and the one thee sent from Poughkeepsie was not very interesting—thee did not say one word about thyself, nor make the least inquiry after Sarah, which I consider a great slight to her mother." Spouses expected letters to demonstrate proper levels of affection not only for each other but also for their children. "Your account of the prattle of my sweet little cherubs concerning their father makes my heart overflow with tenderness," William Munford wrote approvingly to his wife. Yet, ironically, spouses could feel slighted if the children received the lion's share of attention. Anne Parker informed her husband that their daughter Sarah was "highly favored to have received three letters to mama's one," although Anne herself was "not at all pleased at being neglected."[41]

While it was perhaps expected that men would travel for work, women often left home to engage in out-of-town visits with family and friends. Although relatively common, a wife or mother's absence from home represented a symbolic disruption of the family circle. As Elizabeth Shippen noted during one of her mother's trips, "dear Mama's absence is greatly felt by us all, and there is a vacuum in our domestic circle which she only can fill." Although cultural ideals urged women to put their husbands and children first, some married women were determined to maintain close ties with their natal families. During a visit to her parents, Lucy Pierce "for a few minutes repented my resolution to leave my own dear fireside, and *more* dear family."

As she reflected on her situation, Lucy admitted "that in visiting my parents, I not only fulfilled a *duty*, but should highly gratify myself." To conduct such visits, women left their "own dear fireside"—and often their husbands and children—behind.[42]

After she became a mother, Jane's family continued to actively encourage her visits to New York, in essence competing with Reuben for her time and affection. In 1817, Jane's father visited Philadelphia, with the intention of taking Jane and her daughter back to New York with him. Eager to visit with Jane, her family seemed a bit indifferent to the feelings of her husband. "I hope Br. Reuben will try to come along," her sister wrote, "but if he cannot—he surely loves to give pleasure too well—to disappoint us." In an effort to balance her sense of duty to her father and her husband, Jane delayed her visit so that Reuben could accompany her. Her family admitted that they "were not a little disappointed, at finding thy visit was deferred to a later period—as we had all anticipated the pleasure of seeing thee and thy little Sarah." Her family hoped "it will not be long before Reuben can make it convenient to accompany you on."[43] Jane's natal family exerted continued pressure, creating tension in the Haines' marriage—was Jane's primary loyalty to her parents or to her husband?

One particularly tense exchange occurred during spring 1818, while Jane was in New York and Reuben was tending to the cares of their farm in Germantown, on the outskirts of Philadelphia. Reuben remarked on the changes that occurred during Jane's absence: "I can not resist the inclination I feel to assure thee that although I am very happy indeed in my new occupation my wife and children *sometimes* flit across my mind, accompanied by a fervent wish for their preservation and happiness. Indeed yesterday particularly whilst *triumphantly* driving my ox cart...with my old straw hat and the old coat I wore last summer...I doubted whether thee would *acknowledge me* should I unexpectedly had the pleasure of meeting thee."[44] Despite the playful tone of his writing, Reuben's remarks reflected a growing rift in their marriage. Reuben's suggestion that Jane might fail to recognize his new appearance as a farmer suggested a level of both emotional and physical distance that betrayed the couple's sense of intimacy.

Jane's reply indicated that Reuben's distant tone hit its mark:

I hope my dear Reuben that this letter may reach thy hand at some leisure moment or that thee will abstract thy attention a little while from thy farm and oxen and listen to me. I feel that it is a long time since I have seen thee and our letters on either side have been very common place—or at least—not a faithful transcription of feelings—for I do not wish to believe that thou hast engrossed so much larger portion of my thoughts than I have of thine—especially as connected with thy recollection of me there are such interesting objects as our precious children.[45]

Jane's letter provided a gentle yet forceful reminder to Reuben that he had failed to demonstrate a proper level of affection toward her and the children. The idea that their letters had become merely "common place" contrasted sharply with the ideals of heartfelt, candid communication prized between loving partners. Letters shared between married couples were supposed to reflect what William Munford referred to as "the spontaneous effusions of my heart."[46]

Jane's reproach to Reuben succeeded in reopening the lines of communication. Perhaps to smooth the waters, Reuben confessed that his slight was intentional, designed to elicit a strong reaction from Jane: "It was just such a letter as I had been anticipated and just such a one as I should have been *disappointed* not to have received." Reuben tried to ease the tension by suggesting he expected Jane's strong response: "I should have concluded that I did not know my wife as well as I *thought* I did, had I found she could receive with indifference, continued accounts that my Farm and other occupations kept me so interestingly employed that the void made by the loss of both wife and children was scarcely felt."[47] Reuben implied that his initial letter was a deliberate attempt on his part—a test to see how Jane would react to his purported declarations of indifference. Having received assurances of Jane's continued affections, Reuben felt free to engage in more expressive writing:

And yet the reproof was so gentle in affection and so delicate; so like thy self in thy *best* dress—that it touched a cord, that vibrates to no hand but thine, and awakened all my former feelings of affection and love to the dear children and her to whom I owe them. Yes my love now that I have thy confession that I "occupy a large portion of thy thoughts" that thee does "so much want to be with me again" I will acknowledge that I do miss thee *very much* both in the city and the country, in the garden and the fields, each scene where I have been accustomed to be met by the hand of affection and surrounded by the gambols of playful innocence, is now a dreary Solitude to me.[48]

It is significant that Reuben wrote these heartfelt, affectionate musings only after and in response to Jane's criticism of his previous, more distant letter. Reuben's initial reserve, although cloaked in the guise of humor, signaled a breakdown in his expressive communications. Jane responded to his teasing with a serious, hurtful tone rather than interpreting his letter with humor and good nature. The gravity with which Jane responded to his initial letter, along with the subsequent level of regret and affection demonstrated in Reuben's follow-up letter, suggests the importance that married couples placed on affectionate communication—or at least the appearance of it. In his reply to Jane, Reuben was more candid, admitting that her continued devotion to her family in New York created tension in their marriage:

> Nothing reconciles me to these privations but the reflection that our children are lighting up the faces of their aged grandparents with smiles of joy, and that thou thyself are paying a visit of affection and duty to thy beloved parents, on which in all probability memory will long continue to dwell with feelings of the tenderest and dearest recollections. Nothing would give me more pleasure than to be thy companion in this visit but it is impossible. I have other duties to perform, and I am entirely satisfied that the path I am persuing is the right one.[49]

Devoted to his own mother (who began living with the couple in 1816), Reuben must have understood Jane's lingering sense of "affection and duty" for her parents—even if it in some measure conflicted with her role as his devoted wife. Reuben himself felt torn between his role as Jane's husband and traveling companion, and his various duties at the farm. Committed to egalitarian principles, Reuben always granted Jane the autonomy to make decisions respecting the frequency and duration of her visits to New York. "Whether it be thy duty to join me at the appointed time or not I leave to *thy better judgment to decide,*" he insisted. "And if it be my destiny to be still longer deprived of thee, I shall submit to my fate with cheerful resignation, and in the active duties and useful occupations of the Farm, leave no time for unfounded anxieties for my children or useless regrets for the loss of my companion."[50] By stressing the emotional void he felt during her absences, Reuben attempted to influence, rather than directly control, her decisions. When to return home rested entirely with Jane's "better judgment to decide." Inspired by the companionate ideal, Reuben and Jane Haines viewed their marriage as a partnership between equals. Accordingly, they both assumed responsibility for maintaining domestic harmony and for settling conflict.

Although some prescriptive authors urged wives to obey their husbands, the companionate model inspired women to live as the mere equals of their spouses. The companionate ideal enabled women to exert autonomy, especially if they had supportive husbands who subscribed to egalitarian understandings of married life. As Lucy Pierce, reflected, some husbands remained reluctant to experiment with forms of mere equality in marriage: "Mrs. D. said she greatly rejoiced that I could leave home, to visit Northampton. I answered, 'Mr. Pierce was quite willing to take charge of the children, to let me enjoy my friends here a short time.' 'Well' said Mr. Dwight, 'I suppose you would like to have such a husband.' Addressing his wife. She answered in a mild tone of voice, 'Mr. Pierce's habits and yours, my *dear,* are very different.' I was delighted with *her* manner."[51] As this anecdote suggests, a married woman's ability to leave home to visit her parents depended largely on her husband's support. Some husbands, as Mr. Dwight's reaction suggests, were not willing to "take charge of the children" or make concessions so that their wives could leave home, sometimes on their own, on extended visits. Yet men like John Pierce and Reuben Haines, who subscribed to the companionate ideal, gave their wives freedom to make such decisions. In the process, these couples experimented with egalitarian understandings of marriage that could create both possibility and tension.

"My Views on the Matrimonial State"

Throughout their marriage, Jane and Reuben Haines attempted to put the ideals of mere equality into practice. Finding ways to cope with their regular geographical separations remained a recurring source of negotiation. Jane's frequent trips to New York suggest her desire to exert agency and equality within her marriage, even when her husband objected to the frequency and length of her visits. Typically, the couple handled their separations with "cheerful resignation," evoking the ideals, if not the practice, of companionship. During one visit to New York in 1819, Jane left their children at home with Reuben. "Although I submit with great cheerfulness to a temporary privation of thy society," he mused to Jane, "and although my children meet me with smiles of joy, and are every thing I could wish them to be, good hearty and happy, yet we miss thee at every turn in the garden, at every hour in the day, and I feel as though I wanted thy council in every domestic arrangement I am about to make."[52] Reuben continued to stress his desire for Jane's presence without attempting to directly control her actions.

As time progressed, the couple relied on letter writing to reinforce the ideals of togetherness. Perhaps their quarrel in 1818 served to remind them of the symbolic importance of written communication to sustain bonds of affection during geographical separations. Writing in 1820, Jane remarked, "I too long to see [you] more than ever before—tho' I am so happy with my friends here—I look forward with joyful anticipation to our winter comforts when *we* and *our* children shall be gathered together—without intruders or complaints."[53] Such refrains became common in their correspondence, enabling the couple to diffuse the strain caused by Reuben's insecurity and by Jane's frequent absences from home. Evoking such idealized sentiments provided a way of making their frequent absences from each other more acceptable. Instead of changing the frequency or length of Jane's visits to her parents, Jane and Reuben adopted their patterns of written communication to bring to mind the ideals, if not the actualization, of companionship.

In 1824, after twelve years of marriage, Jane and Reuben experienced another moment of strain, occasioned once again by one of her extended visits to New York. In discussing whether Jane should take this particular trip, Reuben apparently responded with a tone that Jane read as "indifference." Reuben insisted that "it was not a feeling of indifference that dictated my language, but a wish not to alloy the pleasure of thy visit, by a knowledge of how much privation I suffered." The timing of this visit—occurring during major renovations to their Germantown home—accounted for Reuben's sense of "privation." Reuben thought Jane should have remained at home to assist in making the various decisions involved in the renovations: "Not a day passes but I want thy opinion upon some point…upon which no other person but thyself can possibly judge."[54] The timing of Jane's visit created another breakdown in their communication patterns. Indeed, during the first month of her absence, it appears that the couple communicated only indirectly, through letters that Jane exchanged with Reuben's cousin Ann Haines (who was staying with him in Germantown). Ann felt awkward in her role as mediator, apologizing to Jane "at seeing my handwriting instead of thy R. H.'s." Ann insisted that Reuben was merely "too much engaged to write"—but the truth was more complicated. As Reuben later admitted, he resented that Jane "ran away," leaving him "to get through the repairs as well as I could without thee." Upset by her decision, Reuben deliberately avoided writing to Jane, "determined not to let thee know how we were getting along or consult thee." He eventually changed his mind, but only after Jane had expressed "some interest in our proceedings and showing some disposition to return to thy deserted husband."[55] As during their earlier rift, Reuben sought proof of Jane's affection before he felt comfortable communicating more candid expressions of disappointment.

Two weeks later, Reuben wrote to Jane about their current separation, admitting that it was a "sacrifice" for him to allow Jane to leave "at the very time when *above all others I thought thee* ought not to have cherished the wish of deserting me." Reuben initially downplayed his sense of disappointment and abandonment. As during previous moments of discord, Reuben used humor to mask his true feelings, only to find that Jane mistook his efforts at lightheartedness as apathy. "And however I may have joked upon the subject," he tried to explain, "I have never thought of thy leaving me but with regret that thy views and mine so entirely differed on that point." Reuben wished Jane would return home, but he insisted that the decision remained hers to make. "Thee must not therefore expect me to *solicit* thy return. This is what I believe I never yet have done, and I should justly incur the sentence of what I sincerely deprecate, *inconsistency with my principles,* were I do to it." Clinging to egalitarian principles even in the face of his emotional turmoil, Reuben insisted that the decision to return was "entirely in thy own hands." The couple's dedication to an egalitarian partnership in some measure contributed to their tensions. Reuben could not bring himself to command Jane's return but, rather, attempted to convey an urgent sense of the importance of her duty to her husband and home. Reuben implored Jane to put aside the "gratification" she took from visiting her family to end the "privations" that they were experiencing as a couple.[56]

The circumstances surrounding this misunderstanding occasioned Reuben to take a retrospective look at their marriage. "Let our reunion my dear Jane be a season of additional happiness to us both," he wrote. "I trust that during our separation we have each resolved and in practice I hope we shall invariably act upon the plan of increasing the sum of our *mutual* happiness by constant sacrifices of personal feeling [in] favor of the other." Keeping central the goal of "mutual happiness," Reuben insisted, would strengthen their marriage: "If this be our constant aim the very sacrifice will become pleasant whilst it will be more than doubly repaid by the kindness and affection of the other and thus the highest summit of connubial felicity be our portion. This is no fancied picture it *may* be realized." Reuben reminded his wife that marriage required mutual "sacrifices" and called on Jane to do her part, perhaps by limiting the number or length of her visits from home. In effect, Reuben entreated Jane to put aside her desire to spend time with her family to focus on their mutual happiness. Reuben's wishes reflected prescriptive advice about married women's duties within their own homes, "the peace and harmony of which, it should be their particular study to promote," as John Burton, author, stressed.[57] Jane, however, maintained a strong sense of loyalty to her natal family, even when it disturbed the peace and harmony of her own home.

Despite their challenges, Reuben maintained ardent faith in the companionate ideal: "My views on the matrimonial state *may* be too exalted, but the more I reflect upon them the more rational they appear. And a few leading points being kept constantly in view, I see no reason why two amiable and congenial minds may not be cemented into a union productive of the greatest possible state of enjoyment. But there must be mutual condescension, unbounded confidence, and profound respect. No such idea should be cherished as a separate responsibility, or individual interest."[58] Reuben articulated his ideal understandings of marriage as a union of "two amiable and congenial minds"—privileging a "rational," rather than truly romantic, view of married life. Such phrasing suggests that he viewed Jane as his equal in understanding and intellect, rather than expecting deference or obedience from his wife.

Reuben's sentiments also captured both the persistent optimism and inevitable tension that characterized the couple's expectations of and experiences with companionate marriage. "Mutual condescension, unbounded confidence, and profound respect" were essential elements to the companionate ideal, providing men and women with a deep sense of affinity and mutuality. Reuben suggested that a married couple avoid areas "separate responsibility, or individual interest," but the reality proved more complex. Jane and Reuben experienced unavoidable moments of conflict when their individual duties, demands, and wishes were not in perfect harmony. A discord in individual priorities (as evident in Jane visiting her family when Reuben wished her to remain at home) or a failure to convey one's wishes and needs (Reuben's reluctance to ask Jane to stay or return home) precipitated these points of tension. Mutuality of thought, feeling, and action was an elusive goal, and accordingly, the Haineses continually dealt with the resulting patterns of strain and accommodation.

Jane could have avoided these conflicts by not visiting her parents as often as she did or by waiting for opportunities when Reuben could accompany her. But she did not defer to her husband's authority—largely because her husband did not command obedience or compliance from her on these matters. Instead, Jane exercised a degree of autonomy within her marriage, creating a role for herself that enabled her to be a loving wife and mother—and a devoted daughter. Even in the face of repeated strain, Jane achieved a measure of mere equality within marriage. She directed her "intelligent firmness and that enlightened zeal" not just toward becoming "an affectionate wife," as her former teacher predicted, but also toward her family and friends in New York. Even though her articulations of equality did not extend beyond this particular goal, they remain significant. Under a more patriarchal model of marriage, Jane would have been expected to leave behind her family and friends to focus *all* her efforts on her husband and children. Instead, she negotiated a more fluid role for herself within a marriage defined by and committed to egalitarian principles.

"Marriage Is the Bond of Society"

Writing to a friend in 1816, Reuben referred to Jane as "a companion whose soft attentions and persuasive accents are ever steady to inspire me with proper confidence in myself. Great reason have I my friend to be thankful for the blessing, and the conviction still rests indelibly on my heart that 'heaven directed my choice.'"[59] Despite their conflicting views on Jane's repeated absences from home, Reuben never expressed regret in his choice of a partner. He did not criticize Jane's strong sense of self but, rather, viewed her as an ideal, devoted wife. The realities of married life proved more complex than Reuben's warm description implied. In their efforts to maintain mere equality, the Haines marriage was characterized by a carefully orchestrated dance of acceptance, resignation, and hopefulness. Despite these tensions, Reuben and Jane continued to privilege the companionate ideal, even when episodes of discord complicated its actualization.

The companionate ideal shaped men and women's expectations and experiences of married life, and as scholars have suggested, also influenced social and political constructions of a virtuous, harmonious republic. As a freely entered union between equals, marriage set the standard for both personal and political interactions. "Conjugal affection," as one author insisted, was the inspiration for national stability: "all civilized societies have conspired to hail thee, as the divinity, on whom their perpetuity, peace, and happiness depend." Marriage served as model and metaphor for articulating citizenship and political participation in the young republic: "Marriage is the bond of society, and therefore the most important object of the politician's investigation."[60] But the idealization of egalitarian unions established between equal partners perhaps promised more than could be actualized in real life. Whenever discord and disharmony became an inevitable part of life, the focus shifted to the sacrifices necessary to maintain harmony and accord despite moments of strife. How to maintain a companionate union in the face of repeated tensions occupied the hearts and minds of both married couples and political participants.

As Jane Bowne Haines's example suggests, married women's experiences of mere equality remained limited to individual expressions of autonomy that did little to fundamentally change the legal or political constructs of marriage. For many women, motherhood further complicated these matters, presenting additional challenges to women seeking to live merely as the equals of man.

CHAPTER 6

"So Material a Change"

Revisiting Republican Motherhood

In the eyes of her son-in-law Samuel B. How, Jane Bayard Kirkpatrick "came as near to perfection as any human being I ever knew." Jane fulfilled her various roles "as daughter, sister, wife, mother, and mistress of a family" with "propriety and grace." Samuel reserved particular praise for Jane's intellectual attainments: "Her mind was naturally strong, and she had diligently cultivated and improved its powers. She was remarkable for the union of a lively imagination, with a solid judgment." Through all stages of her life, "at all times, and in all places and company, she was the accomplished lady." As the quintessential "accomplished lady," Jane Bayard Kirkpatrick's intellectual development did not end when she finished her education or on her marriage. Throughout her life, Jane "was incessantly engaged in some necessary or useful occupation." As a wife and mother, she devoted her educational energies to raising her children and creating a warm circle of family sociability. Jane was also active in the work of benevolence, supporting a variety of educational and charitable endeavors in her home city of New Brunswick, New Jersey. As she engaged in these various activities, Jane found time for literary expression, either in her journal or, as her daughter recalled, by "committing to paper sketches of interesting events which came under her observation."[1]

Samuel How's admiring description suggests that Jane Bayard Kirkpatrick was an ideal "republican mother" who devoted her intellectual and moral energies toward her family and community. As Linda Kerber notes, the idiom of republican motherhood was an ideological response to the American Revolution that sought to constrain women within the domestic sphere. Historians have expanded and challenged Kerber's model to include evidence of women's participation in the vibrant political and print cultures of the era, reminding us that motherhood was one of many possible roles for early national women. Yet the intersections between the prescriptive models and women's lived experiences as mothers remain relatively underexplored. How did women respond to the contradictory messages inherent in republican motherhood, which advocated advancements in women's education while simultaneously promoting a prescribed sphere of domesticity?[2]

Was republican motherhood compatible with educated women's search for mere equality? As we have seen, educated women approached their various personal and social relationships with a sense of optimism, confident in the egalitarian rhetoric of the era. Yet, for many women, the duties of motherhood tested their youthful claims to mere equality. Although determined to pursue lives marked by continued intellectual development, motherhood compelled educated women to confront the realities of difference. Their everyday experiences of family life—childrearing was mother's work, whereas breadwinning was father's work—often contrasted sharply with their visions of mere equality and shared experience.

The experiences of Jane Bayard Kirkpatrick illustrate the key tensions that women experienced—as mothers and in their other social roles—as the early national experimentation with mere equality buttressed against the nineteenth-century rhetoric of difference and separate spheres. In her efforts to enact the role of an "accomplished lady" to perfection, Jane Kirkpatrick developed a model of womanhood increasingly shaped by difference. In both its rhetoric and practices, motherhood presented challenges to any woman seeking to live merely as the equals of man.

"The Improvement of the Mind and Heart"

A brief examination of Jane Bayard's childhood and youth allows us to trace how early national notions of equality, education, and difference shaped her transition into marriage and motherhood. Jane Bayard was the eldest daughter of Martha Hodge Bayard and Colonel John Bayard, a successful merchant noted for his patriotism during the Revolutionary War.[3] The Bayards made their home in Philadelphia and the surrounding Pennsylvania countryside. As a young girl, Jane received "the best education" available at the time. Her father employed a teacher for his children and several neighboring families.

As Jane later recalled, "It was a great matter in those days of desolation to have such a resource." Jane also studied "languages and music from private teachers in New York" while on an extended visit with relatives. Jane was an "an apt scholar, possessing unusual powers of mind, a quick perception, fine imagination, and a very retentive memory."[4]

In 1788, when Jane was sixteen, John Bayard moved his family to New Brunswick, New Jersey. The following year, Jane's younger sisters, Margaret and Anna (ages eleven and ten at the time), began attending the Moravian Female Seminary in Bethlehem, Pennsylvania. As Jane explained to her friend Sally Wister, "Papa was solicited to put my sisters, to a very fashionable Boarding school in NY which is in great repute, but I think he has very wisely preferred Bethlehem." By providing both financial and philosophical support, fathers such as John Bayard helped promote new attitudes toward women's education. Writing to his daughter Lucy, John Pierce conveyed the sentiments of a growing number of early national parents: "I hope, for some good purpose; perhaps, to see his dear children become good, and useful, happy. What greater happiness, my child, can parents feel, than to observe their children thoughtful of serious things, [and] attentive to their studies."[5] Such fathers regarded the proper education of both sons and daughters as an essential family value. Although Jane did not join her sisters at Bethlehem, she expressed approval of her father's decision. As she explained to Sally, "I have always thought the improvement of the mind and heart, of more material consequence than the polish of person and manners." Jane's comments reveal the value she placed on intellectual aspirations while also reflecting emerging criticisms of boarding schools for paying more attention to personal polish than academic achievement.[6]

Jane's "improvement of the mind and heart" shaped her sense of self, but the death of her mother in 1780, when she was just eight years old, was a transformative event. Her father remarried twice (in 1781 and again in 1788), and Jane enjoyed warm relationships with her stepmothers. Yet she carried with her a wistful sense of maternal loss: "Oh, what a loss! I feel as if I should have been another creature had she been spared to me, for then I should have believed that I was truly beloved." Her mother's death created a void that left Jane feeling "differently constituted from others." Prone to what she called "joyless apathy and inactive solitude," Jane struggled, as she confessed to her friend Sally, to melt "the ice around my heart." To counter her melancholy, Jane turned to faith as a source of comfort. As she reflected just days before her nineteenth birthday, "the principles implanted by early education pointed to a surer road to peace—They directed to the blest asylum of Religion." Along with her cultivated mind, Jane developed a strong religious commitment, "determining no longer to depend on earth for my felicity—but to look to a higher and better source for happiness."[7]

Jane sought comfort in religion, but she also longed for more earthly connections. "How often has my heart, either when glowing by the view of some cheering animating prospect—or sinking beneath the weight of some discouraging apprehension—sigh'd—and longed for a congenial spirit—that would participate with me—one that could soothe and bid me be at peace with myself."[8] Her desire for intimate companionship reflected the reigning influence of the culture of sensibility. Like other women in this study, Jane was inspired by cultural values that stressed shared experiences and sentimental communications with like-minded individuals. Jane expressed her longing for a "congenial spirit" to her friend Sally, but such sentimentality undoubtedly shaped her expectations for both friendship and romantic love. In New Brunswick, she met her future husband, Andrew Kirkpatrick, a successful lawyer. Family lore referred to Jane and Andrew as "the best match in New Jersey." Yet as Jane admitted to Sally, her decision to marry Andrew created a sense of anxiety: "I have pass'd thro' a delicate important and trying period.—Weak and timid surrounded with intricacies, which I knew not to develop—dubious which path to choose. Fearful to decide."[9] Jane's choppy, vague language (especially compared with her flowing lines on sensibility, also written to Sally) reflected her unease and hesitancy to commit her feelings about marriage to paper, even to a close friend.

"That heart must be differently formed from mine," Jane confessed to Sally, "which in contemplation of so material a change—can feel a joy unchastized by fear!" Despite her mixed emotions, Jane remained cautiously optimistic about married life: "yet (I will not say there are none) but I believe there are not many—whose prospects promise fairer or more competent and rational satisfaction." In contemplating "so material a change" that marriage would bring to her life, Jane privileged the promise of "rational satisfaction" rather than romantic bliss. She expressed a desire for a union of reason and love, with perhaps more weight given to reason. In her choice of a husband, Jane sought "the society and unbounded confidence of a mind of worth and intelligence." Intellectual compatibility was central to her vision of a happy marriage. "It is a 'bold experiment,'" Jane admitted to Sally, and "more than ever I need your good wishes." Even couples strongly committed to companionate ideals, such as Benjamin Ward and Linda Raymond or Jane Bowne and Reuben Haines, commonly expressed mixed emotions before their weddings. A woman's transition from sister and daughter to wife and mother was indeed "so material a change." Many women shared Jane's trepidation, wondering how marriage would affect their sense of self. "Ah, my dear and amiable friend," she entreated Sally, "love me not the less for tho' I change my name."[10] The change in name signaled greater changes yet to come.

Jane Bayard and Andrew Kirkpatrick married on November 1, 1792, and despite her fears, the bold experiment seemed successful. Writing to Jane in 1821, on the eve of their twenty-ninth wedding anniversary, Andrew mused about their long married life together. "Our course has not been brilliant, but it has been better: it has been calm and peaceful, and undisturbed." Calm, peaceful, undisturbed—the Kirkpatricks sustained a rational marriage rooted in domestic harmony. "Their connexion was a source of happiness to both," according to their son-in-law Samuel How. "He found in her a strongly attached wife, and his children a mother, whom they revered and loved."[11]

Those calm, peaceful years brought material changes to Jane's life—in particular, motherhood. Between 1793 and 1810, Jane gave birth to seven children, two of whom died in infancy.[12] In January 1823, just after her twenty-first birthday, her youngest daughter Elizabeth died "after a linger-ing illness." Her four surviving children—Mary Ann, John Bayard, George Littleton, and Jane Eudora—remained single far past the demographic norms for their peers. Littleton and Jane Eudora married at thirty-five and thirty-eight, respectively, and Jane's two eldest children, Mary Ann and Bayard, did not marry until their late forties.[13] Jane maintained close ties to her children throughout their prolonged periods of singlehood, particularly to her daugh-ters, who continued to live at home. Throughout these years, Jane's domestic, social, and intellectual pursuits were shaped primarily by her identity as a mother. How did "so material a change" shape Jane's understanding of her-self, the world around her, and the notion of mere equality?

"The Path of Duty and Happiness"

Jane Bayard Kirkpatrick settled into her roles as wife and mother, adapting to the material and maternal changes that accompanied marriage. In a letter to a mutual friend, Reverend Samuel Miller expressed his admiration for Jane: "I rejoice that you are favored with the society, the counsels, and the prayers of Mrs. Kirkpatrick, and Miss Bayard, who have minds adorned with piety, as well as enlightened with knowledge, and indeed with that practical wisdom and tender sensibility, which render them invaluable friends and guides to those who are anxiously seeking the path of duty and happiness."[14]

Jane Kirkpatrick and her younger sister Anna Bayard served as shining examples for other women "seeking the path of duty and happiness." Jane's strong intellect was balanced by her sensibility and piety, enabling her to cultivate a model identity as a republican mother. Samuel Miller's admiring description of the Bayard sisters underscores how prescriptive models of womanhood shaped individual perceptions of women's social and domestic duties. Although he praised their knowledge and wisdom, Samuel Miller particularly approved of how Jane and Anna employed their intellectual powers in order to help guide others. "My prayer is, that their conversation and example may be a blessing to you," he wrote to Fanny Martel.[15]

Jane Kirkpatrick enacted the ideals of republican motherhood by sustaining quiet patterns of enlightened sociability. As her daughter Jane Eudora later recalled, "She was fitted to be the intelligent companion of persons of science and erudition." Under Jane's careful efforts, the Kirkpatrick home in New Brunswick offered family and friends a warm social circle rooted in the calm pursuit of rational pleasures. Describing a typical evening at home, Jane wrote, "Mr. K. fixed himself with his stand and book in one corner... and the girls and myself were around our table—they at work and I reading to them." Surrounded by her family and engaged in typical "occupations" of "reading—writing—sewing," Jane cultivated scenes of domestic harmony: "Happy together the hours glided away in peace." Although Jane's husband enjoyed a long career as a New Jersey state Supreme Court judge, discussions of politics rarely seemed to disturb the family's peace. When "the cannon were fired in honour of the Orleans Hero," Jane remained focused on the comforts of home: "The day to me was a day of calm enjoyment." Her "family arrangement, book, pen and needle" produced "a mind composed and cheerful." While the town publicly celebrated Andrew Jackson's election, in the Kirkpatrick home, "the hours pass sweetly without any extraneous amusement."[16]

As a mother, Jane privileged domestic tranquility, selflessly devoting her energies to her family. In both fact and fiction, educated women who channeled their intellectual energies toward their domestic and social duties earned approbation. Writing to his fiancée, Benjamin Ward praised one acquaintance, "Mrs. W.," as "one of the best of women—She is intelligent, and kind and social; possessing a very amiable disposition, with that turn of mind which is inclined to make all around her happy." Margaret Manigault expressed admiration for one of her friends, who "passes her time in a very respectable manner in educating her children." Harriet Margaret Wharton warmly described one family friend, Mrs. L., as "universally pleasing by her cultivated mind and charming manners." These ideals also informed literary representations of motherhood. "Hortensia Mildmay," a character sketch published in the *Weekly Visitor,* "had been well instructed in every useful art and liberal accomplishment." Eager "to cultivate her mind, and improve her manners," Hortensia embraced the educational opportunities made available to her. Once married, Hortensia directed her accomplishments toward a single goal—becoming "a happy wife and mother." Her "natural vivacity" found fullest expression in the care of her family and the education of her children. Her only wish was to have her children "all creditably and agreeably settled in life."[17]

As a generation of educated women transitioned from their roles as students and daughters to wives and mothers, they were encouraged to follow the examples of real and idealized women such as Jane Kirkpatrick and Hortensia Mildmay. Harriet Margaret Wharton drew inspiration from a character sketch that she copied into her journal: "Arabella was one of the kindest daughters without forgetting she was a wife, one of the most attentive wives without forgetting she was a Mother, and the tenderest of Mothers without a breach of the social, the domestic, the friendly, or even the elegant duties of the individual." Arabella represented the epitome of an educated woman who continually put her powers to good use toward serving others: "she could *animate, regulate, compassionate, instruct, serve, and sympathize* by the easiest transitions." Reflecting on this "charming character," Harriet expressed her "wish if I am ever placed in this situation...that I may fulfill them as well."[18]

How could women assure that their own "path of duty and happiness" would follow the same easy course as depicted in idealized representations of womanhood? Proper education was vital. Throughout the early nineteenth century, educators boldly proclaimed that a woman was "permitted by right, and bound by duty, to pursue her own happiness," including "the highest attention upon the development of her mind." A woman's pursuit of happiness, however, was never meant to be purely individualistic but, rather, directed toward serving others: "But the most exalted element of woman's happiness lies in her power of communicating happiness to others." Especially once she became a mother, a woman's energies "must be subordinate to that of home." Creating a happy home life was a mother's primary goal: "Nothing must supersede her constant endeavor to render herself 'intelligent and agreeable in the parlor, companionable in the sitting-room, happy in the nursery, and mistress in the kitchen.'"[19]

Women's pursuit of happiness could best be achieved through selfless devotion to their families rather than any desire to live merely as the equals of man. By infusing motherhood with lofty purpose, prescriptive thinkers sought to persuade women to seek something greater than mere equality. "Would every mother in this intelligent and free nation thus carefully train up her children," Sarah Pierce of the Litchfield Female Academy argued, "we should soon feel its beneficial effects, not only in private life, but in society." As Joseph Emerson asserted in his 1822 essay on *Female Education,* "Surely the mother has more influence in forming the rising generation, than is possessed by any other character." By shaping the next generation of leaders and citizens, mothers held the key to their children's—and the nation's—future. Yet such influence came at a price. Nineteenth-century educators increasingly abandoned the idea of mere equality to promote a hierarchical ordering of the family, insisting that mothering remained "subordinate, as it respects the father." This prescriptive model rooted women's lives within an ideological framework of difference rather than the promise of mere equality. "Though her station is subordinate," Emerson rationalized, "yet in a great measure, she carries in her heart, and holds in her hand, the destinies of the world."[20]

As educators gave increased responsibility and respect to well-educated mothers, they reinforced a patriarchal ordering of family life. "Most men are so entirely engrossed by business," Sarah Pierce reasoned, that the proper training of children's character "can be done only by the mother." Although many early national fathers played active roles in their children's upbringing, most agreed that mothers had a unique role to play, particularly in the education of daughters. "For girl children there can be no substitute, tutor or friend fully to supply the place of mother," Daniel Parker wrote to his wife. "No one but yourself can make Sarah what she should be and what she is capable of being in a few years." Like Jane Kirkpatrick, Anne Parker lost her mother at a young age and was raised by her father. "Although he made you very perfect in all that a man could teach or superintend in a female child," Daniel mused, "still there are parts of education you never thought of till called to exercise them as mistress." The belief that mothers played vital roles in raising children, particularly their daughters, helped constrain women to maternal roles rooted in sexual difference. Even the most well-meaning father could not take the place of a republican mother.[21]

In order to properly fulfill their duties as mothers, women's intellectual energies had to be properly directed. Thus, although Daniel Parker praised his wife's "powers of mind and the superiority of your accomplishments," he worried that Anne did not put those powers to use in her mothering. "Do my dear Anne rouse yourself and exert your fine taste and talents in commanding and instructing them." Daniel's criticisms centered not on Anne's intellectual capacities (which he admired) but, rather, on her failure to properly direct those accomplishments. Yet, in repeatedly urging his wife to "attend a little more to your children," Daniel offended Anne, who resented his frequent reproaches. "Pray do not trouble yourself about looking after the children and servants for me," she curtly wrote in response to one of Daniel's letters. "The children were never as well, so happy, or so good, as they have been for the last four months"—that is, since Daniel's extended absence from home on business. Insisting that he sought "only to excite your pride and your ambition," Daniel continued to offer Anne unsolicited advice, recommending that she read the *Private Journal of Madame Campan,* as "this little treatise confirms the remark you have often heard me make that it is to mothers that we are most indebted for our characters." After perusing Campan's book, Anne replied that "her ideas respecting children, are completely in unison with my own—and her method is what I aim at in educating them."[22] Anne Parker resented her husband's constant reminders of what constituted good mothering because she had already adopted her own methods.

Although Anne Parker responded to her husband's advice with indignation, confident in her maternal abilities, other women wondered if they could live up to idealized accounts of motherhood. "I am so far from discharging the duties of my station or from meeting the high responsibilities which devolve on me as a mother," Abigail Bradley Hyde confessed to her parents, "that the conviction of my deficiencies which sometimes forces itself on me is almost overwhelming."[23] Anne Parker and Abigail Hyde may be seen to represent two opposing responses to ideological constructions of republican motherhood. When faced with challenges to her mothering, Anne Parker's voice remained defiant, retaining assertive qualities that her husband found ill-suited to her primary responsibilities as a mother. Yet if Anne Parker can be seen as remaining too self-centered, Abigail Hyde appears too hesitant to embrace the duties of mothering. Abigail had attended Sarah Pierce's Litchfield Female Academy, one of the most highly regarded female academies in New England. Despite her educational accomplishments, she questioned her mothering abilities and felt overwhelmed by the duties entrusted to her. Both reactions suggest the powerful ways in which motherhood reshaped educated women's sense of themselves. Women's efforts at self-expression reflected their responses to the various depictions of mothering they encountered in both fact and fiction.

"Her Active and Energetic Mind Found Full Employ"

Jane Bayard Kirkpatrick approached her duties as a wife and mother without Anne Parker's overconfidence or Abigail Hyde's tentativeness. "I live for my children," Jane wrote in her journal, "and their happiness must be my object and motive." Jane's understanding of selfless motherhood shaped her identity, as well as the values she sought to pass on to her daughters. "While you cultivate your talents, and polish your manners," she advised in one letter, "study to acquire those graces which are above all price, meekness, gentleness, and charity."[24] Rather than encouraging her daughters to pursue expressions of mere equality, Jane socialized them to embody passive, feminine traits that reflected the power of prescription.

Jane's understanding of proper womanhood underscored the contradictions inherent in republican motherhood. She stressed the importance of female meekness but also constantly sought ways to exercise her mental powers. As her daughter Jane Eudora recalled, Jane "held the pen of a ready writer." Yet for Jane intellectual capacity did not translate into explicit calls for mere equality. Despite her literary talents, Jane "ever shrunk from display, and her modesty equaled her talent." When urged to submit her writings for publication, Jane insisted "her only inducement so to do would be the hope of doing good by them." Unconvinced that "such an end could be effected by her compositions," Jane declined repeated solicitations. After Jane's death in 1851, Jane Eudora published a selection of her mother's writings, "with a view to keep alive her memory."[25]

Among Jane Kirkpatrick's posthumously published writings was a novella titled, *The Light of Other Days,* a fictional account of "past times" based in fact—"the leading events actually took place," Jane insisted in the introduction. In her novella, Jane presents the story of three sisters and their experiences with marriage, motherhood, and domesticity. Her description of Mary, the eldest sister (modeled after Jane's stepmother), provides a representative view of her ideals of womanhood: "Her active and energetic mind found full employ. So adequate was she to every duty that every difficulty disappeared. Order reigned in every department of the house. There was time for everything, no hurry, no delay. Cheerfulness shed a charm over every repast. The parlor was a scene of hilarity, animated conversation, and the cordial reciprocity of kindness."[26] Mary directs her intellectual energies toward her family and friends, creating a warm circle of domestic sociability in which harmony and cheerfulness reigned. "Her energy infused spirit in every department of her household," Jane recalled with admiration. Mary possessed "talents to command an empire," yet was content to focus those talents within her family circle.[27]

Mary provides a model of female excellence rooted not in mere equality but, rather, in domestic tranquility. Her younger sister Eliza, however, fails to follow her wise example. Widowed young, Eliza remains attached to the "high life" and fails to give proper attention to her children, who remain under the care of their grandparents. "Self—self—was the supreme object to which all else must yield," Jane wrote with a disapproving air. Eliza's selfishness stands in stark contrast to Mary's selfless devotion to her family. "Had she restrained her views and wishes to the situation which Providence assigned to her," Jane noted, Eliza "might have been the happiest wife, and the glad mother of her family." Instead, Eliza suffered through a disappointing second marriage with an "improper" man, before succumbing to a debilitating fatal illness. "The delusions of the world cheated her of substantial happiness," Jane reflected, "and brought grief, disappointment, and misery on those who loved her purely and sincerely."[28]

As a young girl, Susan, the third sister, longed for "every pleasure" but has "good sense enough to check these vain repinings." Susan marries a minister and lives a long life "marked by piety, benevolence, and the discharge of every duty."[29] In describing the three sisters' experiences, Jane's novella sought to transform family history into instructive example. She admired Mary's cheerful command of her family circle and Susan's ability to find contentment in a quiet life as a minister's wife. Eliza, by contrast, presents a cautionary tale through her selfish pursuits and desires for autonomy. There was little room for female ambition or mere equality in Jane's understanding of womanhood. "What happiness can the ambitious, the worldly-minded enjoy," she concluded, "compared to the peace and elevated serenity of those who walk in the paths of wisdom and purity?" For Jane, the answer was clear: "Let the course pursued by Eliza and Susan decide the question."[30]

Jane chose the path of motherhood, but her younger sister pursued a different course. Margaret Bayard Smith was the author of two published novels, several essays, and children's stories, and by the 1830s, she was a regular contributor to *The Ladies' Magazine*. Living in Washington, D.C., Margaret Bayard Smith was inspired by the parlor politics that provided Washington women "a station in society which is not known elsewhere." As Margaret noted in an 1814 letter to Jane, Washington women freely occupied public spaces, underscoring the inextricable connections between sociability and politics that prevailed in the national capital: "On every public occasion, a launch, an oration, an inauguration, in the court, in the representative hall, as well as the drawing room, they are treated with mark'd distinction." These activities, Margaret asserted, elevated women "not only to an equality but I think to a superiority to the other sex." Washington women enjoyed "more ease, freedom and equality" than their counterparts elsewhere.[31]

Inspired by such ease, freedom, and equality, Margaret Bayard Smith actively pursued her literary aspirations. While Jane strove to live as an ideal republican mother, her sister confessed a decided aversion to domesticity: "How insignificant and how wearisome do these domestic employments seem." Instead, Margaret "longed to soar in to the regions of intellectual existence." Despite her ambition, Margaret struggled with the "variance between my duties and inclination." Although she enjoyed considerable opportunities to experience a sense of mere equality, Margaret nonetheless felt constrained by early national gender prescriptions. "The limited circle it is prescribed for woman to tread," she wrote, stood in stark contrast to "the unlimited sphere of man... [that] has no bounds offered to the expansion and exercise of his powers."[32] Margaret Bayard Smith understood that her desires for intellectual expression and elevated status contrasted sharply with how the era—and her sister—defined selfless motherhood. Margaret put the promise of mere equality into practice by maintaining a literary career, but she also recognized that gendered constraints limited the full exercise of her ambition.

Although Jane did not seek literary fame for herself, she supported her sister's burgeoning career as writer. When Margaret Bayard Smith's first novel, *Winter in Washington,* was published in 1824, Jane was thrilled to receive "the New Book—we have been anticipating with so much pleasure and solicitude." In her journal, Jane noted that her sister's novel "afforded us a great deal of entertainments—and tho' it has some faults it has many beauties— One who writes so well with care might write better. Practice will make perfect." While shunning the spotlight for herself, Jane eagerly helped Margaret perfect her writing, editing her manuscripts and freely offering constructive criticism. "I sent *Lucy* to the care of S. Southard Esq.," Jane wrote in reference to one of her sister's unpublished manuscripts. "I feel apprehensive that I have written too plainly—yet I could not do less with truth." On reviewing another of Margaret's manuscripts, Jane noted that "it interested and pleased me a great deal yet I dread its appearance in print—I know not how it will take with the publick."[33] Jane's apprehension regarding the public reception of her sister's writings may explain her reluctance to seek publication of her own writings—perhaps she dreaded the criticism that might be directed at her literary efforts. Faced with a choice between "duties and inclination," Jane chose the duties of motherhood over any inclination for literary fame. Unlike her sister, Jane avoided public expressions of mere equality and conformed to prescriptive models of motherhood.

Such tensions shaped the experiences of other early national women who attempted to navigate their desires for literary expression with the duties of domesticity. Gertrude Meredith occasionally wrote for the *Port Folio,* which was edited by her friend Joseph Dennie, but she carefully insisted that her energies remained focused on family: "When I am home, every thing is within my power." Home represented her true "sphere of action"; Gertrude assured her husband, William, "To be happy, to make my husband so, and see my daughter well engross almost all my attentions." When William complimented her writing, she admitted that such praise was "flattering indeed," but informed him, "I should be more delighted, did you tell me I was an *attentive* wife, and a *good* mother—herein consists my ambition." Gertrude defined her literary efforts as secondary to her roles as wife and mother. "Willingly would I resign all my *literary* merit," she wrote to William, in favor of cultivating "domestic affections."[34] It is difficult to assess how sincere Gertrude was in such proclamations. She may have been telling her husband what she imagined he wanted to hear—that being a wife and mother was her first priority. Maintaining her identity as a literary woman was undoubtedly important to Gertrude, but she clearly recognized cultural prescriptions that viewed home as her proper "sphere of action."

Women such as Gertrude Meredith and Margaret Bayard Smith were able, in varying degrees, to balance their literary ambitions with domestic duties, even as they acknowledged persistent conflicts between home and work. Their desire to live as mere equals found expression not just in the domestic sphere but also in the literary public sphere. Jane Bayard Kirkpatrick did not seek publication of her writings, but her pen remained in hand. Journal writing offered an alternate way to voice her experiences with motherhood.

"My Heart Has Been Too Much Occupied"

Evidence suggests that Jane Bayard Kirkpatrick regularly kept a journal from the age of sixteen until her death, indicating her strong commitment to self-expression through writing. Unfortunately, only one volume of her journals, covering a ten-year period from 1824 to 1834, remains extant. Excerpts from January 1824, the beginning of this volume, provide insights into her experiences as a wife and mother:

> –I spent the morning most pleasantly reading and writing. In the afternoon we sat in the parlour all together—in the evening Mr. K. went to his office—Bayard supp'd at Mr. E. M. Kay's and L. at Ross Hall. Mr. Van Keuren sat an hour in the evening with us—I read Las Casas.
> –I do not remember that for years I have felt so much of my natural flow of spirit as I did for the first part of the evening.
> –I went out to return and make a few visits.
> –For a week past I have given Louisa a regular lesson—I want to see if I can teach her to read.
> –I have finished Las Casas.
> –I had some pleasant conversation—and felt my mind cheer'd.[35]

Jane's daily experiences revolved around sociability, reading, and writing, including providing instruction to Louisa, a servant in the Kirkpatrick household. Although still grieving the loss of her daughter Elizabeth, who had died a year earlier, Jane experienced moments of tranquility as she engaged in favored activities. Her journal entries from January 1824 reveal a thoughtful woman whose daily pursuits revolved around the regular exercise of her intellectual powers, especially in the company of family and friends. Yet as time progressed, Jane's articulation of the self through journal writing underwent a subtle, but profound, shift. Here is a similar sampling of her journal entries from January 1827:

–We prepared for company.

–In the evening we resumed our book.

–In the evening we were just fixed round our table beginning to read— a fine glowing fire—thinking we should certainly see no one that night—when we heard an unusual noise at the door—and to our surprise—Mr. & Mrs. Edward Boyd entered—We did all we could to make them comfortable after such a cold ride.

–I was occupied in my own room all the morning reading & writing & teaching Louisa—to whom I give a lesson everyday.

–We invited a few of our neighbors to spend a sociable evening with us.[36]

Although Jane continued to engage in similar activities as she had in 1824, including tutoring Louisa, she increasingly articulated these experiences with the plural *we* instead of the singular *I*. Jane's growing use of the pronoun *we* in her journal writing underscores her shifting sense of identity and experience. As time went on, Jane viewed her journal writing not primarily as an articulation of the self but as a "collective narrative" of her family's activities. Although she still used the singular *I* to record certain events, her journal reflected a loss of individual expression. Jane did not completely disappear as an individual, but her identity became increasingly subsumed within her experiences of motherhood.[37]

This shift was particularly evident in late 1827, when Jane stopped writing in her journal for a month when her adult children were away from home. As she explained on resuming her writing, "Many sad and anxious days here intervene. . . . I have not been able to write in my journal—for my heart has been too much occupied. I hope I shall now be able to do better." Without her children at home, Jane found it difficult to give voice to her daily activities. When her children returned home, Jane expressed a renewed sense of self as she took up her pen again: "I am happy to have my children again with me—may we live in peace and love." Yet the following year, when her daughter Jane Eudora left home for another extended visit with friends, Jane again neglected her journal, noting, "A variety of occupations prevented me from keeping up my journal." During her children's absences (particularly her daughters'), Jane felt less inclined to record her daily experiences. Her silence may have reflected an increase in Jane's domestic duties without her daughters at home to assist her. Jane may have simply been too busy to write; but as she confessed, it was her "heart" that was "too much occupied." Jane felt "lonely and dejected" whenever her "dear girls" were away from home.[38] Their absences from the family circle created a physical and emotional void that Jane found difficult to express in writing.

Through its silences and shifting voices, Jane's journal suggests some of the ways in which motherhood transformed the lives and writings of early national mothers. In the archives, the strong voices of young, educated women often fade as the cares and duties of motherhood increasingly shaped their everyday lives. Young women who wrote expressive diaries and letters during their school days and courtships rarely continued the practice with the same vigor once they became wives and mothers. Although some women, including Margaret Bayard Smith and Gertrude Meredith, achieved a measure of success as published authors, many mothers put down their pens altogether. "Marriage induced silence" as the emotional and physical demands of domesticity "created emotional discontinuity" for women. Marriage and motherhood also created intellectual discontinuity. The ardent acquisition of education that marked women's single, youthful days became difficult to sustain once they became mothers. Finding time to write at all was a challenge for many mothers, leaving gaps in the archival records of women's experiences. Historians are much more likely to discover deeply expressive diaries written by single women than ones kept by mothers. Martha Tomhave Blauvelt notes the example of Sarah Connell Ayer, who wrote 340 pages in her diary in the seven years before her marriage but produced only 47 pages during her fifty years as a wife and mother.[39] Such silences present challenges for historians seeking to trace how marriage and motherhood affected individual women's emotional and intellectual lives.

Some women expressed a determination to balance mothering and literary expression. Writing to Jane in 1805, Margaret Bayard Smith described her surroundings: "I have the stand placed beside the fire in the parlour and the children playing round me. I shall accustom myself to write and read with them in the room and I shall soon find it easy, tho' at present," as she admitted, "it somewhat disturbs me." Yet once they became mothers, many women found it challenging to engage in regular intellectual pursuits. As Sarah Ripley Stearns noted in her journal, "the cares of my Babes, takes up so large a portion of my time and attention, that I have not much time for reading or reflecting." Margaret Manigault's experiences were similar: "in the morning, my little children are running about me, and chattering, and playing, and making such a noise that it is difficult to attend to anything but them." Over a decade later, Margaret still struggled to "write regularly." As she lamented, "I cannot draw forth my book in the face of the whole family assembled—'Mama, are you writing a book?'—'Mama, is that your journal?'—would inevitably be said by half a dozen little curious darlings."[40] Without a room—or time—of their own, many mothers constrained or silenced their literary expressions.

We can glimpse traces of silencing in the letters of early national mothers. Writing to her friend Weltha Brown, Eliza Perkins insisted, "my long silence is wholly out of my power." As Eliza explained, "when you are a wife, and a mother of a crying babe, and feel it necessary to curtail your expenses, as it respects help, your own feelings will supply a sufficient excuse." Motherhood transformed Eliza, by her own admission, into "so very bad a correspondent," as time to write expressive letters was in short supply. "Oh dear Weltha," Eliza sighed, "great is the change." The duties of motherhood interfered with women's efforts at literary self-expression. "I know you would not wonder, at my not writing oftener," Sarah Tappan Pierce began one letter to her sister, "if you could see, how my time is occupied." The cares of tending for her infant daughter, who "is seldom quiet out of my arms," accounted for Sarah's epistolary silence. "I have made several attempts, Eliza, to write to you when the child is asleep," Sarah explained, "but have always been obliged to take her before I could write a page." Motherhood took up considerable time and energy, as Lowry Wister wrote to her sister, "The various duties that daily press upon me, for my own family, or for my children, leave me but little leisure to devote to my pen." Cynthia Pease called on her friend for understanding her failure to write sooner: "Nothing but a multitude of cares, which have occupied my time and attention, has caused this *long, long* silence. Could you call in and see me a little while and know how much my time is taken up with domestic cares, &c.," she pleaded, "you would almost wonder *I ever wrote a letter.*"[41]

Lengthy silences and countless unwritten letters suggest some of the transformations that motherhood brought to women's lives. Even when they found time to write, some women found it difficult to express their interior lives as mothers. "The day passed in domestic quiet—nothing new," Jane wrote in her journal. "In the evening we read and worked as usual." Daily patterns of domestic life often warranted little commentary in women's writings. "Since the departure of my dear Charles," Sarah Bancker wrote to her husband, "nothing material has occurred." "What shall I write about my dear

William?" Gertrude Meredith mused in one letter to her husband. "Nothing has occurred to amuse you, and my brain affords nothing to interest you." Although Gertrude frequently discussed literary matters with her husband, she assumed her daily domestic routines were of little interest. "Our life has since your departure has been unusually dull," she informed her husband. "I can have no news to communicate," Gertrude remarked in another letter. "I devote my time to writing, working, playing with my babes, and reading the Encyclopedia." Even as they recorded days marked by a careful balance of domestic duties and intellectual pursuits, women downplayed their everyday activities. "The day passed as usual," Jane wrote in 1824, "unmarked by events." Two years later, her tone was identical: "Nothing remarkable has marked this day thus far."[42]

Women's characterization of their daily lives as unremarkable suggests how the physical and emotional duties of motherhood transformed their efforts at self-expression. Undoubtedly, women's everyday domestic experiences sometimes failed to match the idealistic visions of motherhood articulated in prescriptive writings. Writing about her sister Jane Bayard Kirkpatrick, Anna Maria Bayard reflected, "I believe her patient and quiet endurance conceals much of the inconvenience and anxiety which she experiences." Jane devoted her energies toward maintaining an exterior sense of calm. "Her husband and children are well and happy about her and bless her," Anna noted, as if in consolation of her sister's struggles. If women addressed the "inconvenience and anxiety" of motherhood, it was often with ambivalence. "I ought not to complain," one woman wrote to a friend: "Yet at times I often catch myself exclaiming Oh My Children!" At times, mothers expressed an anxiousness that betrayed the ideals of domestic tranquility. "I have many trials to endure," Maria Cornell confessed to her daughter. "How little do children know what parents feel," she reflected in another letter. "Every thing—even what to them seems of no consequence—is a subject of anxiety to parents." Gertrude Meredith agreed, writing to her son William that there was "an anxious spirit my dear boy, always at work in the maternal mind."[43]

The anxiety that mothers experienced refocused the "maternal mind" from intellectual expression to emotional work. When her elder son, Bayard, embarked on a voyage to South America in 1825, Jane constantly awaited letters and news of his well-being. In one remarkable passage, she recorded a dream about her absent son: "This morning I had a sweet vision of my dear Bayard—I saw him just as he looked in his picture—I thought I was sitting on a sofa—and he came behind—and leaned his head on my shoulder—and with an expression of tenderness & sensibility uncommon in him said to me 'dear mother, how happy I am in the persuasion of your love'—I laid my

FIGURE 7. Jane Bayard Kirkpatrick, journal, 1825. Among her journal writings from April 1825 is a lengthy entry dated April 20, 1825, in which Jane recorded a dream about her son Bayard, then away from home on a voyage to South America. Special Collections and University Archives, Rutgers University Libraries.

cheek by his—and waked—There seems to me as if there was some communion between his spirit and mind—altho' we are so far distant."[44] In recording her dream, Jane provided a rare glimpse into her unconscious expressions of maternal desire. Jane longed for emotional intimacy and effusive expression from her adult son—to be assured that he was "happy in the persuasion of [her] love." Jane wanted Bayard to recognize her devoted mothering and to respond with corresponding affection and appreciation—traits that she wistfully recognized as "uncommon" in her son. Bayard's frequent travels and professional pursuits created anxiety for Jane, and she repeatedly expressed her desire to see him "settle down in some regular business."[45] Significantly, Jane's dream revolved not around Bayard's professional struggles but, rather, on her experiences of mothering.

Jane's intense reactions to her children's absences from home—from neglecting her journal to recording her dreams—indicate her reluctance to part with her children or with her primary identification as their mother. Her daughter Elizabeth's death in 1823 may have made it more difficult for Jane to relinquish her strong attachment to her surviving children (and her children's sense of duty and loyalty to Jane may explain why they all married so late in life). Elizabeth's death weighed heavily on Jane Kirkpatrick's heart and pen, underscoring the inextricable connections between mothering and mourning that gave meaning to many women's experiences during this era.

"Grief Has Paralyzed My Mental Powers"

Repeatedly returning to her journal, even after periods of disruption, Jane inscribed value to her writing as a means "to keep up the remembrance of past life." Remembrance was essential to Jane's sense of self as a mother, particularly after Elizabeth's death in 1823. Jane already experienced the loss of two infants, Sarah and Charles, between 1802 and 1810. The death of three children in one family was not uncommon; it reflected the demographic realities of early national America. Throughout the early nineteenth century, infant mortality rates remained high, and nearly 25 percent of infants died before their first birthday. Yet the idiom of republican motherhood, along with sentimental conceptions of family life, stressed unique bonds between mothers and children. These ideological shifts in early national families increasingly privileged strong mother-child relationships, infusing the death of children with heightened emotional weight. Seeking to console Maria Cornell after two of her children died within the span of one month, her sister Catherine wrote, "I have often heard a friend of mine say who has lost her father mother and sister, that she thought when she lost her child she felt more, than for all she had lost in a dear and good father, a tender mother and affectionate and beloved sister, so strong is the tie between parents and children."[46]

Although Jane previously had lost her parents and two infants, Elizabeth's death at age twenty-one devastated her. Parents braced themselves for infant mortality, but they expected children who survived past early childhood to be "safe" from further harm. "I too have buried two lovely infants," Elizabeth Bowne wrote in consolation to her daughter Jane Bowne Haines. The earlier loss of her infant children, Elizabeth insisted, was nothing compared to the recent death of her adult son. "At the time [I] thought no heavier affliction could assail me," Elizabeth reflected, "but Oh my child if thee should live to my years and have to part with a Son a Darling son in the Bloom of life, thou will find thy late tryal light in comparison."[47]

Religious prescriptions urged parents to accept their children's deaths with calm resignation, yet such loss was often hard to bear. While her daughter Elizabeth was gravely ill, Jane expressed her "desire to be prepared to meet and to submit to the will of the Lord, however it may be manifested." She sought comfort in the doctrine of resignation but also experienced "the keenest anguish in view of her sufferings and apprehension of my final separation from my Elizabeth." Echoing Jane's anguish, Gertrude Meredith described the experiences of one mother who was "quite inconsolable and from the violence of her grief it is feared her own safety is endangered." Gertrude sympathized deeply with her friend: "I cannot conceive of a situation more agonizing than that of Poor Gitty." Such a loss, Gertrude reflected, "almost staggers reason from its throne, and defies the power of Christian resignation to endure."[48]

The force of her grief temporarily silenced Jane Kirkpatrick's journal writing. "After a long interval I resume my pen," she reflected. "The withering hand of grief has paralyzed my mental powers. Some can give an account of what they have felt. But I am sank in grief, I cannot rise. My heart is bowed down." Overcome by sorrow, many early national mothers found it difficult to express their acute sense of loss. "Since closing my last journal," Sarah Connell Ayer wrote in 1815, "I have been the mother of four children, which now lay side by side in the grave-yard."[49] The emotional trauma of losing four children in as many years could not be expressed—nor assuaged—through writing.

Just as the loss of her mother imbued Jane's childhood with a sense of melancholy, Elizabeth's death cast a mournful shadow over her experiences as a mother. Jane noted the anniversary of her daughter's death each year as a "day of sad remembrance!" The day, as she wrote in 1825, "must always be sad and solemn to me." Jane made a slow, reluctant return to society for the benefit of her surviving daughters. "I should vastly have preferred being in my lonely chamber," she confessed, "but the girls urged me so much— I made the exertion to please them." Yet as guests once again began to fill the Kirkpatrick home, Jane often found it difficult to enjoy their company: "Many tender and sad thoughts came to mind—when I recollected the long interval of sorrow which had intervened since the gay and joyous hours my dear girls used to have with their young friends around them I seem'd the more to miss the darling who used to unite in their mirth and frolick.—But she is at rest!"[50] Attending a neighbor's party in April 1824, Jane felt uncomfortable in the midst of such "gaiety." The lively setting "assorted not with the state of my feelings—but I did all I could to maintain a cheerful exterior." Jane repeatedly expressed unease in large gatherings: "Years of mourning that have been spent in retirement," she mused. "It will be long ere I can enjoy the change." After attending the wedding of a family friend in March 1825, Jane "felt so much indisposed that I retired very early . . . the excitement had been more than I could bear—and a fever attended with delirium set in that night." Once again unable to write in her journal, Jane spent weeks physically recovering from the emotional strain of attending the wedding. "I love to see others gay and enjoying themselves," she later reflected, "but for myself my heart is in the grave.—I feel more and more that I am but a sojourner."[51]

Death and mourning shaped women's experiences with motherhood in profound and powerful ways. For Jane Kirkpatrick, her youthful propensity to melancholy only intensified after Elizabeth's death. As her daughter Jane Eudora recalled, Jane "dwelt on the shadows of the past, rather than on the opening vistas of the future." To help counter her sorrows, Jane strove to live "a life of exemplary piety and usefulness."[52]

"The Exercise of Female Charity"

Throughout her life, Jane embraced opportunities to engage in a variety of charitable and benevolent activities. Reform provided a more "acceptable" activity for women than any desire for literary fame. According to Sarah Sleeper, educator, "It was a sentiment of Miss Hannah More, that the great work of female education is, to annihilate selfishness, and establish in its place principles of benevolence, which prompt to the finding of happiness by contributing to the happiness of others." Reform provided women an unselfish way to put their education to good use. "To literary distinction few may aspire," Sleeper continued, "but to become celebrated for good-ness, to be renowned for usefulness and honoured for moral influence, is in the power of almost any of us." As several scholars have noted, reform enabled women to exercise their "moral influence" to assume a variety of public roles in American society. By the 1840s, thousands of women sustained active presences in the fields of abolition, temperance, and moral reform.[53]

Jane Bayard Kirkpatrick was among the growing number of women attracted to the work of benevolence. In November 1813, Jane founded the Dorcas Society of New Brunswick, serving as its "First Directress" every year until her death in 1851. The Dorcas Society devoted its efforts toward widowed women and the sick, activities "peculiarly suited to the exercise of female charity." Its relief efforts tended to be modest and immediate. The society provided clothing, linens, and small cash allowances to recipients. In 1820, "Mrs. Reed, a widow with two small children" was given "$2.77 for the past six months [that] has served to make them comfortable." That same year, "a coloured woman Margaret—very poor and sick"—received relief in the "amount of 26 cents." To support these relief efforts, the Dorcas Society relied on materials donated by supportive community members; in addition, each year, they asked a local minister to deliver a sermon, which typically generated approximately fifty dollars in annual donations.[54]

As its founder and first directress, Jane infused the Dorcas Society with an air of respectability. Although made up of local women who knew one another socially, the Dorcas Society maintained a degree of formality in its organization and conduct. The society drafted its own constitution, which its members persuaded the local printer to publish free of charge. Female officers and managers ran the society and supervised the work of its female visitors. Meetings were held regularly throughout the year, at which "some instructive work that the Society shall select and approve shall be read for the entertainment and edification of the Ladies while they work." Each November, an anniversary meeting was held, at which Jane often delivered an "affecting and animating Address... calculated to inspire us with zeal in our benevolent efforts."[55]

Although the society maintained its independence as a female-run charity, the organization reflected a gendered division of labor that defined the work of benevolence. Shortly after its establishment, the Dorcas Society "appointed a committee to confer with the gentlemen of the Humane Society" to coordinate their efforts. Members from the New Brunswick Dorcas Society and Humane Society met together to decide "the manner in which the two Societies should mutually aid each other in the distribution of their charity." The Dorcas Society maintained its original intention to "limit their exertions to furnishing articles of cloathing and comforts for the sick," and it relied on the Humane Society to "procure fuel and provision" outside its stated mission. To coordinate relief efforts, the Dorcas Society resolved, "to confirm our Wards to those the Gentlemen have lately arranged."[56] Although this decision suggested a level of deference to male authority, the Dorcas Society maintained its autonomy as a female-led organization without any direct male oversight. Its day-to-day operations rested entirely in the Dorcas Society female managers and visitors.

Through her longstanding commitment to the Dorcas Society, Jane became known throughout New Brunswick for her charitable and educational work. Members of the community regularly sought Jane's assistance and advice in their charitable endeavors. In August 1814, Jane reported to the Dorcas Society that she "had been waited on by Col. Neilson with a proposition from the Lancaster School requesting their aid in catchesing the children." The officers "unanimously agreed to the proposition, and very cheerfully determined to enter on the business." When the women of New Brunswick wanted to promote their "Infant School," they turned to Jane for help. "It was agreed that some little publication should be made to awaken the attention of the publick," Jane noted after a meeting of the Dorcas Society, "and I was requested to prepare it." Although she typically shunned the literary spotlight, she agreed to the request and prepared the address the next morning.[57]

Reform work enabled women to play active, influential roles in their communities. In 1829, Jane and her daughters helped organize a fundraising fair on behalf of the Pines Society, another local charitable organization. The fair was scheduled to coincide with the commencement at Queens College, in "expectation of a great many strangers to attend commencement." The fair was a great success. "The crowd was immense," Jane reported, "and the sales exceeded our expectations." Jane and her daughters raised "near $100," and the event as a whole generated "upwards of $300." Yet the next year, plans to hold another fair generated a small controversy in town. "The Faculty and Dutch oppose it," Jane noted in her journal, and the society "held a special meeting" in which the members considered canceling the event. "The Managers made some little alterations to humour them," she noted, "but would not relinquish the project." Although deferential to male authority, the women involved in this enterprise insisted on a maintaining a degree of autonomy. "It is quite laughable the great stir it has made," Jane noted wryly—and with a touch of pride—in her journal.[58]

Through her involvement in benevolent and reform activities, Jane experienced a sense of usefulness and accomplishment. After hosting a meeting of the Missionary Society to "make up a box of cloathing for the Chickasaw Indians," Jane expressed contentment that "this commencing week of the Year has been marked by pleasures both social and benevolent."[59] The work of benevolence gave her a sense of purpose and identity that extended beyond her familial duties, yet remained compatible with her primary roles as wife and mother. Jane's benevolent work nearly always included her daughters, enabling them to cultivate a shared sense of purpose. Her experiences help illustrate why reform was so meaningful to many nineteenth-century women. Although mere equality seemed unattainable and even contrary to the duties of motherhood, reform work encouraged women to engage in useful work, albeit in a gendered sphere increasingly defined by difference.

"An Exemplary Woman"

In 1826, Jane Bayard Kirkpatrick reflected on the death of a family friend, "She was an exemplary woman and has brought up a large family with great credit—and has formed them for usefulness—Her daughters will arise and call her blessed." In eulogizing her friend's excellent mothering, Jane revealed her own ideals of womanhood. After Jane's death in 1851, her family and friends praised Jane's life as "an exemplary woman." Her son-in-law

Samuel How published his funeral sermon, and her daughter edited a collection of her writings. Family friend Lydia H. Sigourney wrote a poem, "On the Death of a Christian Lady," in Jane's honor. Nearly twenty years after her death, the family kept her memory alive. Her granddaughter's husband James Grant Wilson printed the *Memorials of Andrew Kirkpatrick, and His Wife Jane Bayard,* which contained excerpts from Jane's unfinished autobiography. In 1877, Wilson also included a tribute to Jane in his entry on Andrew Kirkpatrick in the *Appleton Cyclopædia of American Biography.* In all these accounts, Jane Bayard Kirkpatrick received praise for "her accomplishments, benevolence, and beautiful Christian character."[60] These writings all made note of her cultivated mind and manners while celebrating a life of selfless service to others.

Throughout her adult life, Jane Bayard Kirkpatrick seemed content to devote herself to others rather than to seek mere equality. Her desire to be useful found expression in a variety of outlets, including her mothering, her writings, and her reform work. The paths available to Jane indicate both the possibilities and limitations that shaped nineteenth-century womanhood. Republican motherhood elevated women's status as primary caregivers, giving them a sense of cultural and moral authority. Yet, by insisting on women's inherent nurturing skills, maternal ideals often silenced the tensions that women experienced while performing the physical and emotional work of mothering. Writing enabled women to give voice to their aspirations, but many women were not as comfortable as Margaret Bayard Smith in seeking publication of their literary efforts. Reform work provided women with an acceptable "sphere of influence," but the nature of women's reform remained constrained by a gendered ideology that stressed women's work on behalf of others rather than the pursuit of individual ambitions. In all these activities, strong articulations of sexual difference increasingly defined women's experiences and identities.

By the time of Jane Bayard Kirkpatrick's death in 1851, the early national promise of mere equality had been largely eclipsed by prescriptive rhetoric that emphasized sexual difference and separate spheres. Although largely prescriptive in nature, this ideological shift from equality to difference reflected the complex realities of educated women's lives as mothers. As the nineteenth century progressed, increased access to educational institutions opened doors for women to pursue meaningful work as educators, authors, and reformers. By the 1830s, according to Martha Hazeltine, educator, "the sphere of woman" was "far more extended than at any previous period." Yet, as a woman's sphere expanded, notions of mere equality contracted. Even the strongest supporters of women's education increasingly relied on a gendered language of difference to make claims for women's educational opportunities. "Such is the destiny of woman," Hazeltine concluded, "and such the spheres for which she must be fitted by education."[61] The enlightened idea that women possessed intellectual capacity equal to that of men became less important than a constant reiteration of sexual difference. The tributes honoring Jane Bayard Kirkpatrick reflect this shift, privileging antebellum constructions of separate spheres and Victorian womanhood rather than early national expressions of mere equality. Within their own homes, many educated women had learned a final lesson—that the promise of mere equality was perhaps no match for motherhood.

Conclusion
Education, Equality, or Difference

Pray you excuse me, if I have gone too far
In telling you what we've learnt: and what we are
We'll strive to show, if you will deign to hear us;
If worthy, let your approbation cheer us.[1]

Miss A. M. Burton read this poem at commencement exercises held at Susanna Rowson's Female Academy in October 1803. The poem was published in the *Boston Weekly Magazine,* making Burton's acquisition of education at once a lived experience and a literary representation. The interplay between the personal and prescriptive was also reflected in the poem itself, which asserted women's steadfast determination to acquire and demonstrate knowledge ("we'll strive to show"), along with persistent concerns about male reception ("if you will deign to hear us"). Such worries about male criticism were not unfounded, but the story is more complicated than that. As early national women acquired education, many advocates expressed confidence that women would easily achieve a state of near, or mere, equality with men. "By giving *mind* to the fair sex," as one author asserted, "we shall make them equal to any thing that is attainable by rational beings." Another essayist proudly noted that human qualifications, "when properly cultivated and exerted, put men and women nearly on an equal footing with each other, and share the advantages and disadvantages of life impartially between them."[2]

Left unresolved were more precise discussions of what it meant for women to live merely as the equals of man—how near an equal footing was possible, given the legal, political, and economic realities of early American life? Many women succeeded, as one essayist noted, in achieving "moments of transient equality," demonstrating intellectual "ability equal to ours."[3] But those moments remained transient. After promoting women's intellectual capacities and celebrating their importance to civic society, prescriptive writers failed to advocate for women's legal, political, and professional equality with men. Unable to concede the possibility of women's full participation in political and economic spheres, social and political thinkers instead relied on the murky notion of mere equality in an effort to contain the potentially liberating aspects of their own rhetoric. Educated women learned to settle for social and cultural expressions of "approbation" rather than more expansive opportunities to fully utilize their intellectual capacities.

Despite these tensions, early national Americans clearly recognized that women's acquisition of education represented a critical step in their path to equality. Yet more than fifty years later, the subject of women's intellectual equality remained open to debate. In an 1840 essay published in *Godey's Lady Book,* author Mary Hale echoed sentiments expressed half a century earlier, insisting, "with proper cultivation, with the enjoyment of equal advantages, the intellectual attainments of women may equal those of men." Over the course of fifty years, educated women had proven their intellectual capacities in ever-increasing numbers and in an ever-expanding variety of subjects. "Has the short space of a half century given woman new powers," Hale wondered, "or is the spirit of our institutions more favourable to an enlarged cultivation of those she already possessed?" According to Hale, the answer was obvious: expanded access to educational opportunities had clearly led to women's increased attainment of knowledge and understanding.[4]

Women had repeatedly demonstrated that they possessed intellectual capacity equal to that of men; why, then, did Hale still have to defend this assertion? Moreover, why had expanded access to education not led to even more expansive opportunities for women? In 1840, when Hale's article was published, only a handful of colleges admitted women. The clergy, law, and legislature all remained closed to women. Women continued to occupy "a less *public* station" than men, not from lack of intellectual capacity but from lack of access and opportunity. Despite her ardent support of women's educational capacities, Hale largely accepted these constraints as the will of Providence. Yet her essay also pointed to a more secular explanation— the continued criticism leveled against "a literary lady." Any woman who appeared too interested in education risked being tainted with the stain of

Lith. of Endicott & Swett.

THE CIRCULATING LIBRARY.

Published by J.N.Toy & W.R.Lucas, Balto.

FIGURE 8. "The Circulating Library," 1831. This woman could be a pedant, as she fashions books from the library into an affected display of learning. The Library Company of Philadelphia.

"pedantry, self-sufficiency and insipidity."[5] Nineteenth-century Americans remained deeply suspicious of women's intellectual accomplishments.

Reading Hale's essay, we may wonder whether little had actually changed in the course of fifty years. Fears of educated women continued to proliferate in the literary public sphere, perhaps in part because women's access to education continued to expand exponentially. By 1840, scores of academies, seminaries, and collegiate institutes existed, offering a variety of advanced educational opportunities for women. Schools such as the Troy Female Seminary (founded by Emma Willard in 1821), the Hartford Female Seminary (founded by Catherine Beecher in 1823), and Mount Holyoke (founded by Mary Lyon in 1837) offered women the equivalent of a college education—although without explicitly referring to it as such. In 1837, Oberlin College admitted its first female students, paving the way for women's admission to other colleges in the decades to follow. Well-educated women filled the ranks of teachers, authors, missionaries, and reformers.[6] In essence, educated women attended institutions and engaged in the types of activities proposed in the 1802 "Plan for the Emancipation of the Female Sex"—yet without resolving the thorny issue of mere equality.

As women's access to education expanded, nineteenth-century Americans remained at once celebratory and cautious about educated women's influence in society. Articles proudly boasted that the United States "can vie with any nation on earth in a good proportion of intelligent and pious females." To those skeptics who doubted the need for women's education, one author suggested that such critics undoubtedly held "very limited views" of the importance of education or that they had conflated education with affectation: "Perhaps their idea of an 'educated lady' is associated in their mind with nothing better than some starched nun, or round-mouthed pedant." Despite impressive institutional advancements and individual achievements in women's education, prescriptive writers still relied on the figure of the pedant to discredit women's intellectual ambitions. Improperly educated women could still be dismissed as "trifflers and silly women," as one female essayist noted, "but if any of us have resolution enough to soar beyond those narrow limits, . . . we are called critics, wits, female pedants, &c."[7] For over half a century, women steadfastly acquired education, but the potential uses of their intellectual capacities remained constrained by custom, law, and prejudice. Accordingly, the prescriptive literature continued to define women's education through a series of contradictions—between capacity and utilization, between learning and desirability, between coquetry and pedantry.

In their everyday lives, educated women attempted to sort through competing sets of discourses, resisting negative representations while favoring models that validated their intellectual interests. Skeptical of both the pedant and the coquette, women refashioned narrow representations of womanhood into more expansive models. Women experimented with personal interpretations of print, reshaping discourses to suit their individual needs and aspirations. At every stage of their lives, women explored the boundaries of mere equality. In particular, educated women sought relationships with like-minded individuals willing to accept them as their intellectual and social equals. Women such as Eunice Callender, Sarah Ripley Stearns, Elizabeth and Margaret Shippen, Linda Raymond Ward, Jane Bowne Haines, and Jane Bayard Kirkpatrick all enjoyed platonic or romantic relationships with men who valued their intellectual attainments. Shared intellectual interests became a key means by which men and women crafted fulfilling relationships that celebrated areas of affinity and mutuality, in contrast to prescriptive ideas that insisted on models of gender difference and hierarchy. These women's efforts remind us that prescriptive literature can tell us only part of the history of an era, and they illustrate the continued interplay between prescriptive literature and lived experience that informed women's emotional and intellectual lives.

It is important to underscore, and tempting to celebrate, how early national women achieved some measures of mere equality in their everyday lives and relationships, even as we recognize that their efforts failed to challenge structural systems of inequality and inequity. That early national women did not advocate more fully for political rights may be seen as a lost opportunity, yet the paradoxical nature of mere equality offered them few avenues to pursue such broad goals. The narrow expressions of mere equality that educated women achieved reflected not just their own individual limitations but also larger cultural and prescriptive constraints. Despite their enlightened faith in women's intellectual capacity, early national Americans struggled to sustain the malleable and elusive concept of mere equality. Ultimately, when faced with the fundamental question of whether women could be simultaneously equal to and different from men, nineteenth-century Americans could not square the search for mere equality with their overriding belief in sexual difference. In their own lives, women accepted these constraints even as they bristled against them. "I think if we had the advantages of the other sex, we should be equally as reasonable and orderly a set of beings as they are," Elizabeth Lindsay mused to her friend Apphia Rouzee in 1806. Yet, like most of her contemporaries, Elizabeth stopped short of articulating a more radical call for equality: "but enough on the superiority of the sexes, for after all, I believe it is the best way to content ourselves with the station of life in which we have been placed." To best serve society, Elizabeth reflected, educated women needed to learn a final lesson—to "bend all our ambition on becoming as useful as we can."[8] It can be argued that the women of this study bent their ambition, living quiet lives that until recently warranted little historical inquiry. They were well educated and determined to enact useful lives as learned women, but they had few avenues to directly challenge patriarchal systems of inequity.

The more well-known stories in women's history often revolve around those women who were able to express their desires for equality in more ambitious ways. These women, it should be noted, typically enjoyed access to educational opportunities pioneered by the early national generation. In 1848, Elizabeth Cady Stanton—a graduate of Emma Willard's Troy Seminary—presented her *Declaration of Sentiments* at the Seneca Falls convention. Recognizing the link between knowledge and power, Stanton argued that women's educational status contributed to their subordinated place in American society: "He has denied her the facilities for obtaining a thorough education, all colleges being closed against her." Women's rights activists understood that the franchise was only one path to equality; thus, they sought not only the right to vote but further access to education, reforms to divorce and property rights legislation, and expanded economic opportunities, including "an equal participation with men in the various trades, professions and commerce."[9] Women's rights activists called for something greater than mere equality—they sought a comprehensive vision of gender equality largely unconstrained by narrow representations of difference. Perhaps it was, in part, the limits of mere equality that inspired these activists to develop a more expansive women's rights agenda.

We know that most nineteenth-century Americans sharply resisted women's efforts to claim a more fundamental equality with men, as they evoked reformulated arguments about separate spheres and sexual difference in their efforts to maintain patriarchal systems of power. As the idea of mere equality evolved into struggles for wide-ranging forms of equality, the reactions against women became more vigorous. Indeed, the doctrine of separate spheres found its fullest expression in the prescriptive literature *after* women began to assert larger claims for political and economic equality. Writers articulated a narrowly defined private sphere of domesticity at the very time that numerous women were carving out public roles for themselves and making demands for equal access to educational and economic opportunities. Thus, the notion of separate spheres that has dominated the historiography for decades can be better understood as a *reaction* to early national women's experiments with mere equality rather than as an accurate depiction of women's lives during this time period. The sharp emphasis of the antebellum era on difference came to dominate after women had attempted to live merely—and then more fully—as the equals of man.[10]

Perhaps most worthy of future study are the thorny questions of how and why so many women learned to adopt the rhetoric of difference and, indeed, often did so as a conscious, deliberate strategy to justify their public roles. "On the whole, (even if fame be the object of pursuit)," Hannah More, author, argued, "is it not better to succeed as women, than to fail as men?" A leading advocate of women's education, More promoted a model of female excellence sustained not by mere equality but by sharp delineations of difference. She asked women to consider whether it was better "to shine, by walking honorably in the road which nature, custom, and education seem to have marked out, rather than to counteract them all, by moving awkwardly in a path diametrically opposite?" Like other prescriptive writers, More urged women to find cultural authority by seeking "to be excellent women, rather than indifferent men."[11] Such arguments proved persuasive, and as the nineteenth century progressed, many women rejected the complex challenges of mere equality for such clear articulations of difference.

Why did women retreat from the idea of becoming merely the equals of man and embrace a social order rooted in sexual difference? What did the rhetoric of difference offer women that mere equality failed to provide or sustain? As scholars have shown, the prescriptive rhetoric promoting women's "sphere of influence" enabled women to enact a number of expanded roles for themselves as reformers, missionaries, educators, and authors. "There is an influence spread abroad in society," wrote M. H. S. Brown, a member of the Young Ladies' Association of the New Hampton Female Seminary, in 1840. "It is felt, though it may be unacknowledged, in the halls of legislation, as well as in the drawing room, and exerts itself powerfully upon the most gifted as upon the most unintellectual of men. . . . This influence is woman's."[12] Yet such influence came at a price—it was sustained by the explicit notion that women were acting in these influential roles as *women,* not as the mere equals of men.

The abandonment of mere equality was perhaps inevitable, in that it represented a paradoxical expression of gender identity that simultaneously reified sexual difference even as it promoted intellectual equality. Faced with this contradiction, most early national women were unable to approach the pursuit of mere equality with Eugenia Splatterdash's unchecked confidence and brass. Rather, like Eliza Wharton in *The Coquette,* educated women often experienced a sense of ambivalence that complicated their understandings of the connections among education, equality, and difference. Although their efforts met with only limited success, the stories of how individual women attempted to live merely as the equals of man raise fundamental questions about the place of difference in a nation dedicated to the proposition that all men are created equal. Such questions have resonance today, as we consider the ways in which women continue to achieve certain measures of equality that have not required men to cede significant power or privilege. At stake, then and now, has been nothing less than (mere) equality.

 ARCHIVES

American Antiquarian Society (AAS), Worcester, Mass.

Ephraim Abbot Papers
Gage Family Additional Papers, Series I
Sarah Ripley Stearns Journal (from American Women's Diaries Micro-
film Collection)

American Philosophical Society (APS), Philadelphia, Pa.

Bache Family Papers
Benjamin Vaughan Papers
Catherine Wistar Bache Letters
Charles Nicoll Bancker Papers
Eastwick Collection
Peale-Sellers Family Collection
Shippen Family Papers
Wyck Association Collection

Andover Historical Society, Andover, Mass.

Lydia Clark Abbott Flint Papers

David M. Rubenstein Rare Book and Manuscript Library, Duke University, Durham, N.C.

Eleanor Hall Douglas Papers
Munford-Ellis Family Papers

Historical Society of Pennsylvania (HSP), Philadelphia, Pa.

Biddle Family Papers
Harriet Manigault Wilcocks Diary
John Williams Wallace Collection
Meredith Family Papers
Parker Family Papers

Shippen Family Papers
   Margaret Shippen 1824 Album
Thomas and Henry Wharton Papers

Manuscripts Division, Department of Rare Books and Special Collections, Princeton University Library, Princeton, N.J.

Bache and Hodge Family Papers
Boudinot Family Collection
Stimson Collection of Elias Boudinot
Wolcott Family Papers

New York Historical Society, New York, N.Y.

Miscellaneous Manuscripts—Van Schaack, Catherine

Schlesinger Library, Radcliffe Institute, Harvard University, Cambridge, Mass.

Bradley-Hyde Family Papers
Gertrude Foster Brown Additional Papers
Hooker Collection
Poor Family Papers
Sarah Ripley Stearns Papers

South Carolina Historical Society, Charleston, S.C.

Manigault Family Papers (from microfiche copy held at Princeton University Library, Princeton, N.J.)

Special Collections and University Archives, Rutgers University Libraries, New Brunswick, N.J.

Colt Family Papers
Cornell Family Papers
Dorcas Society and Day Nursery Society of New Brunswick, New Jersey, records
Jane Bayard Kirkpatrick journal
Mary Griffith Letters

Virginia Historical Society, Richmond, Va.

Beverley Family Papers
Clairborne Family Papers

Cocke Family Papers
Hunter Family Papers

William L. Clements Library, University of Michigan, Ann Arbor, Mich.

Sophia Sawyer Papers [online]

❧ NOTES

Preface

1. "On Female Acquirements," *Visitor, or Ladies' Miscellany* (New York), June 4, 1803, 276–77.

2. For useful studies the explore intersections between prescriptive literature and lived experience in the eighteenth century, see Heidi Brayman Hackel and Catherine E. Kelly, eds., *Reading Women: Literacy, Authorship, and Culture in the Atlantic World, 1500–1800* (Philadelphia: University of Pennsylvania Press, 2008); Catherine Kerrison, *Claiming the Pen: Women and Intellectual Life in the Early American South* (Ithaca: Cornell University Press, 2006).

3. Elizabeth Maddock Dillon, *The Gender of Freedom: Fictions of Liberalism and the Literary Public Sphere* (Stanford: Stanford University Press, 2004). For other literary and historical studies detailing representations of women and gender in print culture, see Ruth H. Bloch, "Changing Conceptions of Sexuality and Romance in Eighteenth-Century America," *William and Mary Quarterly* 60, no. 1 (January 2003): 13–42; Ivy Schweitzer, *Perfecting Friendship: Politics and Affiliation in Early American Literature* (Chapel Hill: University of North Carolina Press, 2006); Carole Shammas, *A History of Household Government in America* (Charlottesville: University of Virginia Press, 2002).

4. Mary Kelley, *Learning to Stand and Speak: Women, Education, and Public Life in America's Republic* (Chapel Hill: University of North Carolina Press, 2006); Margaret Nash, *Women's Education in the United States, 1780–1840* (New York: Palgrave Macmillan, 2005). For other accounts of women's education in the early republic, see Nancy Cott, *The Bonds of Womanhood: "Woman's Sphere" in New England, 1780–1835* (New Haven: Yale University Press, 1977); Linda Kerber, *Women of the Republic: Ideology and Intellect in Revolutionary America* (Chapel Hill: University of North Carolina Press, 1980); Jan Lewis, "The Republican Wife: Virtue and Seduction in the Early Republic," *William and Mary Quarterly* 44, no. 4 (October 1987): 689–721; Mary Beth Norton, *Liberty's Daughters: The Revolutionary Experiences of American Women, 1750–1800* (Boston: Little, Brown, 1980). The classic descriptive study on women's educational history and academic curriculum is Thomas Woody, *A History of Women's Education in the United States* (1929; reprint, New York: Octagon Books, 1980).

5. For useful accounts of women's private lives in this era, see Martha Tomhave Blauvelt, *The Work of the Heart: Young Women and Emotion, 1780–1830* (Charlottesville: University of Virginia Press, 2007), which explores the emotional worlds of early national women; and Susan E. Klepp, *Revolutionary Conceptions: Women, Fertility, and Family Limitation in America, 1760–1820* (Chapel Hill: University of North

Carolina Press, 2009), which examines women's attempts to exert control over their reproductive choices.

6. Mary Beth Norton traces how shifting ideologies of gender identity and separates spheres came to define eighteenth-century understandings of public and private life. This book suggests that the early national period represented a challenge to both this earlier model traced by Norton and to the subsequent expressions of separate spheres that came to dominate throughout antebellum America. As I argue, the early republic briefly experimented with new understandings of mere equality, but ultimately it could not resolve the persistent tensions between sexual difference and intellectual equality. See Mary Beth Norton, *Separated By Their Sex: Women in Public and Private in the Colonial Atlantic World* (Ithaca: Cornell University Press, 2011).

Introduction

1. "Plan for the Emancipation of the Fair Sex," *Lady's Magazine and Musical Repository* (New York), January 1802, 43–44.

2. "On Female Authorship," *Ladies' Magazine and Repository of Entertaining Knowledge* (Philadelphia), January 1793, 69.

3. Emma Willard, *An Address to the Public: Particularly to the Members of the Legislature of New York, Proposing a Plan for Improving Female Education* (Middlebury, N.Y.: Printed by J. W. Copeland, 1819; reprint, Marietta, Ga.: Larlin Corporation, 1987), 18–26; Ezra Brainerd, *Mrs. Emma Willard's Life and Work in Middlebury* (1888; reprint, Marietta, Ga.: Larlin Corporation, 1987), 43–44. For background information on Willard and her Troy Female Seminary, see Nina Baym, "Women and the Republic: Emma Willard's Rhetoric of History," *American Quarterly* 43, no. 1 (March 1991): 1–23; Nancy Beadie, "Emma Willard's Idea Put to the Test: The Consequences of State Support of Female Education in New York, 1819–67," *History of Education Quarterly* 33, no. 4 (winter 1993): 543–62; Anne Firor Scott, "The Ever Widening Circle: The Diffusion of Feminist Values from the Troy Female Seminary, 1822–1872," *History of Education Quarterly* 19, no. 1 (spring 1979): 3–25; Anne Firor Scott, "What, Then, Is the American: This New Woman?" *Journal of American History* 65, no. 3 (December 1978): 679–703; Lucy Forsyth Townsend, "Emma Willard: Eclipse or Reemergence?" *Journal of the Midwest History of Education Society* 18 (1990): 279–92.

4. For women's legal status in the early republic, see Joan R. Gundersen, "Independence, Citizenship, and the American Revolution," *Signs* 13, no. 1 (fall 1987): 59–77; Marylynn Salmon, *Women and the Law of Property in Early America* (Chapel Hill: University of North Carolina Press, 1986); Carole Shammas, *A History of Household Government in America* (Charlottesville: University of Virginia Press, 2002). New Jersey constitutes an important exception in the history of women's suffrage; women briefly voted in that state before explicitly losing the right in 1807. See Judith Apter Klinghoffer and Lois Elkis, "'The Petticoat Electors': Women's Suffrage in New Jersey, 1776–1807," *Journal of the Early Republic* 12, no. 2 (summer 1992): 159–93; Jan Ellen Lewis, "Rethinking Women's Suffrage in New Jersey, 1776–1807," *Rutgers Law Review* 63, no. 3 (spring 2011): 1017–35; Rosemarie Zagarri, *Revolutionary Backlash: Women and Politics in the Early American Republic* (Philadelphia: University of Pennsylvania Press, 2007). For recent summaries of women's access to education,

see Mary Kelley, *Learning to Stand and Speak: Women, Education, and Public Life in America's Republic* (Chapel Hill: University of North Carolina Press, 2006); Margaret Nash, *Women's Education in the United States, 1780–1840* (New York: Palgrave Macmillan, 2005).

5. For representations of women in print culture, see Ruth H. Bloch, "Changing Conceptions of Sexuality and Romance in Eighteenth-Century America," *William and Mary Quarterly* 60, no. 1 (January 2003): 13–42; Elizabeth Maddock Dillon, *The Gender of Freedom: Fictions of Liberalism and the Literary Public Sphere* (Stanford: Stanford University Press, 2004); Ivy Schweitzer, *Perfecting Friendship: Politics and Affiliation in Early American Literature* (Chapel Hill: University of North Carolina Press, 2006); Shammas, *History of Household Government*.

6. "Female Education," *Port Folio* (Philadelphia), July 1810; *Pennsylvania Gazette* (Philadelphia), June 7, 1786. For the importance of an educated citizenry, see Richard D. Brown, *Knowledge Is Power: The Diffusion of Information in Early America, 1700–1865* (New York: Oxford University Press, 1989); William J. Gilmore, *Reading Becomes a Necessity of Life: Material and Cultural Life in Rural New England, 1780–1835* (Knoxville: University of Tennessee Press, 1989); Alexandra Oleson and Sanborn C. Brown, eds., *The Pursuit of Knowledge in the Early American Republic: American Scientific and Learned Societies from Colonial Times to the Civil War* (Baltimore: Johns Hopkins University Press, 1976); Jason M. Opal, "Exciting Emulation: Academies and the Transformation of the Rural North, 1780s–1820s," *Journal of American History* 91, no. 2 (September 2004): 445–70; Jason M. Opal, *Beyond the Farm: National Ambitions in Rural New England* (Philadelphia: University of Pennsylvania Press, 2008); James D. Watkinson, "Useful Knowledge? Concepts, Values, and Access in American Education, 1776–1840," *History of Education Quarterly* 30, no. 3 (fall 1990): 351–70.

7. "Present Mode of Female Education Considered," *Lady's Weekly Miscellany* (New York), June 11, 1808, 100.

8. Ibid.; "On Female Acquirements," *Weekly Visitor, or Ladies' Miscellany* (New York), June 4, 1803, 276; "On the Mental Endowments of Women," *Lady's Weekly Miscellany* (New York), November 29, 1806; *Philadelphia Repository and Weekly Register*, May 14, 1803. For summaries of Enlightenment thought, see David Jaffee, "The Village Enlightenment in New England, 1760–1820," *William and Mary Quarterly* 47, no. 3 (July 1990): 327–46; Henry May, *The Enlightenment in America* (New York: Oxford University Press, 1976); Dorinda Outram, *The Enlightenment* (New York: Cambridge University Press, 1995).

9. John Burton, *Lectures on Female Education and Manners*, 1st American ed. (New York: Printed and Sold by Samuel Campbell, 1794), 116.

10. Ibid., 78.

11. "Extracts from the Writings of Madame de Genlis," *Lady's Weekly Miscellany* (New York), February 28, 1807, 129. Excerpts from Genlis's writings were frequently reprinted in American periodicals; she served as a representative educated woman who also promoted women's domesticity. See Anne L. Schroder, "Going Public against the Academy in 1784: Mme de Genlis Speaks Out on Gender Bias," *Eighteenth Century Studies* 32, no. 3 (spring 1999): 376–82; Samia I. Spencer, "Women and Education," in *French Women and the Age of Enlightenment*, ed. Samia I. Spencer (Bloomington: Indiana University Press, 1984), 83–96; Mary Seidman Trouille, *Sexual Politics in the Enlightenment: Women Writers Read Rousseau* (Albany: SUNY Press, 1997).

12. "Alphonzo," "An Address to the Ladies," *American Magazine* (New York), March 1788, 245–46. For useful discussions of how sexual difference has been used to discredit women's intellectual ambitions, see Genevieve Fraisse, *Reason's Muse: Sexual Difference and the Birth of Democracy,* trans. Jane Marie Todd (Chicago: University of Chicago Press, 1994); Outram, *Enlightenment,* esp. chap. 6; Joan Wallach Scott, *Only Paradoxes to Offer: French Feminists and the Rights of Man* (Cambridge, Mass.: Harvard University Press, 1996).

13. "Importance of Female Education—and of Educating Young Men in Their Native Country, Addressed to Every American," *American Magazine* (New York), May 1788, 368; "On Female Acquirements," 276–77; Burton, *Lectures on Female Education and Manners,* 81.

14. "Rudiments of Taste, and Polite Female Education," *Juvenile Portfolio* (Philadelphia), August 7, 1813, 170–71; "On Female Authorship," 72; "Alphonzo," "An Address to the Ladies," 241–46.

15. "Alphonzo," "An Address to the Ladies," 244 (emphasis in original).

16. Ibid., 244–45 (emphasis in original). As Elizabeth Dillon argues, heterosexual desire "tends to emphasize rather than erase sexual difference." Dillon, *Gender of Freedom,* 129. This assertion is certainly present in much of the prescriptive literature; the extent to which individual men and women challenged these essentializing assumptions is discussed further, particularly in chapters 4 and 5.

17. "Frontispiece," *Massachusetts Magazine* (Boston) 3, 1791, iv (emphasis in original). By using a symbolic image of a Massachusetts woman as an idealized woman of the early republic, I do not mean to imply that regional variations did not affect both the lived experiences and ideological constructions of American women; I am suggesting that the discourses and representations examined throughout this study were concerned with mapping the boundaries of "American" or national womanhood. Before 1820, most American magazines and periodicals were published in Boston, Philadelphia, or New York—the three key sites of publishing before the development of improved transportation routes and postal codes led to national mass markets. Many of these periodicals targeted a wide national audience, proudly listing the names of subscribers from other states. The classic work on early republican print culture is Frank Luther Mott, *History of American Magazines, 1741–1850* (New York: D. Appleton & Co., 1930), esp. pts. 1 and 2. See also Herbert Brown, "Elements of Sensibility in the *Massachusetts Magazine,*" *American Literature* 1, no. 3 (November 1929): 286–96; Trish Loughran, *The Republic in Print: Print Culture in the Age of U.S. Nation Building, 1770–1870* (New York: Columbia University Press, 2007); Charles G. Steffen, "Newspapers for Free: The Economies of Newspaper Circulation in the Early Republic," *Journal of the Early Republic* 23, no. 3 (fall 2003): 381–419; Bertha-Monica Stearns, "Before Godey's," *American Literature* 2, no. 3 (November 1930): 248–55; Bertha-Monica Stearns, "Early New England Magazines for Ladies," *New England Quarterly* 2, no. 3 (July 1929): 420–57; Michael Warner, *The Letters of the Republic: Publication and the Public Sphere in Eighteenth-Century America* (Cambridge, Mass.: Harvard University Press, 1990).

18. Daniel Bryan, *Oration on Female Education, Delivered before the Visitors and Students of the Female Academy in Harrisonburg, August 4, 1815* (Harrisonburg, Va.: Lawrence Wartmann, 1816), 12; *Philadelphia Repository and Weekly Register,* November 21, 1801.

19. James Milnor, "On Female Education," *Port Folio* (Philadelphia), May 1809, 382–94.

20. The term *republican mother* was coined by Linda Kerber in *Women of the Republic: Intellect and Ideology in Revolutionary America* (Chapel Hill: University of North Carolina Press, 1980), and was revised to take into account the symbolic and metaphoric centrality of the republican wife in Jan Lewis, "The Republican Wife: Virtue and Seduction in the Early Republic," *William and Mary Quarterly* 44, no. 4 (October 1987): 689–721. See also Ruth Bloch, "The Gendered Meanings of Virtue in Revolutionary America," *Signs* 13, no. 1 (fall 1987): 37–58; Ruth Bloch, "American Feminine Ideals in Transition: The Rise of the Moral Mother, 1785–1815," *Feminist Studies* 4, no. 2 (summer 1978): 100–126; Margaret Nash, "Rethinking Republican Motherhood: Benjamin Rush and the Young Ladies' Academy of Philadelphia," *Journal of the Early Republic* 17, no. 2 (summer 1997): 171–92; Mary Beth Norton, *Liberty's Daughters: The Revolutionary Experience of American Women, 1750–1800* (Boston: Little, Brown & Co., 1980); Rosemarie Zagarri, "Morals, Manners, and the Republican Mother," *American Quarterly* 44, no. 2 (June 1992): 192–215.

21. "On Female Authorship," 68–72; *The American Lady's Preceptor*, 2nd ed. (Baltimore: E. J. Coale, 1811), 24–25.

22. Susanna Rowson, *A Present for Young Ladies, Containing Poems, Dialogues, Addresses, &c., as Recited by the Pupils of Mrs. Rowson's Academy, at the Annual Exhibitions* (Boston: John West, 1811), 151–52.

23. Burton, *Lectures on Female Education and Manners*, 257–60; Samuel Whiting, *Elegant Lessons; or the Young Lady's Preceptor: Being a Series of Appropriate Reading Exercises, in Prose and Verse: Carefully Selected from the Most Approved Authors, for Female Schools and Academies* (Middletown, Conn.: Clark & Lyman, 1820), 104.

24. "Life of a Learned Lady. Written by Herself," *Juvenile Portfolio* (Philadelphia), July 6, 1816, 105–6. This essay was serialized in four weekly issues, appearing July 6, July 13, July 20, and July 27, 1816. The reference to Eugenia's father as a "Grubstreet poet" suggests that this story was either selected from a British publication or, at the very least, set in Britain. But by publishing the piece in a Philadelphia magazine, the editors clearly must have felt that the context was appropriate for America as well. As various authors have pointed out, British works remained popular throughout the early republic and were commonly reprinted in various American publications.

25. Fraisse, *Reason's Muse*, 44. Although her analysis occurs in the context of the French Revolution, Fraisse's work contains the most theoretical analysis of the pedant—what she also refers to as the "fine mind"—that I have come across for discussions of women's education. It should be noted that advancements in women's institutional access to education occurred at a slower rate in France than in America and that any use of French sources or comparative analysis must take these differences into account. For a comparative discussion of French and American Revolution historiography, see Linda S. Popofsky and Marianne B. Sheldon, "French and American Women in the Age of Democratic Revolution, 1770–1815: A Comparative Perspective," *History of European Ideas* 8, no. 4–5 (1987): 597–609.

26. "Life of a Learned Lady," July 6, 1816, 105–6.

27. Ibid., July 6, 1816, 105–6; July 20, 1816, 113–14; July 27, 1816, 117–18.

28. Ibid., July 20, 1816, 113–14. Eugenia's veiled reference to Mary Wollstonecraft came at a time when Wollstonecraft had been discredited and criticized in both

England and America. When the details of Wollstonecraft's "immoral" lifestyle were revealed in William Godwin's memoirs (that she had engaged in extramarital affairs and conceived two children out of wedlock), her reputation was tarnished. The negative press surrounding Wollstonecraft made it nearly impossible to see her as a positive model of womanhood. Indeed, she was proof positive of the dangers inherent in the excesses of women's education. See G. J. Barker-Benfield, *The Culture of Sensibility: Sex and Society in 18th-Century Britain* (Chicago: University of Chicago Press, 1992), esp. chap. 7; Chandos Brown, "Mary Wollstonecraft, or the Female Illuminati: The Campaign against Women and 'Modern Philosophy' in the Early Republic," *Journal of the Early Republic* 15, no. 3 (fall 1995): 389–423.

29. "Life of a Learned Lady," July 27, 1816, 117–18.

30. Whiting, *Elegant Lessons,* 70; "The Speculator," "On Coquetry," *Lady's Miscellany; or Weekly Visitor* (New York), December 1, 1810, 87–89.

31. "Melissa—a Character," *Massachusetts Magazine* (Boston), April 1791, 207–8 (emphasis in original). Of course, as several scholars have noted, the "subversive" elements of novel reading, which enabled women to "narrate" the course of their own lives, help explain why novels remained such popular reading material for early national women. For women's strategic novel reading, see Martha Tomhave Blauvelt, *The Work of the Heart: Young Women and Emotion, 1780–1830* (Charlottesville: University of Virginia Press, 2007); Cathy Davidson, *Revolution and the Word* (New York: Oxford University Press, 1986); Cathy Davidson, "The Novel as Subversive Activity: Women Reading, Women Writing," in *Beyond the American Revolution: Explorations in the History of American Radicalism,* ed. Alfred F. Young (DeKalb: Northern Illinois University Press, 1993), 283–316.

32. "The Spectulator," "On Coquetry," 89; Burton, *Lectures on Female Education and Manners,* 331–32; "On Novels," *Philadelphia Repository and Weekly Register,* October 16, 1802, 332; *American Lady's Preceptor,* 81. For symbolic representations of marriage, see Lewis, "Republican Wife."

33. Hannah Webster Foster, *The Coquette: Or, the History of Eliza Wharton. A Novel Founded on Fact* (1797; reprint, Albany, N.Y.: New College and University Press, 1970). All subsequent page references refer to this edition, edited by William S. Osborne. For scholarly treatments of *The Coquette,* see Julie Sutherland Amberg, "Political and Sentimental Discourse in 1790s America: Judith Sargent Murray's *The Gleaner,* Hannah Webster Foster's *The Coquette,* and Susanna Haswell Rowson's *Reuben and Rachel: Or, Tales of Old Times,*" PhD diss., Tulane University, 1995; Gillian Brown, "Consent, Coquetry, and Consequences," *American Literary History* 9, no. 4 (winter 1997): 625–52; Davidson, *Revolution and the Word;* Ian Finseth, "'A Melancholy Tale': Rhetoric, Fiction, and Passion in *The Coquette,*" *Studies in the Novel* 33, no. 2 (summer 2001): 125–59; Irene Fizer, "Signing as Republican Daughters: The Letters of Eliza Southgate and *The Coquette,*" *Eighteenth Century* 34, no. 3 (autumn 1993): 243–63; Kristie Hamilton, "An Assault on the Will: Republican Virtue and the City in Hannah Webster Foster's *The Coquette,*" *Early American Literature* 24, no. 2 (September 1989): 135–51; Claire C. Pettengill, "Sisterhood in a Separate Sphere: Female Friendship in Hannah Webster Foster's *The Coquette* and *The Boarding School,*" *Early American Literature* 27, no. 3 (December 1992): 185–203; Julia Stern, *The Plight of Feeling: Sympathy and Dissent in the Early American Novel* (Chicago: University of Chicago Press, 1997); David Waldstreicher, "'Fallen under My Observation': Vision and Virtue in *The Coquette,*" *Early American Literature* 27, no. 3 (December 1992): 204–18.

34. Foster, *Coquette,* esp. 135–45.

35. Ibid., esp. 140–73; quotations on 232, 251 (emphasis in original).

36. Hamilton, "Assault on the Will," 148; "On Female Acquirements," 276–77.

37. "The Ladies Vindicated," *Weekly Visitor, or Ladies' Miscellany* (New York), May 28, 1803, 269.

38. For discussions of female genius as masculine, see Fraisse, *Reason's Muse;* Christine Battersby, *Gender and Genius: Towards a Feminist Aesthetics* (Bloomington: Indiana University Press, 1989).

39. "On Female Education, by a Young Lady, a Student in a Seminary in Beekman-Street, New York," *New York Magazine, or Literary Repository,* September 1794.

40. Anna Harrington, "An Apology for Studious Ladies," September 27, 1798, in *Dramatic Dialogues for the Use of Schools,* by Charles Stearns (Leominister, Mass: Printed by John Prentiss, 1798), 499.

Chapter 1

1. Violetta Bancker to Evert Bancker, March 20, 1801; Violetta Bancker to Anne Bancker, December 15, 1802, Charles Nicoll Bancker Papers, American Philosophical Society (APS), Philadelphia. For evidence of various female academies established in Philadelphia in the early national period, see Cornelius William Stafford, *The Philadelphia Directory of 1801* (Philadelphia, 1801).

2. Violetta Bancker to Anne Bancker, December 15, 1802, Charles Nicoll Bancker Papers.

3. For recent research on the history of women's institutional access to education, see Nancy Beadie and Kim Tolley, eds., *Chartered Schools: Two Hundred Years of Independent Academies in the United States, 1727–1925* (New York: Routledge, 2002); Margaret Nash, *Women's Education in the United States, 1780–1840* (New York: Palgrave Macmillan, 2005); essays collected for a symposium on the "Reappraisals of the Academy Movement" and published in *History of Education Quarterly* 41, no. 2 (summer 2001): 216–70.

4. See Mary Kelley, *Learning to Stand and Speak: Women, Education, and Public Life in America's Republic* (Chapel Hill: University of North Carolina Press, 2006); Mary Kelley, "Reading Women/Women Reading: The Making of Learned Women in Antebellum America," *Journal of American History* 83, no. 2 (September 1996): 401–24.

5. Maria Cornell to Margaretta Cornell, May 17, 1813 and May 17, 1814, Cornell Family Papers, Special Collections and University Archives, Rutgers University Libraries, New Brunswick, N.J.

6. Margaretta Cornell to Maria Cornell, May 23, 1814; Maria Cornell to Margaretta Cornell, June 6, 1814; John Cornell to Margaretta Cornell, August 8, 1814, Cornell Family Papers.

7. "The Female Academy," advertisement, *Guardian* (New Brunswick, N.J.), May 12, 1812; Maria Cornell to Margaretta Cornell, May 1815, Cornell Family Papers. For more on New Brunswick schools, see Mary A. Demarest, "Some Early New Brunswick Schools for Girls," *Proceedings of the New Jersey Historical Society* 53 (1935): 163–85; Lucia McMahon, "'A More Accurate and Extensive Education than is Customary': Educational Opportunities for Women in Early Nineteenth-Century New Jersey," *New Jersey History* 124, no. 1 (fall 2009): 1–28.

8. Margaretta Cornell to Maria Cornell, September 7, 1815, Cornell Family Papers. Margaretta wrote this letter as a school composition; it contains minor corrections and comments added by her instructor Isaac N. Wyckoff.

9. "Female Education," *Port Folio* (Philadelphia), July 1810, 85; James Grant Wilson, *Memorials of Andrew Kirkpatrick and His Wife* (New York: Privately Printed for Mrs. Dr. How, 1870), 63; Jane Bayard to Sally Wister, February 1, 1790, Eastwick Collection, APS.

10. For overviews of eighteenth-century women's education, see especially E. Jennifer Monaghan, "Literary Instruction and Gender in Colonial New England," *American Quarterly* 40, no. 1 (March 1988): 18–41; E. Jennifer Monaghan, *Learning to Read and Write in Colonial America* (Amherst: Massachusetts University Press, 2005). See also Jane Greer, ed., *Girls and Literacy in America: Historical Perspectives to the Present* (Santa Barbara, Calif.: ABC-CLIO, 2003); Kevin J. Hayes, *A Colonial Woman's Bookshelf* (Knoxville: University of Tennessee Press, 1996); Kenneth Lockridge, *Literacy in Colonial New England: An Enquiry into the Social Context of Literacy in the Early Modern West* (New York: Norton, 1974); Sheila L. Skemp, *First Lady of Letters: Judith Sargent Murray and the Struggle for Female Independence* (Philadelphia: University of Pennsylvania Press, 2009).

11. "Miss Hay's Boarding School," advertisement, *Fredonian* (New Brunswick, N.J.), April 20, 1815; Catherine Frelinghuysen to Maria Cornell, March 27, 1813, Cornell Family Papers. For other examples of late-eighteenth-century boarding schools, see advertisements in *The Pennsylvania Gazette* (Philadelphia), for example, June 9, 1768; November 17, 1773; October 11, 1786; and August 12, 1789.

12. Rachel Van Dyke, journal, August 19, 1810; October 17, 1810; and February 28, 1811, in *To Read My Heart: The Journal of Rachel Van Dyke, 1810–1811,* ed. Lucia McMahon and Deborah Schriver (Philadelphia: University of Pennsylvania Press, 2000), 113, 165, 245–46.

13. "Education," *Port Folio* (Philadelphia), April 17, 1802, 116. This article included a reprint of a broadside advertisement for the Newark Female Academy. For overviews of women's access to education, see Kelley, *Learning to Stand and Speak;* Nash, *Women's Education in the United States.*

14. For background information on the Litchfield Female Academy, see Lynne Templeton Brickley, "Sarah Pierce's Litchfield Female Academy, 1792–1833," EdD diss., Harvard University, 1985; Lisa Roberge Pichnarcik, "'On the Threshold of Improvement': Women's Education at the Litchfield and Morris Academies," *Connecticut History* 37, no. 2 (fall 1996–spring 1997): 129–58; Theodore Sizer, Nancy Sizer, et al., *To Ornament Their Minds: Sarah Pierce's Litchfield Female Academy, 1792–1833* (Litchfield, Conn.: Litchfield Historical Society, 1993); Emily Noyes Vanderpoel, *Chronicles of a Pioneer School from 1792 to 1833, Being the History of Miss Sarah Pierce and Her Litchfield School* (Cambridge, Mass.: The University Press, 1903); Emily Noyes Vanderpoel, *More Chronicles of a Pioneer School from 1792 to 1833, Being Added History on the Litchfield Female Academy Kept by Miss Sarah Pierce and Her Nephew, John Pierce Brace* (New York: Cadmus Book Shop, 1927). Less scholarly work has been done on Catherine Fiske's academy. For a brief overview, see Gardner Hill, M.D., "A Famous Institution: Miss Catherine Fiske's Boarding School of the Early Days," *Granite Monthly* 39, no. 10 (October 1907): 335–38.

15. See Colin Burke, *American Collegiate Populations: A Test of the Traditional View* (New York: New York University Press, 1982).

16. James A. Neal, *An Essay on the Education and Genius of the Female Sex. To Which is Added, An Account, of the Commencement of the Young Ladies' Academy of Philadelphia, Held the 18th of December, 1794* (Philadelphia: Printed by Jacob Johnson, 1795), 7. For other primary source material on the Young Ladies' Academy, see *The Rise and Progress of the Young Ladies' Academy of Philadelphia: Containing an Account of the Number of Public Examinations and Commencements; the Charter and Bye-Laws; Likewise, A Number of Orations Delivered by the Young Ladies, and Several by the Trustees of Said Institution* (Philadelphia: Printed by Stewart & Cochran, 1794); Benjamin Rush, *Thoughts upon Female Education, Accommodated to the Present State of Society, Manners, and Government in the United States of America* (Boston: Printed by Samuel Hall, 1787); John Swanwick, *Thoughts on Education, Addressed to the Visitors of the Young Ladies' Academy in Philadelphia* (Philadelphia: Printed for Thomas Dobson, 1787). For historical accounts of the Young Ladies' Academy of Philadelphia, see Ann Gordon, "The Young Ladies Academy of Philadelphia," in *Women of America: A History,* ed. Carol Ruth Berkin and Mary Beth Norton (Boston: Houghton Mifflin Company, 1979), 68–91; Margaret Nash, "Rethinking Republican Motherhood: Benjamin Rush and the Young Ladies' Academy of Philadelphia," *Journal of the Early Republic* 17, no. 2 (summer 1997): 171–92; Marion B. Savin and Harold J. Abrahams, "The Young Ladies' Academy of Philadelphia," *History of Education Journal* 8, no. 2 (winter 1957): 58–67; Thelma M. Smith, "Feminism in Philadelphia, 1790–1850," *Pennsylvania Magazine of History and Biography* 68, no. 3 (July 1944): 243–68.

17. Catherine Beecher, quoted in Brickley, "Sarah Pierce's Litchfield Female Academy," 49; Mary Chester to mother, May 29, 1819, in Vanderpoel, *Chronicles,* 189. For background information on Catherine Beecher, see Kathryn Kish Sklar, *Catherine Beecher: A Study in American Domesticity* (New York: Norton, 1973); Vanderpoel, *Chronicles,* 179–83.

18. "Female Schools," *Ladies' Literary Cabinet* (New York), July 15, 1820, 78. See Elizabeth Barrows, *A Memorial of Bradford Academy* (Boston: Congregational S. S. and Publishing Society, 1870); Suzanne Geissler, *A Widening Sphere of Usefulness: Newark Academy, 1774–1993* (West Kennebunk, Mass.: Phoenix Publishing, 1993); Carl F. Kaestle, "Common Schools before the Common School Revival: New York Schooling in the 1790s," *History of Education Quarterly* 12, no. 4 (winter 1972): 465–500; Thomas Woody, *A History of Women's Education in the United States* (1929; reprint, New York: Octagon Books, 1980).

19. Sarah Ripley, diary, May 13, 1800, American Antiquarian Society (AAS), Worcester, Mass. (accessed through *American Women's Diaries Microfilm Collection,* Reel 4); Sarah Ripley, diary, September 8, 1804, Sarah Ripley Stearns Papers, Schlesinger Library, Radcliffe Institute, Harvard University (accessed through *History of Women Microfilm Collection,* Reel 992). (The Sarah Ripley Stearns diaries contain some overlap with each other; the AAS holdings are dated 1799–1801 and 1805–1809, whereas the Schlesinger library holds three volumes, dated 1801–1805, 1808–1812, and 1813–1818.) Linda Raymond to Joel Raymond, May 5, 1815; see also Linda Raymond, school journal, June 28,1814, Gertrude Foster Brown Additional Papers, Carton 5, Folders 129 and 136, Schlesinger Library, Radcliffe Institute, Harvard University; Elizabeth Pierce, journal, April 14, 1818, Poor Family Papers, Box 3, Folder 48, Schlesinger Library, Radcliffe Institute, Harvard University.

20. Charles L. Coon, *North Carolina Schools and Academies, 1790–1840* (Raleigh, N.C.: Edwards & Broughton Printing Co., 1915), 80–81. See also Marian H. Blair, "Contemporary Evidence—Salem Boarding School, 1834–1844," *North Carolina Historical Review* 27, no. 2 (April 1950): 142–61; Adelaide Lisetta Fries, *Historical Sketch of Salem Female Academy* (Salem, N.C.: Crist & Keehln, 1902); Lucy Leinbach Wenhold, "The Salem Boarding School between 1802 and 1822," *North Carolina Historical Review* 27, no. 1 (January 1950): 32–45. For overviews of southern women's educational opportunities, see Christine Anne Farnham, *The Education of the Southern Belle: Higher Education and Student Socialization in the Antebellum South* (New York: New York University Press, 1994); Woody, *History of Women's Education*.

21. John Leyburn to Thomas Preston, January 13, 1808, Cocke Family Papers, Virginia Historical Society, Richmond, Va.; Elizabeth Lindsay to Apphia Rouzee, May 1809, Hunter Family Papers, Series III, Virginia Historical Society, Richmond, Va. See also William W. Pusey, *Elusive Aspirations: The History of the Female Academy in Lexington, Virginia* (Lexington: Washington and Lee University, 1983); Oren F. Morton, *The History of Rockbridge County, Virginia* (Staunton, Va.: McClure Co., 1920).

22. Sophia Sawyer to Linda Raymond, November 31, 1820, Gertrude Foster Brown Additional Papers, Carton 5, Folder 133; Joseph Emerson, *Female Education. A Discourse, Delivered at the Dedication of the Seminary Hall in Saugus, January 15, 1822* (Boston: Published by Samuel T. Armstrong, and Crocker & Brewster, 1823), 31–32. For background information on Sophia Sawyer, who became a teacher and missionary, see Teri L. Castelow, "Creating an Educational Interest: Sophia Sawyer, Teacher of the Cherokee," in Beadie and Tolley, *Chartered Schools*, 186–210.

23. For discussion of the similarities in male and female curricula, see Kelley, *Learning to Stand and Speak;* Nash, *Women's Education in the United States*.

24. John Cosens Odgen, *The Female Guide: Or, Thoughts on the Education of That Sex, Accommodated to the State of Society, Manners, and Government, in the United States* (Concord: George Hough, 1793), 29; Mary Ann Bacon, "From the Diary and Composition and Extract Book of Mary Bacon," 1820, in Vanderpoel, *Chronicles,* 73; Catherine E. Kelly, "Reading and the Problem of Accomplishment," in *Reading Women: Literacy, Authorship, and Culture in the Atlantic World, 1500–1800,* ed. Heidi Brayman Hackel and Catherine E. Kelly (Philadelphia: University of Pennsylvania Press, 2008), 124–43; Margaret Nash, "'A Triumph of Reason': Female Education in Academies in the New Republic," in Beadie and Tolley, *Chartered Schools,* 64–86.

25. Nancy Maria Hyde, "Lecture II," in *The Life and Writings of Nancy Maria Hyde of Norwich, Connecticut, Connected With a Sketch of Her Life,* ed. Lydia Sigourney (Norwich, Conn.: Printed by Russell Hubbard, 1816), 156; "Wesleyan Seminary, New York," *Ladies' Literary Cabinet* (New York), July 1, 1820.

26. Catherine Frelinghuysen to Maria Cornell, July 12 [1804?], Cornell Family Papers; Polly Raymond to Joel Raymond, June 29, 1805, Gertrude Foster Brown Additional Papers, Carton 5, Folder 129.

27. *The American Lady's Preceptor,* 2nd ed. (Baltimore: E. J. Coale, 1811), xi; Mary Wilson to A. Lencrard and Mary Bennet, May 23, 1818, Hooker Collection, Box 1, Folder 28, Schlesinger Library, Radcliffe Institute, Harvard University; Linda Raymond to Mary Raymond, August 10, 1814, Gertrude Foster Brown Additional Papers, Carton 5, Folder 129.

28. Mary Chester, letter to mother, May 29, 1819, in Vanderpoel, *Chronicles,* 190; Violetta Bancker to Anne Bancker, November 8, 1801, Charles Nicoll Bancker Papers; Neal, *Essay on the Education,* 12–13. For further discussion of the ornamental offerings at Litchfield, see Glee Krueger, "Paper and Silk: The Ornamental Arts of the Litchfield Female Academy," in Sizer et al., *To Ornament Their Minds,* 82–100.

29. Jane Swann Hunter, diary, February 6, 1825, Hunter Family Papers, Series XII; Lucy Sheldon, journal, March 12, 1803, and March 26, 1803, in Vanderpoel, *Chronicles,* 52–53; Jane Lewis, "Extracts from Commonplace Book," 1820, in Vanderpoel, *Chronicles,* 223.

30. Linda Raymond, school journal, July 5, 1814, Gertrude Foster Brown Additional Papers, Carton 5, Folder 136; Mary Wilson to A. Lencrard and Mary Bennet, May 23, 1818, Hooker Collection, Box 1, Folder 28; Abigail Bradley to Mrs. Abigail Bradley, May 30 [1814], Bradley-Hyde Family Papers, Box 1, Folder 2, Schlesinger Library, Radcliffe Institute, Harvard University; Margaretta Cornell to Maria Cornell, May 23, 1814, Cornell Family Papers.

31. Rebecca Beverley to Robert Beverley, October 10, 1816; November 16, 1816; and January 10, 1817, Beverley Family Papers, Virginia Historical Society, Richmond, Va.

32. Rebecca Beverley to Robert Beverley, August 31, 1817, and August 2, 1817, Beverley Family Papers. For education as a marker of class status, see Mary Ryan, *Cradle of the Middle Class: The Family in Oneida County, New York, 1700–1865* (New York: Cambridge University Press, 1981).

33. Maria Cornell to Margaretta Cornell, May 1815, Cornell Family Papers; Elisha Boudinot to Julia Boudinot, March 10, 1801, Colt Family Papers, Special Collections and University Archives, Rutgers University Libraries, New Brunswick, N.J.; Mary Raymond to Linda Raymond, May 19, 1815, and Linda Raymond to Mary Raymond, August 10, 1814, Gertrude Foster Brown Additional Papers, Carton 5, Folders 127 and 129; Eliza Odgen, journal, October 13, 1817, in Vanderpoel, *Chronicles,* 171.

34. Eliza Southgate to Octavia Southgate, September 14, 1800, in *A Girl's Life Eighty Years Ago* (1887; reprint, New York: Arno Press, 1974), 30–31; Sarah Bache to Catherine Bache, June 25, 1819, Bache and Hodge Family Papers, Box 1, Folder 16, Manuscripts Division, Department of Rare Books and Special Collections, Princeton University Library, Princeton, N.J.; John Shippen to Elizabeth Shippen, January 27, 1796, Shippen Family Papers, APS. In addition to the collection of Shippen family letters at APS, there is also a collection of Shippen Family Papers at the Historical Society of Pennsylvania (HSP).

35. Abigail Bradley to Mrs. Abigail Bradley, May 30 [1814], Bradley-Hyde Family Papers, Box 1, Folder 2; Jane Bowne to Elizabeth Bowne, August 3, 1804, Wyck Association Collection, Series II, APS; Polly Raymond to Joel Raymond, June 29, 1805, and Linda Raymond to Mary Raymond, June 19, 1815, Gertrude Foster Brown Additional Papers, Carton 5, Folder 129; Elizabeth Pierce, journal, July 23, 1816, Poor Family Papers, Box 3, Folder 45; Eliza Southgate to Mary Southgate, January 23, 1797, in *Girl's Life Eighty Years Ago,* 3.

36. Rachel Van Dyke, journal, January 15, 1811, in McMahon and Schriver, *To Read My Heart,* 223; Abigail Bradley to Mrs. Abigail Bradley, May 30 [1814], Bradley-Hyde Family Papers, Box 1, Folder 2.

37. Caroline Chester, journal, January 1, 1816, in Vanderpoel, *Chronicles*, 152; Mary Ann Bacon, "Upon Education," in Vanderpoel, *Chronicles*, 72; Lucy Sheldon, diary, 1801, in Vanderpoel, *Chronicles*, 43; Eliza Ogden, journal, December 1, 1816, in Vanderpoel, *Chronicles*, 166; Lavinia Stafford to Lydia Clark Abbott, December 5, 1814, Lydia Clark Abbott Flint Papers (Ms S 171), Andover Historical Society, Andover, Mass.

38. Anne Brewer to Mrs. Phebe Ripley, undated [c. 1810s], Gage Family, Additional Papers, Series I, American Antiquarian Society (AAS), Worcester, Mass.

39. Sarah Crawford Cook, diary, [December] 1810; Betsey Melcalf, memoir, 1807–1810, in "'By the Pens of Females': Girls' Diaries From Rhode Island, 1788–1821," ed. Jane Lancaster, *Rhode Island History* 57, no. 3–4 (August–November 1999), 84–93; Sarah Connell, diary, July 25, 1807, in *Diary of Sarah Connell Ayer* (Portland, Maine: Lefavor-Tower Company, 1910), 15; Anna Giles Morris to Ann Haines, undated [c. 1810–1812], Wyck Association Collection.

40. Eliza Pintard Boudinot, letter book, January 6, 1810, Colt Family Papers. Eliza kept this letter book, which contains compositions on various subjects, while a student at the Newark Academy.

41. Timothy Alden, *Quarterly Catalogue of the Names of the Young Ladies, Who Belong to the Newark Academy, under the Instruction of Rev. Timothy Alden* (Newark: Printed by William Tuttle, 1810), esp. nos. I, II, III, and VI. For a detailed description of the merits and commendations awarded to students at the Newark Academy, see Timothy Alden, *Key to Quarterly Catalogues of the Names of the Young Ladies at the Newark Academy: Under the Instruction of Rev. Timothy Alden; with a Historical Sketch of the Academy* (Newark, N.J.: William Tuttle, 1810).

42. "Female Seminary," *Boston Weekly Magazine*, October 29, 1803, 1; Linda Raymond, school journal, October 9, 1814, Gertrude Foster Brown Additional Papers, Carton 5, Folder 136. For examples of the essays, poems, and dialogues performed by female students, see Susanna Rowson, *A Present for Young Ladies, Containing Poems, Dialogues, Addresses, &c., as Recited by the Pupils of Mrs. Rowson's Academy, at the Annual Exhibitions* (Boston: John West & Co, 1811); Charles Stearns, *Dramatic Dialogues for the Use of Schools* (Leominster, Mass.: John Prentiss, 1798). For further description and analysis of these ceremonies, see Kelly, "Reading and the Problem of Accomplishment"; Lucia McMahon, "'Of the Utmost Importance to Our Country': Women, Education, and Society, 1780–1820," *Journal of the Early Republic* 29, no. 3 (fall 2009): 475–506; Jason M. Opal, *Beyond the Farm: National Ambitions in Rural New England* (Philadelphia: University of Pennsylvania Press, 2008), chap. 4. For a compelling analysis of women's oratory in the early republic, see Carolyn Eastman, "The Female Cicero: Young Women's Oratory and Gendered Public Participation in the Early American Republic," *Gender & History* 19, no. 2 (August 2007): 260–83; Carolyn Eastman, *A Nation of Speechifiers: Making an American Public after the Revolution* (Chicago: University of Chicago Press, 2009).

43. Lavinia Stafford to Lydia Clark Abbott, August 7, 1815, Lydia Clark Abbott Flint Papers.

44. Nancy Maria Hyde, journal, August 7, 1811, in Sigourney, *Life and Writings of Nancy Maria Hyde*, 145–46.

45. William Staughton, *An Address, Delivered October 1807, at Mrs. Rivardi's Seminary. On the Occasion of the Examination of the First and Middle Classes* (Philadelphia: Printed by Kimber, Conrad, & Co, 1807), 11.

46. *Rise and Progress,* 47.

47. Neal, *Essay on the Education,* 14.

48. For discussions of the importance of civic society in the early republic, see Cynthia Kierner, "Genteel Balls and Republican Parades: Gender and Early Southern Civic Rituals, 1677–1826," *Virginia Magazine of History and Biography* 104, no. 2 (spring 1996): 185–210; Albrecht Koschnik, "The Democratic Societies of Philadelphia and the Limits of the American Public Sphere, circa 1793–1795," *William and Mary Quarterly* 58, no. 3 (July 2001): 615–36; David Shields, *Civil Tongues and Polite Letters in British America* (Chapel Hill: University of North Carolina Press, 1997); David Waldstreicher, *In The Midst of Perpetual Fetes: The Making of American Nationalism, 1776–1820* (Chapel Hill: University of North Carolina Press, 1997). For descriptions of early national women's participation in the public sphere, see Catherine Allgor, *Parlor Politics: In Which the Ladies of Washington Help Build a City and a Government* (Charlottesville: University of Virginia Press, 2000); Susan Branson, *These Fiery Frenchified Dames: Women and Political Culture in Early National Philadelphia* (Philadelphia: University of Pennsylvania Press, 2001); Jan Lewis, "Politics and the Ambivalence of the Public Sphere: Women in Early Washington, D.C.," in *A Republic for the Ages,* ed. Donald Kennon and Barbara Wolanin (Charlottesville: University of Virginia Press, 1999), 122–51.

49. Stearns, *Dramatic Dialogues,* 479; Betsey Metcalf, memoir, in Lancaster, "By the Pens of Females," 84. For examples of printed school catalogues, see Alden, *Quarterly Catalogue; Catalogue of the Officers and Students of the Bradford Academy, August 1821* ([Haverhill, Mass.]: Burrill and Hersey Printers, 1821); *Rise and Progress.*

50. See Alden, *Quarterly Catalogue;* Alden, *Key to Quarterly Catalogues.*

51. John Brace, journal, October 31, 1814, and November 1, 1814, in Vanderpoel, *More Chronicles,* 103–4; *Rise and Progress,* 17.

52. Rebecca Beverley to Robert Beverley, December 26, 1816, and April 26, 1817, Beverley Family Papers; N. Stocken to Ann Sellers, Peale-Sellers Family Collection, Series I, APS. These prizes could also lead to very competitive behavior among students. See Martha Tomhave Blauvelt, *The Work of the Heart: Young Women and Emotion, 1780–1830* (Charlottesville: University of Virginia Press, 2007), esp. chap. 2.

53. Elias Nason, *A Memoir of Mrs. Susanna Rowson, with Elegant and Illustrative Extracts from Her Writings in Prose and Poetry* (Albany, N.Y.: Joel Munsell, 1870), 121–22; John Brace, journal, August 6, 1814, in Vanderpoel, *More Chronicles,* 99; "Female Academy," *Weekly Recorder* (Chilicothe, Ohio), November 14, 1818, 110; "Waterford Female Academy," *Plough Boy* (Albany, N.Y.), September 30, 1820, 2. For other published accounts of commencement ceremonies, see *Pennsylvania Gazette* (Philadelphia), December 16, 1789; "Useful and Instructing: Mrs. Rowson's Academy," *Boston Weekly Magazine,* October 30, 1802, 2; "Communication," *Philadelphia Repository and Weekly Register,* March 1, 1802, 143; "Notice," *Miscellany* (Trenton, N.J.), June 24, 1805, 11; "Waterford Female Academy," *Plough Boy* (Albany, N.Y.), January 1, 1820, 247; "For the Philadelphia Repository," *Philadelphia Repository and Weekly Register,* May 14, 1803, 158; "Female Schools," *Ladies' Literary Cabinet* (New York), July 15, 1820, 78; "Wesleyan Seminary, New York," *Ladies' Literary Cabinet* (New York), July 1, 1820, 2; "Cincinnati Female Academy," *Cincinnati Literary Gazette,* July 31, 1824, 2.

54. "Analyticus," "For the *Port Folio,*" *Port Folio* (Philadelphia), October 25, 1806, 241.

55. Mary Ann Bacon, "A Composition Written at Litchfield," and "Upon Education," in Vanderpoel, *Chronicles,* 71–72.

56. "Essay on Education," *Massachusetts Magazine* (Boston), January 1789, 29; Rachel Van Dyke, journal, June 12, 1810, and June 20, 1810, in McMahon and Schriver, *To Read My Heart,* 45, 53–54.

57. Maria Taylor to Charles Bancker, July 8, 1802, Charles Nicoll Bancker Papers; Eliza Southgate to Moses Porter, May 1801, in *Girl's Life Eighty Years Ago,* 55–57.

58. Sarah Upshur Teackle, "An Oration Delivered by Sarah Upshur Teackle," undated [c. 1803], Charles Nicoll Bancker Papers.

59. Maria Cornell to Margaretta Cornell, May 1815, Cornell Family Papers.

60. Molly Wallace, "Valedictory Oration," in *Rise and Progress,* 73.

61. Ann Harker, "Salutatory Oration," in Neal, *Essay on the Education,* 17–20.

62. Ibid., 18–19; Wallace, "Valedictory Oration," 74.

63. "Essay on Education," 29.

64. Nancy Maria Hyde to sister, January 5, 1811, in Sigourney, *Life and Writings of Nancy Maria Hyde,* 107–8.

65. Sarah Vaughan to Mrs. R. H. Gardiner, February 27, 1812, Benjamin Vaughan Papers, APS; Maria Cornell to Margaretta Cornell, August 7, 1815, Cornell Family Papers.

66. Violetta Bancker to Anne Bancker, February 21, 1813, Charles Nicoll Bancker Papers.

67. Sarah Bache to Catharine Bache, June 25, 1819, Bache and Hodge Family Papers.

68. Linda Raymond, "Verses Addressed to a Young Lady on her Leaving School," school notebook, Gertrude Foster Brown Additional Papers, Carton 5, Folder 136.

69. Ibid.

Chapter 2

1. Eunice Callender to Sarah Ripley, October 29, 1803, Sarah Ripley Stearns Papers, Schlesinger Library, Radcliffe Institute, Harvard University (accessed through the *History of Women Microfilm Series,* Reel 968). There is only one letter in the collection written *by* Sarah Ripley Stearns *to* Eunice Callender, dated January 19, 1832. Internal evidence in Eunice Callender's letters suggests that their correspondence may have begun some time prior to 1802, but the first extant letter in the collection dates from September 1802. All citations from this collection are cited here as "Eunice Callender to Sarah Ripley (Stearns)" with the date of the letter. I refer to Sarah as "Sarah Ripley" until her marriage in 1812.

2. Carroll Smith-Rosenberg, "The Female World of Love and Ritual: Relations between Women in Nineteenth-Century America," *Signs* 1, no. 1 (autumn 1975), 9. For discussions of female friendship, which are often contextualized within a framework of "woman's culture" or "woman's sphere," see Martha Tomhave Blauvelt, "The Work of the Heart: Emotion in the 1805–35 Diary of Sarah Connell Ayer," *Journal of Social History* 35, no. 3 (spring 2002): 577–92; Martha Tomhave Blauvelt, *The Work of the Heart: Young Women and Emotion 1780–1830* (Charlottesville: University of Virginia Press, 2007); Lee Virginia Chambers-Schiller, *Liberty, a Better Husband: Single Women in America, the Generations of 1780–1840* (New Haven: Yale

University Press, 1984); Nancy Cott, *The Bonds of Womanhood: "Woman's Sphere" in New England, 1780–1835* (New Haven: Yale University Press, 1977); Lillian Faderman, *Surpassing the Love of Men: Romantic Friendship and Love between Women from the Renaissance to the Present* (New York: William Morrow, 1981); Carol F. Karlsen and Laurie Crumpacker, eds., *The Journal of Esther Edwards Burr, 1754–1757* (New Haven: Yale University Press, 1984); Carol Lasser, "Let Us Be Sisters Forever: The Sororal Model of Nineteenth-Century Female Friendships," *Signs* 14, no. 1 (autumn 1988): 158–81; Suzanne Lebsock, *The Free Women of Petersburg: Status and Culture in a Southern Town, 1784–1860* (New York: Norton, 1984); Claire Pettengill, "Sisterhood in a Separate Sphere: Female Friendship in Hannah Webster Foster's *The Coquette* and *The Boarding School*," *Early American Literature* 27, no. 3 (December 1992): 185–203; Carroll Smith-Rosenberg, *Disorderly Conduct: Visions of Gender in Victorian America* (New York: Oxford University Press, 1985); Steven Stowe, "'The Thing Not Its Vision': A Woman's Courtship and Her Sphere in the Southern Planter Class," *Feminist Studies* 9, no. 1 (spring 1983): 113–30.

3. In *The Bonds of Womanhood,* for example, Cott employs a separate spheres argument to suggest that physical and emotional distance was the norm between men and women: "[Women] would find truly reciprocal interpersonal relationships only with other women. They would find answering sensibilities only among their own sex" (168). In their analysis of female friendship, Smith-Rosenberg and other scholars (particularly Faderman, *Surpassing the Love of Men*) also focus largely on the erotic and passionate nature of these relationships, part of the effort to reconceptualize the history of women's sexuality. Although I do not explicitly discuss female sexuality in this chapter, female friends often used the same language as courting couples, suggesting that such relationships were rooted in intense bonds of affinity and affection.

4. For parallel discussions of male friendship, see Caleb Crain, "Leander, Lorenzo, and Castalio: An Early American Romance," *Early American Literature* 33, no. 1 (March 1998): 6–38; Richard Godbeer, *The Overflowing of Friendship: Love between Men and the Creation of the American Republic* (Baltimore: Johns Hopkins University Press, 2009); Anya Jabour, "Male Friendship and Masculinity in the Early National South: William Wirt and His Friends," *Journal of the Early Republic* 20, no. 1 (spring 2000): 83–111; E. Anthony Rotundo, "Romantic Friendship: Male Intimacy and Middle-Class Youth in the Northern United States, 1800–1900," *Journal of Social History* 23, no. 1 (fall 1989): 1–25; E. Anthony Rotundo, *American Manhood: Transformations in Masculinity from the Revolution to the Modern Era* (New York: Basic Books, 1993).

5. Eunice Callender to Sarah Ripley, May 21, 1803; Eunice Callender, diary, esp. June 11, 1809; February 3, 1819; and February 16, 1819, Sarah Ripley Stearns Papers (accessed through *History of Women Microfilm Series,* Reel 967). Eunice Callender (1786–1848) was the daughter of Benjamin Callender and Eunice (Franklin) Callender. Given her ardent interest in education and her residence in Boston, Eunice probably attended school(s) in her youth, but I have not located her specific educational history. Her extant diary begins in 1808 when she was twenty-two years old, after she would have already completed any formal education.

6. Sarah Ripley, diary, esp. July 15, 1799, and May 13, 1800, American Antiquarian Society (AAS), Worcester, Mass. (accessed through *American Women's Diaries Microfilm Collection,* Reel 4). The Sarah Ripley Stearns Papers at Schlesinger Library also contain three volumes of her journals (accessed through *History of Women*

Microfilm Series, Reel 992). The dates and content of these diaries overlap somewhat. The American Antiquarian Society holdings are dated 1799–1801 and 1805–1809, whereas the Schlesinger Library holdings are dated 1801–1805, 1808–1812, and 1813–1818. Sarah Ripley (b. November 26, 1785) was the daughter of Jerome Ripley, a shopkeeper, and Sarah (Franklin) Ripley. Her younger brother George Ripley (1802–1880) became a prominent social reformer and transcendentalist. The academy that Sarah attended in Greenfield was led by Proctor Pierce. At this academy, Sarah and her fellow classmates studied grammar, rhetoric, composition, arithmetic, geography, and astronomy.

7. Eunice Callender to Sarah Ripley, October 29, 1803; Sarah Ripley, diary, May 19, 1804, and August 1804. For information on the Dorchester Academy, founded in 1803, see "Saunders and Beach Academy," *Dorchester Atheneum,* www.dorchesteratheneum.org/page.php?id=1009 (accessed April 2011).

8. Polly Raymond to Joel Raymond, June 29, 1805; Linda Raymond, school journal, October 11, 1814, Gertrude Foster Brown Additional Papers, Carton 5, Folder 129, Schlesinger Library, Radcliffe Institute, Harvard University; Mary Moody Emerson to Anne Brewer, January 29, 1816, Gage Family, Additional Papers, Series I, American Antiquarian Society (AAS), Worcester, Mass.; Godbeer, *Overflowing of Friendship,* 51–52.

9. "Temple of the Muses," *Philadelphia Repository and Weekly Register,* March 12, 1803, 3.

10. Charlotte Hills to Lydia Clark Abbott, May 2, 1815, Lydia Clark Abbott Flint Papers (Ms S 171), Andover Historical Society, Andover, Mass.; Sarah Connell, diary, August 20, 1807, in *Diary of Sarah Connell Ayer* (Portland, Maine: Lefavor-Tower Company, 1910), 17.

11. Eunice Callender to Sarah Ripley, December 21, 1814; September 21, 1809; and June 1810; Harriet Margaret Wharton, journal, September 16, 1813, Thomas and Henry Wharton Papers [Collection 2047a], Historical Society of Pennsylvania (HSP), Philadelphia.

12. Harriet Margaret Wharton, journal, October 1812, Thomas and Henry Wharton Papers; Mary Cogswell to Weltha Brown, April 2, 1822, Hooker Collection, Box 1, Folder 13, Schlesinger Library, Radcliffe Institute, Harvard University; Sarah Vaughan to Mrs. R. H. Gardiner, January 9, 1812, Benjamin Vaughan Papers, American Philosophical Society (APS), Philadelphia.

13. Eunice Callender to Sarah Ripley, August 14, 1811; J. Shotwell to Catherine Wistar Bache, September 14, 1788, Catherine Wistar Bache Letters, APS.

14. For discussions of the culture of sensibility, see G. J. Barker-Benfield, *The Culture of Sensibility: Sex and Society in 18th-Century Britain* (Chicago: University of Chicago Press, 1992); Andrew Burstein, *Sentimental Democracy: The Evolution of America's Romantic Self-Image* (New York: Hill and Wang, 1999); Jay Fliegelman, *Declaring Independence: Jefferson, Natural Language, and the Culture of Performance* (Stanford: Stanford University Press, 1993); John Gillis, "From Ritual to Romance: Toward an Alternative History of Love," in *Emotion and Social Change: Toward a New Psychohistory,* ed. Carol Z. Stearns and Peter N. Stearns (New York: Holmes and Meier, 1988), 87–121; Karen Halttunen, *Confidence Men and Painted Women: A Study of Middle-Class Culture in America, 1830–1870* (New Haven: Yale University Press, 1982); Thomas

Haskell, "Capitalism and the Origins of the Humanitarian Sensibility, Part 2," in *The Antislavery Debate: Capitalism and Abolitionism as a Problem in Historical Interpretation,* ed. Thomas Bender (Berkeley: University of California Press, 1992), 136–60; Sarah Knott, "Sensibility and the American War for Independence," *American Historical Review* 109, no. 1 (February 2004): 19–40; Sarah Knott, *Sensibility and the American Revolution* (Chapel Hill: University of North Carolina Press, 2009); Jan Lewis, *The Pursuit of Happiness: Family and Values in Jefferson's Virginia* (New York: Cambridge University Press, 1983).

15. "Hints; Addressed to Both Sexes," *Massachusetts Magazine* (Boston), April 1793, 231; "Susan" to Jane Bowne, February 15, 1810, Wyck Association Collection, Series II, APS.

16. Eunice Callender to Sarah Ripley, May 24, 1803.

17. Eunice Callender, diary, May 12, 1812.

18. Sarah Ripley, diary, May 17, 1812.

19. Eunice Callender to Sarah Ripley, October 19, 1809, August 12, 1808; Jane Bayard to Sally Wister, August 30 [1792?], Eastwick Collection, APS; "Maria" to Delia Hayes, August 2, 1809, Clairborne Family Papers, Virginia Historical Society, Richmond, Va.

20. "Eliza" to Jane Bowne, February 2, 1807, Wyck Association Collection; Linda Raymond, School Book, 1814, Gertrude Foster Brown Additional Papers, Carton 5, Folder 129.

21. Deborah Norris to Sally Wister, February 27, 1779, Eastwick Collection; "Emma" to Jane Bowne, January 4, 1808, Wyck Association Collection.

22. "Eliza" to Jane Bowne, February 2, 1807, Wyck Association Collection; Eliza Payson to Linda Raymond, August 4, 1814, Gertrude Foster Brown Additional Papers, Carton 5, Folder 133; Lavinia Stafford to Lydia Clark Abbott, April 5, 1815, Lydia Clark Abbott Flint Papers; Maria Wilson to Delia Hayes, November 9, 1813, Claiborne Family Papers; S. H. Young to Ann Haines, September 5, 1814, Wyck Association Collection.

23. Jane Bayard to Sally Wister, February 1, 1790, Eastwick Collection; Eunice Callender to Sarah Ripley Stearns, June 7, 1813. For an interesting account of eighteenth-century French women's use of letter writing as a means of self-reflection and self-expression, see Dena Goodman, *Becoming a Woman in the Age of Letters* (Ithaca: Cornell University Press, 2009).

24. Marcia Hall to Weltha Brown, September 1819, Hooker Collection, Box 1, Folder 14; Eunice Callender to Sarah Ripley Stearns, February 2, 1814. Marcia may have been referring to Mrs. Elizabeth Montagu (1720–1800), a British intellectual and salon hostess, famous for her "bluestocking parties." See Elizabeth Montagu, *The Letters of Mrs. Elizabeth Montagu with Some of the Letters of Her Correspondents* (Philadelphia: Published by Bradford and Inskeep, 1810).

25. Harriet Margaret Wharton, journal, undated [c. 1812]; September 15, 1813; and October 18, 1813, Thomas and Henry Wharton Papers.

26. "On Friendship," *Lady's Magazine and Musical Repository* (New York), November 1801, 246; "Commentator, No. 5," *Philadelphia Repository and Weekly Register,* April 18, 1801, 181; "On Women. An Essay on Friendship with Women," *Massachusetts Magazine* (Boston), August 1796, 440–43. Both personal and published writings

on friendship often quoted Oliver Goldsmith, a member of Samuel Johnson's literary circle, who wrote that friendship was "but a name, a charm that lulls to sleep." See Oliver Goldsmith, *The Vicar of Wakefield: A Tale* (1766; reprint, Edinburgh: Oliver & Co. Netherbow, 1806), 40. For a discussion of the importance of (and difficulty in obtaining) the ideals of sincerity in communications with others, see Fliegelman, *Declaring Independence.*

27. Rachel Van Dyke, journal, June 2, 1810, and June 20, 1810, in *To Read My Heart: The Journal of Rachel Van Dyke, 1810–1811,* ed. Lucia McMahon and Deborah Schriver (Philadelphia: University of Pennsylvania Press, 2000), 33–34, 53–54.

28. "Friendship: A Fragment," *Weekly Visitor; or Ladies' Miscellany* (New York), February 1, 1806, 107; Elizabeth Lindsay to Apphia Rouzee, March [1805?], Hunter Family Papers, Series III, Virginia Historical Society, Richmond, Va.

29. Eunice Callender to Sarah Ripley, March 23, 1809. See February 4, 1809, for the letter that Sarah read as flattery and sarcasm on Eunice's part; in this letter, Eunice discussed a number of literary works and commented that Sarah had not shared her interest in a particular poem.

30. "Susan" to Jane Bowne, February 15, 1810, Wyck Association Collection; Elizabeth Shippen to Margaret Shippen, June 3, 1799, Shippen Family Papers, APS.

31. Eunice Callender to Sarah Ripley, undated [c. 1807].

32. For a discussion of how female friends used poetry and prose as conduits of emotional expression, see Anya Jabour, "Albums of Affection: Female Friendship and Coming of Age in Antebellum Virginia," *Virginia Magazine of History and Biography* 107, no. 2 (spring 1999): 125–58.

33. Eunice Callender to Sarah Ripley Stearns, June 7, 1813. For Walter Scott's popularity in America, see Emily B. Todd, "Walter Scott and the Nineteenth-Century American Literary Marketplace: Antebellum Richmond Readers and the Collected Editions of the Waverley Novels," *Papers of the Bibliographical Society of America* 93, no. 4 (December 1999): 495–517.

34. For discussion of "intensive" reading practices, see Robert Darnton, "Readers Respond to Rousseau: The Fabrication of Romantic Sensibility," in *The Great Cat Massacre and Other Episodes in French Cultural History* (New York: Vintage Books, 1985), 215–56; David D. Hall, "The Uses of Literacy in New England, 1600–1850," in *Printing and Society in Early America,* ed. William L. Joyce, David D. Hall, Richard D. Brown, and John B. Hench (Worcester, Mass.: American Antiquarian Society, 1983), 1–47; Carlo Ginzburg, *The Cheese and the Worms: The Cosmos of a Sixteenth-Century Miller,* trans. John and Anne Tedeschi (1976; reprint, New York: Penguin, 1980).

35. Eunice Callender to Sarah Ripley, August 14, 1811; Ann Haines to Jane Bowne Haines, June 13 [1822]; [Unsigned] to Jane Bowne, March 1811, Wyck Association Collection; Sarah Vaughan to Mrs. R. H. Gardiner, February 27, 1812, Benjamin Vaughan Papers. Descriptions of shared reading practices are common throughout the diaries and letters of early national men and women. For one typical example, see Anthony G. Roeber, "A New England Woman's Perspective on Norfolk, Virginia, 1801–1802: Excerpts from the Diary of Ruth Henshaw Bascom," *Proceedings of the American Antiquarian Society* 88, no. 2 (October 1978): 277–325.

36. S. Minturn to Jane Bowne Haines, undated [February 1821], Wyck Association Collection; Elizabeth Pierce, journal, November 19, 1817, Poor Family Papers, Box 3, Folder 48, Schlesinger Library, Radcliffe Institute, Harvard University.

37. Harriet Burnham to Abigail Bradley, October 3, 1812, Bradley-Hyde Collection, Box 1, Folder 2, Schlesinger Library, Radcliffe Institute, Harvard University; "Eliza" to Jane Bowne, July 2, 1809, Wyck Association Collection; Eunice Callender to Sarah Ripley, February 4, 1809.

38. Mary Kelley, "Reading Women/Women Reading: The Making of Learned Women in Antebellum America," *Journal of American History* 83, no. 2 (September 1996): 401–24 (see esp. 419–24). The parallel process of validating masculinity through shared intellectual pursuits is discussed in Konstantin Dierks, "Letter Writing, Masculinity, and American Men of Science, 1700–1800," *Explorations in Early American Culture: Pennsylvania History* 65 (1998): 167–98; Godbeer, *Overflowing of Friendship.*

39. Catherine Van Schaack to Sarah Jay, August 10, 1811, and August 22, 1811, Miscellaneous Manuscripts—Van Schaack, Catherine, New York Historical Society, New York. Catherine Van Schaack's diverse reading interests were common. See Kelley, "Reading Women/Women Reading"; Lucia McMahon and Deborah Schriver, eds., *To Read My Heart: The Journal of Rachel Van Dyke, 1810–1811* (Philadelphia: University of Pennsylvania Press, 2000; Ronald Zboray, *A Fictive People: Antebellum Economic Development and the American Reading Public* (New York: Oxford University Press, 1993), esp. 156–79; Ronald J. Zboray and Mary Saracino Zboray, "'Have You Read . . . ?': Real Readers and Their Responses in Antebellum Boston and Its Region," *Nineteenth-Century Literature* 52, no. 2 (September 1997): 139–70.

40. Eunice Callender to Sarah Ripley Stearns, March 15, 1817; Sarah Wister to Hannah Fauke, January 20, 1802, Eastwick Collection; Lucy Vaughan to Mrs. R. H. Gardiner, February 20, 1819, Benjamin Vaughan Papers; Ann Haines to Jane Bowne Haines, June 27 [1822], Wyck Association Collection; Catherine Eddowes to Margaret Shippen, February 4, 1809, Shippen Family Papers [Collection 595], HSP. The "worthy women" mentioned in this paragraph were well known throughout the early national period. Isabella Graham (1742–1814) was a noted educator active in several benevolent societies in New York; her memoir was published after her death. Hannah More (1745–1833) was one of the most successful and influential women of the era, known for her numerous writings and charitable activities. Mary Hays (1759–1843) was a British writer, a friend and contemporary of Mary Wollstonecraft. See Isabella Graham, *The Power of Faith Exemplified in the Life and Writings of the Late Mrs. Isabella Graham* (New York: Printed by J. Seymour, 1816); Anne Stott, *Hannah More: The First Victorian* (New York: Oxford University Press, 2003); Mary Hays, *Female Biography, or, Memoirs of Illustrious and Celebrated Women, of All Ages and Countries,* 1st American ed. (Philadelphia: Printed by Birch and Small, 1807).

41. Susanna Rowson, *A Present for Young Ladies, Containing Poems, Dialogues, Addresses, &c., as Recited by the Pupils of Mrs. Rowson's Academy, at the Annual Exhibitions* (Boston: John West, 1811), 83–86, 119–22.

42. Lusanna Richmond, diary, September 14, 1818, in Jane Lancaster, ed., *"By the Pens of Females": Girls' Diaries From Rhode Island, 1788–1821, Rhode Island History* 57, no. 3–4 (August–November 1999), 101. Martha Laurens Ramsey (1759–1811), from South Carolina, was relatively unknown during her own lifetime. Her husband published her memoirs, containing excerpts from her diaries and letters, after her death. See David Ramsey, ed., *Memoirs of the Life of Martha Laurens Ramsay,* 2nd ed. (Charlestown: Printed by Samuel Etheridge, 1812).

43. Rachel Van Dyke, journal, July 11, 1810, in McMahon and Schriver, *To Read My Heart,* 75; "Review of Elizabeth Smith," quoted in *The American Lady's Preceptor,* 2nd ed. (Baltimore: E. J. Coale, 1811), 167–68. Elizabeth Smith (1776–1806) was a British woman, largely self-educated, who translated works in several languages. Her memoirs, published after her death in 1806, went through several editions in England and America. See Elizabeth Smith, *Fragments in Prose and Verse by Miss Elizabeth Smith. With Some Account of Her Life and Character: by H. M. Bowdler (Burlington, N.J.: D. Allinson & Co., 1811).*

44. Eunice Callender to Sarah Ripley Stearns, February 2, 1814.

45. Eunice Callender to Sarah Ripley, February 7, 1810. The book referred to by Eunice was Anne MacVicar Grant, *Memoirs of an American Lady* (New York: S. Campbell, 1809), a memoir about Catalina Schuyler (1701–1779?).

46. Sarah Ripley Stearns, diary, May 1, 1814; Eunice Callender to Sarah Ripley Stearns, August 13, 1814. Sarah had recommended the memoir of Harriett Newell, a young woman who had died while engaged in missionary work in India with her husband. See Leonard Woods, *A Sermon Preached at Haverhill, in Remembrance of Mrs. Harriet Newell, Wife of the Rev. Samuel Newell, Missionary to India. Who Died at the Isle of France, November 30, 1812, Aged 19 Years. To Which Are Added Memoirs of Her Life,* 2nd ed. (Boston: Printed by Samuel T. Armstrong, 1814).

47. Eunice Callender to Sarah Ripley, December 30, 1808, and February 4, 1809. The book referred to by Eunice was Elizabeth Singer Rowe, *Friendship in Death* (New York: Evert Duyckinck and Co., 1795). This book was organized as a collection of letters "written" in the voices of deceased persons on various moral subjects. Rowe (1674–1737) was a respected member of Isaac Watts's literary circle, and her book remained popular throughout the eighteenth century. For one example of how the lives of such women were presented in a variety of published formats, see "Biography," *Boston Weekly Magazine,* February 26, 1803, 74. The epistolary form of this book may have served to reinforce Eunice's own thoughts about her correspondence with Sarah being potentially publishable material.

48. "Sarah" to Jane Bowne, undated [c. 1808–1811], Wyck Association Collection. For a discussion of how women were socialized to avoid conflict and maintain harmony, see Blauvelt, *Work of the Heart.*

49. Eunice Callender to Sarah Ripley, August 14, 1811.

50. Eunice Callender to Sarah Ripley, August 3, 1807. The book mentioned by Eunice was Charles Rollin, *Ancient History* (reprint, London: Mundell & Son, 1790), one of the most popular and widely read works of history in early national America.

51. Charles Peirce, *The Portsmouth Miscellany, or Lady's Library Improved* (Portsmouth, N.H.: Peirce, Hill, and Peirce, Printers, 1804), vi. For discussions of women's novel reading, see Blauvelt, *Work of the Heart;* Cathy N. Davidson, "The Novel as Subversive Activity: Women Reading, Women Writing," in *Beyond the American Revolution: Explorations in the History of American Radicalism,* ed. Alfred F. Young (DeKalb: Northern Illinois University Press, 1993), 283–316; Cathy N. Davidson, *Revolution and the Word: The Rise of the Novel in America* (New York: Oxford University Press, 1985); Catherine Kerrison, *Claiming the Pen: Women and Intellectual Life in the Early American South* (Ithaca: Cornell University Press, 2006).

52. Elizabeth Lindsay to Apphia Rouzee, May 15, 1810, Hunter Family Papers; Harriet Margaret Wharton, journal, February 15, 1813, Thomas and Henry Wharton

Papers. See Hannah More, *Coelebs in Search of a Wife,* 11th ed. (London: T. Cadell and W. Davies, 1809).

53. Eunice Callender to Sarah Ripley, March 23 1809, and September 1, 1809; "Sarah" to Jane Bowne, April 1809, and undated [c. 1809], Wyck Association Collection. Like other social commentators of the era, John Bennett was critical of novel reading and recommended that women read history and biography instead. See John Bennett, *Letters to a Young Lady, on a Variety of Useful and Interesting Subjects: Calculated to Improve the Heart, to Form the Manners, and Enlighten the Understanding* (1789; reprint, Hartford: Printed by Hudson and Goodwin, 1791).

54. "Novels and Romances," *Weekly Visitor, or Ladies' Miscellany* (New York), December 10, 1803, 412; Eunice Callender to Sarah Ripley, September 1, 1809.

55. Harriet Manigault, diary, July 29, 1814 [Am. 18837], HSP; Anna Maria Cornell to Margaretta Cornell, January 8, 1818, Cornell Family Papers, Special Collections and University Archives, Rutgers University Libraries, New Brunswick, N.J.; Eunice Callender to Sarah Ripley, December 30, 1808; Lucy Vaughan to Mrs. R. H. Gardiner, March 9, 1819, Benjamin Vaughan Papers.

56. David Hume, "History a Proper Object of Female Pursuit (extracted from the writings of Hume)," *Lady's Magazine and Musical Repository* (New York), February 1801, 91–95. For women readers, history typically did not focus on those "truths" most relevant to their lives (whereas novels were more likely to center on women's experiences). For women seeking validation of their own intellectual ambitions or personal experiences, traditional histories often failed to accomplish what novels "founded on fact" could.

57. Ibid., 91.

58. Eunice Callender to Sarah Ripley, August 3, 1807.

59. Ibid.

60. Eunice Callender to Sarah Ripley, October 19, 1808.

61. Eunice Callender to Sarah Ripley Stearns, April 2, 1813, and April 29, 1813.

62. Eunice Callender to Sarah Ripley Stearns, March 15, 1817, and May 30, 1817.

63. Eunice Callender to Sarah Ripley Stearns, October 20, 1815; Rebecca Root to Weltha Brown, December 2, 1817, Hooker Collection, Box 1, Folder 8; Elizabeth Lindsay Gordon to Apphia Rouzee, November 5, 1816, Hunter Family Papers; H. Ryers to Catherine Wistar Bache, July 12, 1799, Bache Family Papers, APS.

64. Eunice Callender to Sarah Ripley Stearns, October 23, 1830, and February 10, 1830.

65. Eunice Callender to Sarah Ripley Stearns, February 10, 1830, and August 12, 1815; Deborah Norris to Sally Wister, February 27, 1779, Eastwick Collection; Harriet Margaret Wharton, December 9, 1817, Thomas and Henry Wharton Papers.

66. Eunice Callender to Sarah Ripley Stearns, October 2, 1827; February 10, 1830; and October 23, 1830.

Chapter 3

1. John Shippen to Elizabeth Shippen, January 27, 1796, Shippen Family Papers, American Philosophical Society (APS), Philadelphia. John, Elizabeth, Margaret, and their siblings were the children of Jane Galloway Shippen (1745–1801) and Joseph Shippen III (1732–1810). For background material on the Shippen family, see John

Jordan, ed., *Colonial and Revolutionary Families of Pennsylvania: Genealogical and Personal Memoirs* (1911; reprint, Baltimore: Genealogical Publishing, 1994), 96–109; Randolph Shipley Klein, *Portrait of an Early American Family: The Shippens of Pennsylvania across Five Generations* (Philadelphia: University of Pennsylvania Press, 1975).

2. James A. Neal, *An Essay on the Education and Genius of the Female Sex. To Which Is Added, an Account, of the Commencement of the Young Ladies' Academy of Philadelphia, Held the 18th of December 1794* (Philadelphia: Printed by Jacob Johnson, 1795), 11.

3. Elizabeth Shippen to Margaret Shippen, June 13, 1799, APS; Elizabeth Shippen to John Shippen, December 21, 1797, APS.

4. See Mary P. Ryan, *Cradle of the Middle Class: The Family in Oneida County, New York, 1790–1865* (New York: Cambridge University Press, 1981). For other representative descriptions of nineteenth-century family life, see Carl Degler, *At Odds: Women and the Family in America from the Revolution to the Present* (New York: Oxford University Press, 1980); John Demos, *Past, Present, and Personal: The Family and Life Course in American History* (New York: Oxford University Press, 1986); Joan Jensen, *Loosening the Bonds: Mid-Atlantic Farm Women* (New Haven: Yale University, 1986); Shawn Johansen, *Family Men: Middle Class Fatherhood in Early Industrializing America* (New York: Routledge, 2001); Nicholas Marshall, "Rural Experience and the Development of the Middle Class: The Power of Culture and Tangible Improvements," *American Nineteenth Century History* 8, no. 1 (March 2007): 1–25; Steven Mintz and Susan Kellogg, *Domestic Revolutions: A Social History of American Family Life* (New York: Free Press, 1988); Robert E. Shalhope, *A Tale of New England: The Diaries of Hiram Harwood, Vermont Farmer, 1810–1837* (Baltimore: Johns Hopkins University Press, 2003).

5. Joseph Shippen (1732–1810) and Jane Galloway Shippen (1745–1801) married in 1768; Jane gave birth to ten children between 1769 and 1788, three of whom died in infancy. Elizabeth (1780–1801) and Margaret (1782–1876) had one older sister Mary (1773–1809), who married Samuel Swift in 1793; their eldest brother Robert (1769–1840) was also married and living away from home at the time the major events covered in this chapter occurred. See Thomas Willing Balch, "The English Ancestors of the Shippen Family," *Pennsylvania Magazine of History and Biography* 28, no. 4 (October 1904): 385–402; Jordan, *Colonial and Revolutionary Families of Pennsylvania*, esp. 96–109; Klein, *Portrait of an Early American Family*, esp. chart B-3.

6. Klein, *Portrait of an Early American Family*, 203–10.

7. Elizabeth Shippen to John Shippen, March 26, 1799, APS.

8. For family life in colonial America, see John Demos, *A Little Commonwealth: Family Life in Plymouth County* (New York: Oxford University Press, 1970); Philip Greven, *The Protestant Temperament: Patterns of Child-Rearing, Religious Experience, and the Self in Early America* (New York: Knopf, 1977); Edmund Morgan, *The Puritan Family: Religion and Relations in Seventeenth-Century New England* (New York: Harper & Row, 1944); Lisa Wilson, *Ye Heart of a Man: The Domestic Life of Men in Colonial New England* (New Haven: Yale University Press, 1999). For discussions of colonial women's experiences, see Kathleen M. Brown, *Good Wives, Nasty Wenches, and Anxious Patriarchs: Gender, Race, and Power in Colonial Virginia* (Chapel Hill: University of North Carolina Press, 1996); Cornelia Hughes Dayton, *Women before the Bar: Gender, Law, and Society in Connecticut, 1639–1789* (Chapel Hill: University of North Carolina

Press, 1995); Mary Beth Norton, *Founding Mothers and Fathers: Gendered Power and the Forming of American Society* (New York: Knopf, 1996); Laurel Thatcher Ulrich, *Good Wives: Image and Reality in the Lives of Women in Northern New England, 1650–1750* (New York: Knopf, 1980).

9. See Jay Fliegelman, *Prodigals and Pilgrims: The American Revolution against Patriarchal Authority, 1750–1800* (New York: Cambridge University Press, 1982); Gordon S. Wood, *The Radicalism of the American Revolution* (New York: Knopf, 1992).

10. See especially Johansen, *Family Men,* 87. For other descriptions of this transition, see Philip Aries, *Centuries of Childhood: A Social History of Family Life,* trans. Robert Baldick (New York: Vintage, 1965); Joseph F. Kett, *Rites of Passage: Adolescence in America 1790 to the Present* (New York: Basic Books: 1977); Jan Lewis, *The Pursuit of Happiness: Family and Values in Jefferson's Virginia* (New York: Cambridge University Press, 1983); Steven Mintz, *Huck's Raft: A History of American Childhood* (Cambridge, Mass.: Belknap Press of Harvard University Press, 2004); Carole Shammas, *A History of Household Government in America* (Charlottesville: University of Virginia Press, 2002).

11. John Burton, *Lectures on Female Education and Manners* (New York: Printed by Samuel Campbell, 1794), 19.

12. Samuel Whiting, *Elegant Lessons, or the Young Lady's Preceptor: Being a Series of Appropriate Reading Exercises, in Prose and Verse: Carefully Selected from the Most Approved Authors, for Female Schools and Academies* (Middletown, Conn.: Clark & Lyman, 1820), 25–26.

13. Henry Shippen to Joseph Shippen, June 2, 1806, Shippen Family Papers [Collection 595], Historical Society of Pennsylvania (HSP), Philadelphia. For Shippen family ties to Princeton, see Balch, "English Ancestors," 738; Jordan, *Colonial and Revolutionary Families of Pennsylvania,* 96–109.

14. See Thomas Augst, *The Clerk's Tale: Young Men and Moral Life in Nineteenth-Century America* (Chicago: University of Chicago Press, 2003); Jason M. Opal, "Exciting Emulation: Academies and the Transformation of the Rural North, 1780s–1820s," *Journal of American History* 91, no. 2 (September 2004): 445–70; Jason M. Opal, *Beyond the Farm: National Ambitions in Rural New England* (Philadelphia: University of Pennsylvania Press, 2008).

15. Elizabeth Shippen to John Shippen, December 5, 1798, APS; Elizabeth Shippen to Jane Galloway Shippen, January 25, 1799, APS.

16. Henry Shippen to Margaret Shippen, March 4, 1807, HSP.

17. "Female Education, Important to the Virtue and Happiness of Society," *Evening Fire-Side* (Philadelphia), February 22, 1806; Catherine E. Kelly, "Reading and the Problem of Accomplishment," in *Reading Women: Literacy, Authorship, and Culture in the Atlantic World, 1500–1800,* ed. Heidi Brayman Hackel and Catherine E. Kelly (Philadelphia: University of Pennsylvania Press, 2008), 129. For other discussions of this trend, see Kathryn Kish Sklar, "The Schooling of Girls and Changing Community Values in Massachusetts Towns, 1750–1820," *History of Education Quarterly* 33, no. 4 (winter 1993): 511–42; Marshall, "Rural Experience"; Maris A. Vinovskis, "Family and Schooling in Colonial and Nineteenth-Century History," *Journal of Family History* 12 (January 1987): 19–37.

18. Elizabeth Shippen to Jane Galloway Shippen, January 5, 1796, APS.

19. For women's access to college in the mid- to late nineteenth century, see Helen Lefkowitz Horowitz, *Alma Mater: Design and Experience in the Women's Colleges*

from Their Nineteenth-Century Beginnings to the 1930s (New York: Knopf, 1984); Barbara Miller Solomon, *In the Company of Educated Women: A History of Women and Higher Education in America* (New Haven: Yale University Press, 1985).

20. Whiting, *Elegant Lessons*, 25–26.

21. Elizabeth Shippen to Margaret Shippen, July 11, 1799, APS.

22. Anna Marie Cornell to Margaretta Cornell, June 21, 1824, Cornell Family Papers, Special Collections and University Archives, Rutgers University Libraries, New Brunswick, N. J.

23. Elizabeth Wister to John Wister, December 18, 1793, Eastwick Collection, APS. For the importance of sibling relations in early national families, see C. Dallett Hemphill, *Siblings: Brothers and Sisters in American History* (New York: Oxford University Press, 2011).

24. Rachel Van Dyke, journal, June 11, 1810, in Lucia McMahon and Deborah Schriver, eds., *To Read My Heart: The Journal of Rachel Van Dyke, 1810–1811* (Philadelphia: University of Pennsylvania Press, 2000), 43; Elizabeth Pierce to John Pierce, December 12, 1813, Poor Family Papers, Box 3, Folder 35, Schlesinger Library, Radcliffe Institute, Harvard University; Eliza Teackle to Sarah Bancker, October 7, 1806, and Violetta Bancker to Charles Bancker, June 21, 1813, Charles Nicoll Bancker Papers, APS.

25. John Shippen to Elizabeth Shippen, November 19, 1797, APS.

26. Elizabeth Shippen to John Shippen, October 27, 1797, APS; John Shippen to Elizabeth Shippen, November 19, 1797, APS.

27. John Shippen to Elizabeth Shippen, June 15, 1799, APS.

28. Elizabeth Shippen to Margaret Shippen, April 26, 1799, HSP.

29. Sally Wister to Elizabeth Wister, undated [c. 1790s], Eastwick Collection.

30. Horace Binney to Susan Binney, May 23, 1800, John Williams Wallace Collection [Collection 686], HSP; Elizabeth Shippen to Margaret Shippen, June 3, 1799, APS.

31. Elizabeth Shippen to Margaret Shippen, April 26, 1799, HSP.

32. Elizabeth Shippen to Margaret Shippen, July 11, 1799, APS.

33. Henry Shippen to Margaret Shippen, February 28, 1802, HSP.

34. Maria Cornell to Margaretta Cornell, December 20, 1817, Cornell Family Papers.

35. Margaret Bayard Smith to J. Bayard Smith, November 23, 1828, in Gaillard Hunt, ed., *Forty Years in Washington: Portrayed by the Family Letters of Mrs. Samuel Harrison Smith* (London: T. Fisher Unwin, 1906), 244.

36. Ibid.

37. Harriet Margaret Wharton, journal, October 8, 1813, Thomas and Henry Wharton Papers [Collection 2047a], HSP; Henrietta Teackle to Sarah Bancker, May 4, 1805, Charles Nicoll Bancker Papers; Mary Cogswell to Weltha Brown, April 2, 1822, Hooker Collection, Box 1, Folder 13, Schlesinger Library, Radcliffe Institute, Harvard University; Eliza Southgate to Mrs. Southgate, July 3, 1800, in *A Girl's Life Eighty Years Ago* (1887; reprint, New York: Arno Press, 1974), 27.

38. Elizabeth Wister, journal, August 20, 1785, Eastwick Collection; Jane Bayard Kirkpatrick, journal, April 27, 1825, Special Collections and University Archives, Rutgers University Libraries, New Brunswick, N. J.; Eliza Southgate to Moses Porter, June 1, 1801, in *Girl's Life Eighty Years Ago*, 62.

39. Samuel Bayard to Sally Wister, July 6, 1787, and undated [c. 1787], Eastwick Collection; William W. Wister to Susan Foulke, March 29, 1802, Eastwick Collection.

40. Elizabeth Shippen to Margaret Shippen, July 11, 1799, APS. For discussions of the culture of sensibility, see especially Lewis, *Pursuit of Happiness*. See also G. J. Barker-Benfield, *The Culture of Sensibility: Sex and Society in Eighteenth-Century Britain* (Chicago: University of Chicago Press, 1992); Andrew Burstein, *Sentimental Democracy: The Evolution of America's Romantic Self-Image* (New York: Hill and Wang, 1999); Jay Fliegelman, *Declaring Independence: Jefferson, Natural Language, and the Culture of Performance* (Stanford: Stanford University Press, 1993); John Gillis, "From Ritual to Romance: Toward an Alternative History of Love," in *Emotion and Social Change: Toward a New Psychohistory*, ed. Carol Z. Stearns and Peter N. Stearns (New York: Holmes and Meier, 1988), 87–121; Karen Halttunen, *Confidence Men and Painted Women: A Study of Middle-Class Culture in America, 1830–1870* (New Haven: Yale University Press, 1982); Thomas Haskell, "Capitalism and the Origins of the Humanitarian Sensibility, Part 2," in *The Antislavery Debate: Capitalism and Abolitionism as a Problem in Historical Interpretation*, ed. Thomas Bender (Berkeley: University of California Press, 1992), 136–60; Sarah Knott, "Sensibility and the American War for Independence," *American Historical Review* 109, no. 1 (February 2004): 19–40; Sarah Knott, *Sensibility and the American Revolution* (Chapel Hill: University of North Carolina Press, 2009).

41. *Philadelphia Repository and Weekly Register*, September 2, 1804, 276–77; "Importance of Female Education—and of Educating Young Men in Their Native Country, Addressed to Every American," *American Magazine* (New York), May 1788; "The Influence of the Female Sex on the Enjoyments of Social Life," *Rural Magazine* (Newark, N.J.), June 9, 1798.

42. Elizabeth Shippen to Jane Galloway Shippen, May 3, 1796, and January 25, 1799, APS; Elizabeth Shippen to Margaret Shippen, January 24, 1799, APS; Elizabeth Shippen to Joseph Shippen, February 8, 1799, APS.

43. "J. M. P.," "On the Influence of Female Society," *Philadelphia Repository and Weekly Register*, April 25, 1801, 188 (emphasis in original).

44. See Lucia McMahon, "'Of the Utmost Importance to Our Country': Women, Education, and Society, 1780–1820," *Journal of the Early Republic* 29, no. 3 (fall 2009): 475–506.

45. Karen Hansen, *A Very Social Time: Crafting Community in Antebellum New England* (Berkeley: University of California Press, 1994); Catherine E. Kelly, *In the New England Fashion: Reshaping Women's Lives in the Nineteenth Century* (Ithaca: Cornell University Press, 1999); Charlene M. Boyer Lewis, *Ladies and Gentlemen on Display: Planter Society at the Virginia Springs, 1790–1860* (Charlottesville: University of Virginia Press, 2001); Claire A. Lyons, *Sex among the Rabble: An Intimate History of Gender & Power in the Age of Revolution, Philadelphia, 1730–1830* (Chapel Hill: University of North Carolina Press, 2005). For other examples of historians who have charted fluid interactions between public and private and/or between men and women, see Paula Baker, "The Domestication of Politics: Women and American Political Society, 1780–1920," *American Historical Review* 89, no. 3 (June 1984): 620–47; Bruce Dorsey, *Reforming Men and Women: Gender in the Antebellum City* (Ithaca: Cornell University Press, 2002); Laura McCall and Donald Yacovone, eds., *A Shared Experience: Women, Men and the History of Gender* (New York: New York University Press, 1998); Nancy Grey Osterud, *The Bonds of Community: The Lives of Farm Women*

in Nineteenth-Century New York (Ithaca: Cornell University Press, 1991); Mary Ryan, *Women in Public: Between Banners and Ballots, 1825–1880* (Baltimore: Johns Hopkins University Press, 1996).

46. For analysis of how the concept of separate spheres has affected the historiography of nineteenth-century America, see Linda Kerber, "Separate Spheres, Female Worlds, Woman's Place: The Rhetoric of Women's History," *Journal of American History* 75, no. 1 (June 1988): 9–39; Susan M. Reverby and Dorothy O. Helly, "Introduction: Converging on History," in *Gendered Domains: Rethinking Public and Private in Women's History* (Ithaca: Cornell University Press, 1992).

47. Elizabeth Shippen to John Shippen, July 12, 1798, APS; Sarah Connell, Diary, July 4, 1808, in *Diary of Sarah Connell Ayer* (Portland, Maine: Lefavor-Tower Company, 1910), 51; Mary Griffith to Arabella Wharton, December 1821, Mary Griffith Letters, Special Collections and University Archives, Rutgers University Libraries, New Brunswick, N.J.

48. John Shippen to Elizabeth Shippen, January 27, 1796, APS.

49. "Female Education."

50. Joshua Francis Fisher, "Excerpts from a Memoir of Joshua Francis Fisher," in *The Diary of Harriet Manigault 1813–1816* (Rockland, Maine: Maine Coast Printers, 1976), 141–42. For salon culture, see Daniel Kilbride, *An American Aristocracy: Southern Planters in Antebellum Philadelphia* (Columbia: University of South Carolina Press, 2006); Daniel Kilbride, "Cultivation, Conservatism, and the Early National Gentry: The Manigault Family and Their Circle," *Journal of the Early Republic* 19, no. 2 (summer 1999): 221–56.

51. Margaret Manigault, diary, November 5, 1805, in Joseph P. Monigle, ed., "The Diaries of Mrs. Gabriel Manigault, 1793–1809," MA thesis, University of Delaware, 1959, 102; Harriet Manigault, diary, January 26, 1815 [Am. 18837], HSP; Alice Izard to Margaret Manigault, March 31, 1811, Manigault Family Papers, Series 55-2, South Carolina Historical Society, Charleston, S.C. (from microfiche copy held at Princeton University Library, Princeton, N.J.).

52. [Unsigned] to Marianne Williams, March 10, 1804, Biddle Family Papers, Series II [Collection 1792], HSP; Mary Cogswell to Weltha Brown, April 2, 1822, Hooker Collection, Box 1, Folder 13; Sarah Connell, diary, June 17, 1810, in *Diary of Sarah Connell Ayer,* 160; Henrietta Teackle to Sarah Bancker, August 6, 1807, Charles Nicoll Bancker Papers.

53. Catherine Eddowes to Margaret Shippen, November 29, 1809; February 3, 1803; and January 24, 1810, HSP; Henry Shippen to Margaret Shippen, January 5, 1818, HSP.

54. For analysis of this trend, see Jeanne Boydston, *Home and Work: Housework, Wages, and the Ideology of Labor in the Early Republic* (New York: Oxford University Press, 1990); Ann Douglas, *The Feminization of American Culture* (New York: Anchor Press, 1988); Jane Tompkins, *Sensational Designs: The Cultural Work of American Fiction, 1790–1860* (New York: Oxford University Press, 1986).

55. "The Influence of Females upon Society in General," *Boston Weekly Magazine,* May 31, 1817, 135.

56. Elizabeth Shippen to John Shippen, March 10, 1798, APS.

57. Elizabeth Shippen to Margaret Shippen, June 13, 1799, and June 3, 1799, APS; Harriet Margaret Wharton, journal, May [1822 or 1823], Thomas and Henry Wharton Papers.

58. Elizabeth Shippen to Margaret Shippen, June 3, 1799, APS; Elizabeth Shippen to John Shippen, March 26, 1799, APS; John Shippen to Margaret Shippen, June 24, 1799, HSP.

59. Elizabeth Foster to Margaret Shippen, September 16, 1799, HSP; John Shippen to Margaret Shippen, February 3, 1800, APS.

60. Elizabeth Foster to Margaret Shippen, September 16, 1799, HSP.

61. Elizabeth Wister to William Wister, June 8 [c. 1804], Eastwick Collection.

62. Ibid. See Randolph C. Randall, "Authors of the *Port Folio* Revealed by the Hall Files," *American Literature* 11, no. 4 (January 1940), 413.

63. Joseph Shippen to Margaret Shippen, January 4, 1802, APS.

64. John Shippen to Margaret Shippen, August 5, 1803, HSP; Henry Shippen to Margaret Shippen, May 26, 1832, HSP.

65. Catherine Eddowes to Margaret Shippen, November 1, 1808, HSP.

66. Harriet Margaret Wharton, journal, December 28, 1817, and February 3, 1818, Thomas and Henry Wharton Papers; "Address to Miss S," in Margaret Shippen, 1824 Album, HSP. For an insightful look at the "emotional work" required of young women in the early national period, see Martha Tomhave Blauvelt, *The Work of the Heart: Young Women and Emotion, 1780–1830* (Charlottesville: University of Virginia Press, 2007); Boydston, *Home and Work.*

Chapter 4

1. Benjamin Ward to Linda Raymond, November 8, 1818, Gertrude Foster Brown Additional Papers, Carton 5, Folder 117, Schlesinger Library, Radcliffe Institute, Harvard University. For Linda Raymond's letters to Benjamin Ward, see Carton 5, Folder 131. All subsequent quotations from Benjamin Ward and Linda Raymond's correspondence are from these two folders in the Gertrude Foster Brown Additional Papers Collection, unless otherwise noted. For various discussions of courtship, romantic love, and the companionate marriage ideal, see Martha Tomhave Blauvelt, *The Work of the Heart: Young Women and Emotion, 1780–1830* (Charlottesville: University of Virginia Press, 2007); Nicole Eustace, "'The Cornerstone of a Copious Work': Love and Power in Eighteenth-Century Courtship," *Journal of Social History* 34, no. 3 (spring 2001): 517–46; C. Dallett Hemphill, "Isaac and 'Isabella': Courtship and Conflict in an Antebellum Circle of Youth," *Early American Studies* 2, no. 2 (fall 2004): 398–434; Anya Jabour, *Marriage in the Early Republic: Elizabeth and William Wirt and the Companionate Ideal* (Baltimore: Johns Hopkins University Press, 1998); Timothy Kenslea, *The Sedgwicks in Love: Courtship, Engagement, and Marriage in the Early Republic* (Boston: Northeastern University Press, 2006); Jan Lewis, "The Republican Wife: Virtue and Seduction in the Early Republic," *William and Mary Quarterly* 44, no. 4 (October 1987): 689–721; Karen Lystra, *Searching the Heart: Women, Men, and Romantic Love in Nineteenth-Century America* (New York: Oxford University Press, 1989); Ellen Rothman, *Hands and Hearts: A History of Courtship in America* (New York: Basic Books, 1984); Steven Stowe, "'The Thing Not Its Vision': A Woman's Courtship and Her Sphere in the Southern Planting Class," *Feminist Studies* 9, no. 1 (spring 1983): 113–30; Samuel Watson, "Flexible Gender Roles during the Market Revolution: Family, Friendship, Marriage, and Masculinity among U.S. Army Officers, 1815–1846," *Journal of Social History* 29, no. 1 (fall 1995): 81–106.

2. Benjamin Ward to Linda Raymond, May 23, 1818. For a discussion of friendship as a metaphor for marriage, see Lewis, "Republican Wife."

3. This neighbor, Sophia Sawyer, later became a missionary to the Cherokee tribe and founded the Fayetteville Female Seminary in Arkansas. See Teri L. Castelow, "Creating an Educational Interest: Sophia Sawyer, Teacher of the Cherokee," in *Chartered Schools: Two Hundred Years of Independent Academies in the United States, 1727–1925,* ed. Nancy Beadie and Kim Tolley (New York: Routledge, 2002), 186–210; Sophia Sawyer Papers, William L. Clements Library, University of Michigan, www.clements.umich.edu/exhibits/online/womened/SawyerRead.html (accessed September 2011).

4. See Ruth H. Bloch, "Changing Conceptions of Sexuality and Romance in Eighteenth-Century America," *William and Mary Quarterly* 60, no. 1 (January 2003), 41. See also Elizabeth Maddock Dillon, *The Gender of Freedom: Fictions of Liberalism and the Literary Public Sphere* (Stanford: Stanford University Press, 2004). For other useful discussions of representations of women and gender in print culture, see Ivy Schweitzer, *Perfecting Friendship: Politics and Affiliation in Early American Literature* (Chapel Hill: University of North Carolina Press, 2006); Carole Shammas, *A History of Household Government in America* (Charlottesville: University of Virginia Press, 2002).

5. Benjamin Ward to Linda Raymond, November 10, 1817; Linda Raymond to Benjamin Ward, December 8, 1817. For background material on Benjamin Ward and Linda Raymond, see Marianna Ward Brown, Raymond-Ward Family History, undated, Gertrude Foster Brown Additional Papers, Carton 5, Folder 112; Ezra S. Stearns, *History of the Town of Rindge, New Hampshire* (Boston: Press of George H. Ellis, 1875), 372, 653–54. Linda Raymond was born on February 23, 1798, the daughter of Captain Joel Raymond (1764–1840) and Mary Ball Raymond (d. 1848). During her courtship with Benjamin, Linda was living with her family in Rindge, New Hampshire, where she taught school. During her youth, Linda attended at least two female academies (see chap. 1 for discussions of her early educational experiences). Benjamin Ward was born in Phillipston, Massachusetts, on January 25, 1793. He was the son of Ithamar Ward (1752–1828) and Anna Powers Ward (d. 1794), and was the grandson of Revolutionary General Artemas Ward of Shrewsbury, Massachusetts. Benjamin studied at the Leicester Academy before attending Harvard in 1815 (according to Harvard records, it does not appear that he graduated—he is listed as a "temporary student"). In 1817, he studied law in Shrewsbury with his uncle, Andrew Ward, and beginning in 1819, he studied under Louis Bigelow of Petersham, Massachusetts.

6. Sarah Connell, diary, June 13, 1809, in *Diary of Sarah Connell Ayer* (Portland, Maine: Lefavor-Tower Co., 1910), 102; Eliza Southgate to Mrs. Southgate, September 9, 1802, in *A Girl's Life Eighty Years Ago* (1887; reprint, New York: Arno Press, 1974), 139.

7. John Douglas to Eleanor Hall, December 26, 1816, Eleanor Hall Douglas Papers, David M. Rubenstein Rare Book and Manuscript Library, Duke University, Durham, N.C.; Benjamin Ward to Linda Raymond, January 18, 1818, and May 23, 1818; Linda Raymond to Benjamin Ward, June 9, 1818. In their letters, both Benjamin and Linda frequently referred to Linda as "Adnil" (her name spelled backward). For discussions of nineteenth-century male attitudes toward courtship and work, see Thomas Augst, *The Clerk's Tale: Young Men and Moral Life in Nineteenth-Century*

America (Chicago: University of Chicago Press, 2003); Robert Shalhope, *A Tale of New England: The Diaries of Hiram Harwood, Vermont Farmer, 1810–1837* (Baltimore: Johns Hopkins University Press, 2003).

8. Linda Raymond to Benjamin Ward, August 27, 1819; Benjamin Ward to Linda Raymond, January 14, 1818.

9. Linda Raymond to Benjamin Ward, July 4, 1818. Undoubtedly, Benjamin was pleased with Linda's sentiment because in his next letter he repeated it verbatim, and in quotation marks, to describe a walk he had taken with some friends (changing only "Linda" for "Benjamin"). See Benjamin Ward to Linda Raymond, July 22, 1818.

10. Benjamin Ward to Linda Raymond, June 30, 1818; Ephraim Abbot to Mary Holyoke Pearson, October 24, 1811, Ephraim Abbot Papers, American Antiquarian Society (AAS), Worcester, Mass.

11. Benjamin Ward to Linda Raymond, August 19, 1818.

12. Lystra, *Searching the Heart,* 4; Ephraim Abbot to Mary Holyoke Pearson, March 14, 1811, Ephraim Abbot Papers; George Munford to Lucy Taylor, August 6, 1828, Munford-Ellis Family Papers, David M. Rubenstein Rare Book and Manuscript Library, Duke University, Durham, N.C.

13. George Munford to Lucy Taylor, September 26, 1826, Munford-Ellis Papers; John Douglas to Eleanor Hall, March 4, 1817, Eleanor Hall Douglas Papers; Ephraim Abbot to Mary Pearson, October 12, 1808, Ephraim Abbot Papers; Benjamin Ward to Linda Raymond, August 19, 1818.

14. Benjamin Ward to Linda Raymond, June 30, 1818; Linda Raymond to Benjamin Ward, October 17, 1818. For discussions of the private, privileged nature of courting couples' correspondence, see Lystra, *Searching the Heart;* Rothman, *Hands and Hearts.*

15. Benjamin Ward to Linda Raymond, October 10, 1819, and July 12, 1819.

16. Benjamin Ward to Linda Raymond, July 12, 1819; Linda Raymond to Benjamin Ward, October 28, 1820, and May 20, 1823.

17. John Burton, *Lectures on Female Education and Manners* (New York: Printed and Sold by Samuel Campbell, 1794), 147; Dr. John Gregory, "Friendship, Love, Marriage," in *The Lady's Pocket Library,* 4th American ed. (Philadelphia: Mathew Carey, 1809), 145; Charles Bancker to Sarah Upshur Teackle, May 16, 1803, Charles Nicoll Bancker Papers, American Philosophical Society (APS), Philadelphia. Dr. John Gregory was a Scottish physician and moralist, and the author of the popular work, *A Father's Legacy to His Daughters,* first published in 1774. Throughout the early national period, excerpts from his writings were reprinted in several guidebooks and periodicals.

18. Harriet Manigault, diary, July 28, 1814, and April 14, 1815 [Am. 18837], Historical Society of Pennsylvania (HSP), Philadelphia; Sarah Connell, diary, September 3, 1809, in *Diary of Sarah Connell Ayer,* 124–25.

19. Christine Williams to Thomas Biddle, June 26, June 15, and December 14 [c. 1805], Biddle Family Papers, Series I [Collection 1792], HSP.

20. Benjamin Ward to Linda Raymond, December 8, 1819; Linda Raymond to Benjamin Ward, December 19, 1819. For mail delivery, see Richard John, *Spreading the News: The American Postal System from Franklin to Morse* (Cambridge, Mass.: Harvard University Press, 1995).

21. Thomas Biddle to Christine Williams, undated [c. 1805], Biddle Family Papers; Linda Raymond to Benjamin Ward, March 5, 1821; Benjamin Ward to Linda Raymond, February 19, 1821; March 21, 1821; and March 25, 1821.

22. Linda Raymond to Benjamin Ward, February 8, 1822; Benjamin Ward to Linda Raymond, March 2, 1822.

23. Benjamin Ward to Linda Raymond, January 14, 1818.

24. "Real and Pretended Love Contrasted," *Lady's Weekly Miscellany* (New York), January 17, 1807, 92; "On Delusions in Courtship," *Weekly Visitor or Ladies' Miscellany* (New York), July 9, 1803. For discussions of sincerity and duplicity in mid-nineteenth-century culture, see Jay Fliegelman, *Declaring Independence: Jefferson, Natural Language, and the Culture of Performance* (Stanford: Stanford University Press, 1993); Karen Halttunen, *Confidence Men and Painted Women: A Study of Middle-Class Culture in America, 1830–1870* (New Haven: Yale University Press, 1982).

25. Linda Raymond to Benjamin Ward, March 5, 1821; Mary Guion, diary, March 7, 1805, in Martha Tomhave Blauvelt, "Women, Words, and Men: Excerpts from the Diary of Mary Guion," *Journal of Women's History* 2, no. 2 (fall 1990), 183.

26. "Real and Pretended Love Contrasted," 92; Charles Peirce, *The Portsmouth Miscellany, or Lady's Library Improved* (Portsmouth, N.H.: Peirce, Hill and Peirce, Printers, 1804), 118. For discussions of seduction in early national literature, see especially Rodney Hessinger, *Seduced, Abandoned, and Reborn: Visions of Youth in Middle-Class America, 1780–1850* (Philadelphia: University of Pennsylvania Press, 2005). See also Blauvelt, *Work of the Heart*, esp. chap. 3; Catherine Kerrison, "By the Book: Eliza Ambler Brent Carrington and Conduct Literature in Late Eighteenth-Century Virginia," *Virginia Magazine of History and Biography* 105, no. 1 (winter 1997): 27–50; Lewis, "Republican Wife"; Sarah Emily Newton, "Wise and Foolish Virgins: 'Usable Fiction' and the Early American Conduct Tradition," *Early American Literature* 25, no. 2 (September 1990): 139–67.

27. Linda Raymond, "Verses Addressed to a Young Lady on Her Leaving School," in school notebook, Gertrude Foster Brown Additional Papers, Carton 5, Folder 136.

28. Linda Raymond to Benjamin Ward, September 5, 1818.

29. Benjamin Ward to Linda Raymond, November 8, 1818; Linda Raymond to Benjamin Ward, December 12, 1818.

30. Benjamin Ward to Linda Raymond, May 23, 1818.

31. Linda Raymond to Benjamin Ward, June 9, 1818. Here I rely on the work of several literary critics and historians on reader's response theory, particularly the idea that readers bring their own subjective ideas to texts and that interactions between readers and texts shape the individual meanings derived from particular works. For an overview of reader response theory in the context of nineteenth-century history and literature, see Heidi Brayman Hackel and Catherine E. Kelly, eds., *Reading Women: Literacy, Authorship, and Culture in the Atlantic World, 1500–1800* (Philadelphia: University of Pennsylvania Press, 2008); James L. Machor, ed., *Readers in History: Nineteenth-Century American Literature and the Contexts of Response* (Baltimore: Johns Hopkins University Press, 1993), especially the essay by Susan K. Harris, "Responding to the Text(s): Women Readers and the Quest for Higher Education" (259–82). For historical applications of reader response theory, see Robert Darnton, "Readers Respond to Rousseau: The Fabrication of Romantic Sensibility," in *The Great Cat Massacre and Other Episodes in French Cultural History* (New York: Vintage Books, 1985), 215–56; Cathy N. Davidson, ed., *Reading in America: Literature and Social His-*

tory (Baltimore: Johns Hopkins University Press, 1989); Carlo Ginzburg, *The Cheese and the Worms: The Cosmos of a Sixteenth-Century Miller,* trans. John and Anne Tedeschi (1976; reprint, New York: Penguin, 1980); Mary Kelley, "Reading Women/ Women Reading: The Making of Learned Women in Antebellum America," *Journal of American History* 83, no. 2 (September 1996): 401–24; Janice Radway, *Reading the Romance: Women, Patriarchy, and Popular Literature* (Chapel Hill: University of North Carolina Press, 1991).

32. Benjamin Ward to Linda Raymond, November 9, 1819; Linda Raymond to Benjamin Ward, November 24, 1819.

33. Linda Raymond to Benjamin Ward, December 12, 1818.

34. Benjamin Ward to Linda Raymond, June 3, 1821.

35. Linda Raymond to Benjamin Ward, June 9, 1818. See Johann George Zimmerman, *Solitude Considered with Respect to Its Influence upon the Mind and Heart,* [originally in German] trans. from the French of J. B. Mercier (New York: Printed by Mott and Lyon for Evert Duyckinch, 1796). For a related discussion of Zimmerman's ideals about true friendship, see Lucia McMahon, "'While Our Souls Together Blend': Narrating a Romantic Readership in the Early Republic," in *An Emotional History of the United States,* ed. Peter N. Stearns and Jan Lewis (New York: New York University Press, 1998), 66–90.

36. Benjamin Ward to Linda Raymond, June 22, 1818. For the emergence of romanticism as a literary and cultural movement, see Meyer H. Abrams, *Natural Supernaturalism: Tradition and Revolution in Romantic Literature* (New York: Norton, 1971); Leon Chai, *The Romantic Foundations of the American Renaissance* (Ithaca: Cornell University Press, 1987); Charles Chapper, *Margaret Fuller: An American Romantic Life* (New York: Oxford University Press, 1992); Anne Mellor, ed., *Romanticism and Feminism* (Bloomington: Indiana University Press, 1988); Marlon Ross, *The Contours of Masculine Desire: Romanticism and the Rise of Women's Poetry* (New York: Oxford University Press, 1989).

37. See Lystra, *Searching the Heart.* Although she focuses largely on mid- to late-nineteenth-century America, Lystra provides useful evidence that couples privileged an ideal of romantic love that focused on achieving a sense of shared selfhood. My aim here is not to argue whether or not such a "true self" actually existed but, rather, to explore the belief systems and performative processes that men and women enacted in an effort to meet specific cultural and emotional standards associated with the companionate ideal.

38. Benjamin Ward to Linda Raymond, June 3, 1821; Ephraim Abbot to Mary Holyoke Pearson, December 29, 1811, Ephraim Abbot Papers.

39. "On Masculine Manners in the Fair Sex," *Boston Weekly Magazine,* May 5, 1804, 109; "Eugenius," "For the Visiter," *Ladies' Visiter* (Marietta, Pa.), May 27, 1819, 3.

40. For a review of the scholarship and a useful analysis of how the concept of separate spheres has affected the historiography of nineteenth-century America, see Linda Kerber, "Separate Spheres, Female Worlds, Woman's Place: The Rhetoric of Women's History," *Journal of American History* 75, no. 1 (June 1988): 9–39. For a discussion of changing cultural standards of patriarchy and paternalism, see Jay Fliegelman, *Prodigals and Pilgrims: The American Revolution against Patriarchal Authority, 1750–1800* (New York: Cambridge University Press, 1982); Jan Lewis, *The Pursuit of Happiness: Family and Values in Jefferson's Virginia* (New York: Cambridge University Press, 1983); Lewis, "Republican Wife."

41. "Philo. No. II," *Massachusetts Magazine* (Boston), October 1789, 647–48; Gregory, "Conduct and Behavior" in *Lady's Pocket Library,* 123–24 (emphasis in original).

42. Linda Raymond to Benjamin Ward, July 4, 1818; Benjamin Ward to Linda Raymond, November 9, 1819; Ephraim Abbot to Mary Holyoke Pearson, October 28, 1808, Ephraim Abbot Papers; Harriet Manigault, diary, July 10, 1815; Charles Bancker to Sarah Upshur Teackle, May 16, 1803, Charles Nicoll Bancker Papers.

43. Catherine Judd to Anna Maria Cornell, March 8, 1822; Maria Cornell to Frederick Frelinghuysen Cornell, July 14, 1826, Cornell Family Papers, Special Collections and University Archives, Rutgers University Libraries, New Brunswick, N.J.; John Teackle to Charles N. Bancker, January 24, 1810, Charles Nicoll Bancker Papers; A. B[rown] to Susan Binney, undated [c. 1806], John Williams Wallace Collection [Collection 686], HSP. These examples suggest the various ways that friends and family members supported the educational aspirations of women. For further examples of intellectual exchange that were rooted in general patterns of heterosociability (that is, not exclusively in courtship), see Catherine O'Donnell Kaplan, *Men of Letters in the Early Republic: Cultivating Forums of Citizenship* (Chapel Hill: University of North Carolina Press, 2008); Bryan Waterman, *The Republic of Intellect: The Friendly Club of New York City and the Making of American Literature* (Baltimore: Johns Hopkins University Press, 2007), esp. chap. 3; Ronald J. Zboray and Mary Saracino Zboray, *Everyday Ideas: Socioliterary Experience among Antebellum New Englanders* (Knoxville: University of Tennessee Press, 2006).

44. Benjamin Ward to Linda Raymond, September 22, 1818.

45. Linda Raymond to Benjamin Ward, May 20, 1823.

46. Linda Raymond to Benjamin Ward, March 13, 1820; Benjamin Ward to Linda Raymond, April 15, 1820. Before receiving Linda's March 13, 1820, letter, Benjamin wrote to her on March 26, 1820, and made brief reference to the "fiendlike slander of which I spoke to you." He also informed Linda that he had received supportive "letters from [his cousins] Sarah and Catherine and others" and expressed confidence that the rumor "never would gain ground again." See Benjamin Ward to Linda Raymond, March 26, 1820. Linda did not directly reply to this letter, either because it arrived after she had sent her March 13, 1820, letter or because the couple may have resolved the issue face to face during Benjamin's next visit.

47. Sarah H. and Caroline Ward to Benjamin Ward, January 21, 1820, Gertrude Foster Brown Additional Papers, Carton 5, Folder 118. For further clues, see Henry David Ward to Benjamin Ward, July 30, 1820, Carton 5, Folder 119; Benjamin Ward to Linda Raymond, March 26, 1820, and April 15, 1820. There is also an earlier incident related in Benjamin and Linda's letters that may or may not be related to this scandal. On June 22, 1819, Benjamin wrote Linda to discuss "rumors of my partiality for some other besides your self. I understand such a rumor has been—I hope, Adnil, to see you before long, and if I think of it I will relate the circumstances to you." It is unclear whether the allegations that occurred in early 1820 were related to this earlier rumor or not, but the repeated accusations of Benjamin's misconduct points to the possibility that there may have been some truth to the allegations.

48. Benjamin Ward to Linda Raymond, May 8, 1820, and June 18, 1820; Linda Raymond to Benjamin Ward, May 23, 1820. The book referred to was Walter Scott, *The Bride of Lammermoor,* ed. J. H. Alexander (1819; reprint; New York: Columbia University Press, 1995). For evidence of Scott's American popularity, see Emily B. Todd,

"Walter Scott and the Nineteenth-Century American Literary Marketplace: Antebellum Richmond Readers and the Collected Editions of the Waverley Novels," *Proceedings of the Bibliographical Society of America* 93, no. 4 (December 1999): 495–517. Despite the contemporary assumption that women were most typically associated with novels (an assumption that has carried into many historical treatments of novel reading), evidence suggests that both men and women read novels and that, further, both men and women read from a variety of sources and genres.

49. See Darnton, "Readers Respond to Rousseau," for evidence of individuals' often intense, personal responses to particular authors and texts.

50. Benjamin Ward to Linda Raymond, May 8, 1820; Linda Raymond to Benjamin Ward, May 23, 1820. See Mary Wollstonecraft, *A Vindication of the Rights of Woman* (1792; reprint, New York: Penguin Books, 1985). In this letter, Benjamin transcribed a quotation from a history book he had read, which noted, "Mary Ann Wollstonecraft, who produced as a counterpart to the '*Rights of Man*' (an infamous work of Tom. Paine) a performance entitled the '*Rights of Woman*.'"

51. "New Publications," *Baltimore Weekly Magazine,* July 5, 1800, 82; Eliza Southgate to Moses Porter, June 1, 1801, in *Girl's Life Eighty Years Ago,* 61–62. For a discussion of Wollstonecraft's declining reputation, see G. J. Barker-Benfield, *The Culture of Sensibility: Sex and Society in 18th-Century Britain* (Chicago: University of Chicago Press, 1992), esp. chap. 7; Chandos Brown, "Mary Wollstonecraft, or the Female Illuminati: The Campaign against Women and 'Modern Philosophy' in the Early Republic," *Journal of the Early Republic* 15, no. 3 (fall 1995): 389–423.

52. Benjamin Ward to Linda Raymond, April 15, 1820; Linda Raymond to Benjamin Ward, May 23, 1820. See Lystra, *Searching the Heart,* esp. chap. 6. In her study of mid- to late-nineteenth-century courtship, Lystra maintains that women tested their partners more "intensely" and "routinely" than men did. As I suggest in this chapter, Benjamin and Linda both engaged in episodes of testing—but, if anything, Benjamin tested Linda more than she tested him (or at least he seemed to express more insecurity and doubt about their relationship).

53. Benjamin Ward to Linda Raymond, October 10, 1819, and April 16, 1819; Linda Raymond to Benjamin Ward, April 12, 1819.

54. Ephraim Abbot to Mary Holyoke Pearson, July 13, 1813, Ephraim Abbot Papers. For discussions of failure and masculinity, see Toby Ditz, "Shipwrecked; or, Masculinity Imperiled: Mercantile Representations of Failure and the Gendered Self in Eighteenth-Century Philadelphia," *Journal of American History* 81, no. 1 (June 1994): 51–80; Scott Sandage, *Born Losers: A History of Failure in America* (Cambridge, Mass.: Harvard University Press, 2005). For representative works on masculinity, see Mark C. Carnes and Clyde Griffen, eds., *Meanings for Manhood: Constructions of Masculinity in Victorian America* (Chicago: University of Chicago Press, 1990); Konstantin Dierks, "Letter Writing, Masculinity, and American Men of Science, 1700–1800," *Explorations in Early American Culture: Pennsylvania History* 65 (1998): 167–98; Jane Kamensky, "Talk like a Man: Speech, Power, and Masculinity in Early New England," *Gender and History* 8, no. 1 (April 1996): 22–47; Dana Nelson, *National Manhood: Capitalist Citizenship and the Imagined Fraternity of White Men* (Durham, N.C.: Duke University Press, 1998); E. Anthony Rotundo, *American Manhood: Transformations in Masculinity from the Revolution to the Modern Era* (New York: Basic Books, 1993).

55. Sarah Ripley Stearns, journal, November 10, 1812, Sarah Ripley Stearns Papers, Schlesinger Library, Radcliffe Institute, Harvard University (accessed through *History of Women Microfilm Series,* Reel 992).

56. Benjamin Ward to Linda Raymond, November 10, 1821, and January 13, 1822; Linda Raymond to Benjamin Ward, February 8, 1822.

57. Linda Raymond to Benjamin Ward, February 8, 1822; Benjamin Ward to Linda Raymond, March 2, 1822.

58. Benjamin Ward to Linda Raymond, May 26, 1822; Linda Raymond to Benjamin Ward, October 16, 1821.

59. Linda Raymond to Benjamin Ward, June 2, 1822. For discussions of patriarchal authority and parents' involvement in their children's marital plans, see Fliegelman, *Prodigals and Pilgrims.*

60. Benjamin Ward to Linda Raymond, June 15, 1822.

61. Benjamin Ward to Linda Raymond, July 14, 1822.

62. Linda Raymond to Benjamin Ward, August 11, 1822.

63. "Rules and Maxims for Promoting Matrimonial Happiness," *Philadelphia Minerva,* February 1795.

64. Linda Raymond to Benjamin Ward, August 11, 1822; Benjamin Ward to Linda Raymond, May 26, 1822, and July 14, 1822.

65. Sophia Sawyer to Linda [Ward], May 24, 1824, Sophia Sawyer Papers.

66. See Benjamin and Linda Ward, Commonplace Book, Gertrude Foster Brown Additional Papers, Carton 5, Folder 137v.

67. "Rudiments of Taste, and Polite Female Education," *Juvenile Portfolio* (Philadelphia), August 7, 1813, 170–71.

68. "Rational Love," *Saturday Evening Post* (Philadelphia), July 5, 1823 (emphasis in original).

69. Linda Raymond to Benjamin Ward, October 16, 1821. With the exception of a few scattered letters, Benjamin and Linda's correspondence did not extend into their married years because the couple no longer faced long periods of physical separation. In 1825, the couple's first (and only surviving) daughter was born (Linda subsequently gave birth to two daughters who both died in infancy). Unfortunately, their engagement lasted longer than their marriage. Benjamin continued to suffer from ill health and passed away in 1828.

Chapter 5

1. John Griscom to Jane Bowne Haines, May 16, 1812, Wyck Association Collection, Series II, American Philosophical Society (APS), Philadelphia. All correspondence cited in this chapter written to or by Jane Bowne Haines or Reuben Haines is from this collection, unless otherwise noted.

2. Anya Jabour's work on marriage in the early republic provides a compelling case study of how the ideals of companionate marriage were enacted and experienced during this period; Anya Jabour, *Marriage in the Early Republic: Elizabeth and William Wirt and the Companionate Ideal* (Baltimore: Johns Hopkins University Press, 1998). For other accounts of nineteenth-century marriage, see Timothy Kenslea, *The Sedgwicks in Love: Courtship, Engagement, and Marriage in the Early Republic* (Boston: Northeastern University Press, 2006); Peg Lamphier, *Kate Chase and William Sprague:*

Politics and Gender in a Civil War Marriage (Lincoln: University of Nebraska Press, 2003); Karen Lystra, *Searching the Heart: Women, Men, and Romantic Love in Nineteenth-Century America* (New York: Oxford University Press, 1989); Ellen Rothman, *Hands and Hearts: A History of Courtship in America* (New York: Basic Books, 1984).

3. "Conjugal Love, Exemplified in the History of Florio and Elvira," *Philadelphia Repository, and Weekly Register,* June 9, 1804, 177. For the shift against patriarchal models of marriage and family, see especially Jay Fliegelman, *Prodigals and Pilgrims: The American Revolution against Patriarchal Authority, 1750–1800* (New York: Cambridge University Press, 1982); Carl N. Degler, *At Odds: Women and the Family in America from the Revolution to the Present* (New York: Oxford University Press, 1980); Daniel Blake Smith, "The Study of the Family in Early America: Trends, Problems, Prospects," *William and Mary Quarterly* 39, no. 1 (January 1982): 3–28.

4. Daniel Parker to Anne Collins, March 26, 1817, Parker Family Papers [Collection 1802], Historical Society of Pennsylvania (HSP), Philadelphia; John Burton, *Lectures on Female Education and Manners* (New-York: Printed and Sold by Samuel Campbell, 1794), 60; "Conjugal Affection, Exemplified in the Story of Cyrus, King of Persia," in *The American Lady's Preceptor,* 2nd ed. (Baltimore: E. J. Coale, 1811), 28.

5. Several scholars have examined how both legal and prescriptive constructions of marriage functioned in the early republic. See Norma Basch, "Marriage, Morals, and Politics in the Election of 1828," *Journal of American History* 80, no. 3 (December 1993): 890–918; Ruth H. Bloch, "Changing Conceptions of Sexuality and Romance in Eighteenth-Century America," *William and Mary Quarterly* 60, no. 1 (January 2003): 13–42; Elizabeth Maddock Dillon, *The Gender of Freedom: Fictions of Liberalism and the Literary Public Sphere* (Stanford: Stanford University Press, 2004); Jan Lewis, "The Republican Wife: Virtue and Seduction in the Early Republic," *William and Mary Quarterly* 44, no. 4 (October 1987): 689–721; Marylynn Salmon, *Women and the Law of Property in Early America* (Chapel Hill: University of North Carolina Press, 1986); Carole Shammas, *A History of Household Government in America* (Charlottesville: University of Virginia Press, 2002).

6. Reuben Haines to Jane Bowne, November 20, 1811. At the time of her engagement, Jane Bowne was twenty years old and lived in New York City with her parents, Elizabeth and Robert Bowne (1744–1818). Jane attended at least two boarding schools in New York State, as well as a female academy in New York City under the direction of John Griscom, and she also frequently attended various lectures held in the city. Jane's parents had twelve children, at least seven of whom survived to adulthood. Her father, Robert Bowne, was a member of the Society of Friends in New York. He also served as governor of New York Hospital and as a member of the Board of Directors for the Bank of New York. In 1812, Reuben Haines was twenty-six years old and living in Philadelphia with his widowed mother, Hannah Marshall Haines. Reuben's father, Casper Wistar Haines (1762–1801), married Hannah Marshall (1765–1828) in 1785. Casper and Hannah had four children, but only Reuben, their oldest, survived to adulthood. Reuben was educated in Philadelphia and Burlington, New Jersey, and his parents made their home in both Philadelphia and Germantown, just northwest of Philadelphia, where many Quakers settled. Reuben's wealth came primarily from real estate and other investments, enabling him to retire early from business to cultivate the status of "gentleman farmer." For background and genealogical material on the Bowne and Haines families, see Wyck Association

Collection, Miscellaneous Genealogy Papers, Series I, APS; John M. Groff, Stephanie Grauman Wolf, and Sandra Mackenzie Lloyd, "Wyck: Witness to a Way of Life,"
Pennsylvania Heritage 29, no. 1 (2003): 22–29.

7. Karin Wulf, *Not All Wives: Women of Colonial America* (Ithaca: Cornell University Press, 2000), esp. 59. For Quaker views of marriage, see also Jacques Tual,
"Sexual Equality and Conjugal Harmony: The Way to Celestial Bliss. A View of
Early Quaker Matrimony," *Journal of the Friends' Historical Society* 55, no. 6 (1988):
161–74. For discussions of how Quaker theology afforded women opportunity and
empowerment, see Margaret Hope Bacon, *Mothers of Feminism: The Story of Quaker
Women in America* (San Francisco: Harper & Row, 1986); Margaret Morris Havi-
land, "Beyond Women's Sphere: Young Quaker Women and the Veil of Charity in
Philadelphia, 1790–1810," *William and Mary Quarterly* 51, no. 3 (July 1994): 419–46;
Rebecca Larson, *Daughters of Light: Quaker Women Preaching and Prophesying in the
Colonies and Abroad, 1700–1775* (New York: Knopf, 1999); Joan Jensen, "Not Only
Ours but Others: The Quaker Teaching Daughters of the Mid-Atlantic, 1790–1850,"
History of Education Quarterly 24, no. 1 (spring 1984): 3–19. For general information
on Quaker family life, see J. William Frost, *The Quaker Family in Colonial America: A
Portrait of the Society of Friends* (New York: St. Martin's Press, 1973); Barry Levy, *Quak-
ers and the American Family: British Settlement in the Delaware Valley* (New York: Oxford
University Press, 1988); Michael Zuckerman, ed., *Friends and Neighbors: Group Life in
America's First Plural Society* (Philadelphia: Temple University Press, 1982).

8. John Merrick to Benjamin Vaughan, April 5, 1798, Benjamin Vaughan
Papers, APS; Frederick Wolcott to Betsey Huntington, June 27, 1800, Wolcott Family Papers, Box 1, Manuscripts Division, Department of Rare Books and Special
Collections, Princeton University Library, Princeton, N. J.; Lystra, *Searching the Heart,*
42. Although the time frame of Lystra's study is the mid- to late nineteenth century,
the emphasis on mutuality and shared identity can also be found in the courting and
marital experiences of early national men and women.

9. "The Duties of Married Females," *Weekly Visitor; or Ladies' Miscellany* (New
York), October 4, 1806, 388.

10. A. B[rown] to Susan Binney, undated [c. 1806], John Williams Wallace
Collection [Collection 686], HSP; Elias Boudinot to Hannah Stockton Boudinot,
December 12, 1785, Stimson Collection of Elias Boudinot, Box 1, Folder 10, Man-
uscripts Division, Department of Rare Books and Special Collections, Princeton
University Library, Princeton, N. J.; Hannah Wister to Susan Foulke, December 24
[1803], Eastwick Collection, APS; John Teackle to Charles Bancker, March 9, 1804,
Charles Nicoll Bancker Papers, APS.

11. "An Address to Young Married Men," *Visitor, or Ladies' Miscellany* (New
York), May 11, 1804, 252; "Thoughts on Marriage, Addressed to a Lady, Attached
to a Person Very Much Her Inferior," *Lady's Weekly Miscellany* (New York), September 12, 1807, 363.

12. Burton, *Lectures on Female Education,* 62; "An Essay on the Studies Proper
for Women," in *The American Lady's Preceptor,* 28; "Picture of a Wife," *Ladies' Weekly
Miscellany* (New York), August 15, 1807, 333.

13. Samuel Whiting, *Elegant Lessons; or the Young Lady's Preceptor: Being a Series of
Appropriate Reading Exercises, in Prose and Verse: Carefully Selected from the Most Approved
Authors, for Female Schools and Academies* (Middletown, Conn.: Clark & Lyman, 1820),

69–70,103–4; "Philadelphia Ladies," *Ladies' Literary Museum* (Philadelphia), January 26, 1817, 216; John Brace, journal, February 28, 1814, in Emily Noyes Vanderpoel, *More Chronicles of a Pioneer School from 1792 to 1833, Being Added History on the Litchfield Female Academy Kept by Miss Sarah Pierce and Her Nephew, John Pierce Brace* (New York: Cadmus Book Shop, 1927), 87.

14. "Thoughts on Marriage," 362–63; Harriet Manigault, diary, October 31, 1814 [Am. 18837], HSP; Margaret Manigault to Mrs. Lewis (Elizabeth) Morris, May 15, 1814, Manigault Family Papers, Series 55-2, South Carolina Historical Society, Charleston, S.C. (accessed from microfiche copy held at Princeton University Library, Princeton, N.J.).

15. "On the Choice of a Husband," *Columbian Magazine* (Philadelphia), February 1788, 66–67; Christine Williams to Thomas Biddle, August 7 [c. 1805], Biddle Family Papers, Series I [Collection 1792], HSP; Elizabeth Griffith, *Letters Addressed to Young Married Women* (Philadelphia: John Turner, 1796), 37.

16. "Advice to Husbands," *Lady's Miscellany, or Weekly Visitor* (New York), June 6, 1812, 41; Mary Moody Emerson to Anne Brewer Sargent Gage, January 13, 1822, Gage Family, Additional Papers, Series I, American Antiquarian Society (AAS), Worcester, Mass.

17. Frederick Wolcott to Betsey Huntington, June 27, 1800, Wolcott Family Papers. For representative works on masculinity, see Thomas Augst, *The Clerk's Tale: Young Men and Moral Life in Nineteenth-Century America* (Chicago: University of Chicago Press, 2003); Mark C. Carnes and Clyde Griffen, eds., *Meanings for Manhood: Constructions of Masculinity in Victorian America* (Chicago: University of Chicago Press, 1990); Shawn Johansen, *Family Men: Middle Class Fatherhood in Early Industrializing America* (New York: Routledge, 2001); E. Anthony Rotundo, *American Manhood: Transformations in Masculinity from the Revolution to the Modern Era* (New York: Basic Books, 1993); Robert Shalhope, *A Tale of New England: The Diaries of Hiram Harwood, Vermont Farmer, 1810–1837* (Baltimore: Johns Hopkins University Press, 2003).

18. "Portrait from Life, of an Amiable Female," *Weekly Visitor; or Ladies' Miscellany* (New York), January 15, 1803, 116; "Duties of Married Females," 388; "Maxims for Promoting Matrimonial Happiness," *Lady's Miscellany, or Weekly Visitor* (New York), September 26, 1812, 359–60. For insightful analyses of women's emotional and domestic contributions to family life, see Martha Tomhave Blauvelt, *The Work of the Heart: Young Women and Emotion, 1780–1830* (Charlottesville: University of Virginia Press, 2007); Jeanne Boydston, *Home and Work: Housework, Wages, and the Ideology of Labor in the Early Republic* (New York: Oxford University Press, 1990).

19. [John Aikin], "On the Choice of a Wife, from Dr. Aikin's Letters to His Son," *Lady's Monitor* (New York), May 15, 1802, 310–11; May 22, 1802, 316–17. Aikin's writings were a popular source of marital advice and were reprinted frequently in various early national periodicals. See John Aikin, *Letters from a Father to His Son, on Various Topics, Related to Literature and the Conduct of Life* (Philadelphia: Printed for Mathew Carey, 1796). For analysis of the prescriptive literature on marriage, see Bloch, "Changing Conceptions"; Dillon, *Gender of Freedom;* Lewis, "Republican Wife."

20. Reuben Haines to Jane Bowne, March 10, 1812. Reuben Haines and Jane Bowne both came from Quaker backgrounds, and accordingly, they used the terms *thee* and *thy* in place of *you* and *yours* throughout their letters.

21. "Thoughts on Marriage," 362. In the early nineteenth century, divorce was still uncommon but was slowly becoming more accessible and acceptable. As Glenda Riley argues, "many Americans began to believe that divorce was a citizen's right in a democratic country dedicated to principles of freedom and happiness." *Divorce: An American Tradition* (New York: Oxford University Press, 1991), 34. See also Norma Basch, *Framing American Divorce: From the Revolutionary Generation to the Present* (Berkeley: University of California Press, 1999); Nancy Cott, "Divorce and the Changing Status of Women in Eighteenth-Century Massachusetts," *William and Mary Quarterly* 33, no. 4 (October 1976): 586–614; Mary Beth Sievens, *Stray Wives: Marital Conflict in Early National New England* (New York: New York University Press, 2005).

22. John Griscom to Jane Bowne Haines, May 16, 1812; [unsigned] to Anne Abbott, October 5, 1793, Lydia Clark Abbott Flint Papers (Ms S 171), Andover Historical Society, Andover, Mass.; Jane Bowne to Reuben Haines, November 24, 1811. For expressions of female ambivalence about marriage, see Nancy Cott, *The Bonds of Womanhood: "Woman's Sphere" in New England, 1780–1835* (New Haven: Yale University Press, 1979), esp. chap. 2; Anya Jabour, "'It Will Never Do for Me to Be Married': The Life of Laura Wirt Randall, 1803–1833," *Journal of the Early Republic* 17, no. 2 (summer 1997): 193–236; Lee Virginia Chambers-Schiller, *Liberty, a Better Husband: Single Women in America: The Generations of 1780–1840 (New Haven: Yale University Press, 1984).* Women's concerns may have also reflected the financial and social status of their new husbands. See Nicole Eustace, "'The Cornerstone of a Copious Work': Love and Power in Eighteenth-Century Courtship," *Journal of Social History* 34, no. 3 (spring 2001): 517–46.

23. Sarah Ripley Stearns, journal, November 10, 1812, Sarah Ripley Stearns Papers, Schlesinger Library, Radcliffe Institute, Harvard University (accessed through *History of Women Microfilm Series,* Reel 992).

24. Frederick Wolcott to Betsey Huntington, June 27, 1800, Wolcott Family Papers.

25. Jane Bowne Haines to Eliza H. Bowne, May 22, 1812; Eliza H. Bowne to Jane Bowne Haines, May 24, 1812. Eliza was married to Jane's brother John Bowne.

26. "Duties of Married Females," 388; Eliza Southgate Bowne to Octavia Southgate, June 6, 1803, in *A Girl's Life Eighty Years Ago* (1887; reprint, New York: Arno Press, 1974), 152.

27. See Jane Bowne Haines, diary, esp. June 19, 1812, June 24, 1812; Hannah Haines to Abraham M. Garigues, July 9, 1812, Wyck Association Collection. For descriptions of these extended visits, sometimes called "bridal tours," see Rothman, *Hands and Hearts,* esp. 81–83, 175–76.

28. "Susan" to Jane Bowne, May 25, 1810; "Advice to Husbands by a Lady," *Lady's Weekly Miscellany* (New York), December 13, 1806, 52.

29. Charles Bancker to Sarah Bancker, June 25, 1805, Charles Nicoll Bancker Papers; Reuben Haines to Jane Bowne Haines, September 15, 1812.

30. Reuben Haines to Jane Bowne Haines, October 1, 1812.

31. Jane Bowne Haines to Elizabeth Bowne, January 26, 1813.

32. E. W. Ware to Ann Haines, May 3, 1818, Wyck Association Collection. Ware may have been referring to Anne Collins, also from Philadelphia, who married Daniel Parker in 1817. See later in this chapter for a brief discussion of the Parker marriage.

33. Blauvelt, *Work of the Heart,* 177. As Blauvelt continues, early national "women enjoyed a sense of self-distinction and agency that often plummeted after marriage." In light of Blauvelt's findings, it is significant that Jane Bowne Haines was able to maintain such a strong sense of autonomy and agency within her marriage.

34. Sarah Ripley Stearns, journal, November 10, 1812, and January 1, 1815, Sarah Ripley Stearns Papers; Harriet Manigault Wilcocks, diary, June 6, 1816, HSP; Polly Cutler to Linda Raymond, January 20, 1812, Gertrude Foster Brown Additional Papers, Carton 5, Folder 130, Schlesinger Library, Radcliffe Institute, Harvard University. Women's changes in self-expression after motherhood are addressed more fully in chapter 6. Sarah Connell Ayer and Hannah Callender Sansom are examples of two women who kept diaries before their marriages and then neglected to write in them for several years during their childbearing years. *Diary of Sarah Connell Ayer* (Portland, Maine: Lefavor Tower Company, 1910); Susan E. Klepp and Karin Wulf, eds., *The Diary of Hannah Callender Sansom: Sense and Sensibility in the Age of the American Revolution* (Ithaca: Cornell University Press, 2010).

35. Reuben Haines to Robert Vaux, October 15, 1812.

36. Gertrude Meredith to William Meredith, September 19, 1800; and August 29, 1802, Meredith Family Papers [Collection 1509], HSP; Charles Bancker to Sarah Bancker, June 25, 1805, Charles Nicoll Bancker Papers.

37. Coleman Sellers to Sophonisha Sellers, September 26, 1816, Peale-Sellers Family Collection, APS; Rachel Boudinot to Elisha Boudinot, May 1800, Stimson Collection of Elias Boudinot, Box 1, Folder 35; Sarah Bancker to Charles Bancker, August 18, 1811, and May 4 [1805], Charles Nicoll Bancker Papers; Gertrude Meredith to William Meredith, September 11, 1800, Meredith Family Papers; William Munford to Sarah Munford, April 2, 1803, and February 19, 1803, Munford-Ellis Family Papers, David M. Rubenstein Rare Book and Manuscript Library, Duke University, Durham, N.C.

38. See Daniel Parker to Anne Parker, February 16, 1825, and March 3, 1825; Anne Parker to Daniel Parker, February 21, 1825, Parker Family Papers.

39. Anne Parker to Daniel Parker, November 13, 1824, Parker Family Papers.

40. Gertrude Meredith to William Meredith, February 26, 1797, Meredith Family Papers; Daniel Parker to Anne Parker, March 3, 1825, Parker Family Papers; Margaret Manigault to Mrs. Lewis (Elizabeth) Morris, November 19, 1809, Manigault Family Papers.

41. Jane Bowne Haines to Reuben Haines, July 17, 1813, and July 20, 1813; William Munford to Sarah Munford, December 22, 1805, Munford-Ellis Family Papers; Anne Parker to Daniel Parker, November 23, 1824, Parker Family Papers. As Karen Lystra argues, courting couples routinely engaged in moments of "testing" the strength of one another's commitment to each other (see chap. 4). Lystra also suggests that, "the ritualistic cycle of doubt, testing, and reassurance, which was central in nineteenth-century courtship letters, largely disappeared from marital exchanges." Lystra, *Searching the Heart,* 205–6. As shown in this chapter, episodes of testing continued to occur in the writings of some married couples.

42. Elizabeth Shippen to Mrs. Joseph Shippen, July 27, 1797, Shippen Family Papers, APS; Lucy Pierce to John Pierce, February 16, 1815, Poor Family Papers, Box 1, Folder 4, Schlesinger Library, Radcliffe Institute, Harvard University.

43. Hannah Collins to Jane Bowne Haines, April 21, 1817; Eliza H. Bowne to Jane Bowne Haines, May 5, 1817.

44. Reuben Haines to Jane Bowne Haines, April 12, 1818. Wyck, their family home in Germantown, was part of Reuben's family since 1689; it is now a historic site. See Groff, Wolf, and Lloyd, "Wyck." For background information on Germantown, see Stephanie Grauman Wolf, *Urban Village: Population, Community, and Family Structure in Germantown, Pennsylvania 1683–1800* (Princeton: Princeton University Press, 1976).

45. Jane Bowne Haines to Reuben Haines, April 27, 1818.

46. William Munford to Sarah Munford, February 26, 1803, Munford-Ellis Family Papers.

47. Reuben Haines to Jane Bowne Haines, April 29, 1818.

48. Ibid.

49. Ibid.

50. Ibid.

51. Lucy Pierce to John Pierce, February 16, 1815, Poor Family Papers, Box 1, Folder 4.

52. Reuben Haines to Jane Bowne Haines, May 30, 1819.

53. Jane Bowne Haines to Reuben Haines, October 25, 1820.

54. Reuben Haines to Jane Bowne Haines, June 4, 1824.

55. Ann Haines to Jane Bowne Haines, April 22, 1824; Reuben Haines to Jane Bowne Haines, May 23, 1824.

56. Reuben Haines to Jane Bowne Haines, June 4, 1824. This incident revealed the persistence of Jane's competing loyalties. "And my only consolation," Reuben noted, "was that thee was enjoying thyself with thy friends; and having the children with thee, would pay so long and so satisfactory a visit that thee would not for a long time wish to leave me again."

57. Reuben Haines to Jane Bowne Haines, June 13, 1824; Burton, *Lectures on Female Education,* 63.

58. Reuben Haines to Jane Bowne Haines, June 13, 1824.

59. Reuben Haines to James P. Parke, September 10, 1816.

60. "Albert," "A Panegyric on the Delights of Matrimony," *Massachusetts Magazine* (Boston), October 1793, 610–12; Leander," "Marriage," *Weekly Visitor; or Ladies' Miscellany* (New York), September 13, 1806, 364. For a discussion of marriage as political model and metaphor, see Lewis, "Republican Wife."

Chapter 6

1. Samuel B. How, *A Tribute of Filial Affection. A Sermon, Preached in the First Reformed Dutch Church of New Brunswick, NJ, April 5, 1851 on the Occasion of the Death of Mrs. Jane Kirkpatrick* (New Brunswick, N.J.: A. Ackerman, 1851), 10–20; Jane Eudora Kirkpatrick Cogswell, ed., *The Light of Other Days: Sketches of the Past, and Other Selections from the Writings of the Late Mrs. Jane Kirkpatrick* (New Brunswick, N.J.: Press of J. Terhune, 1856), v. I am indebted to Lisa Purcell, who generously shared with me her earlier research on Jane Bayard Kirkpatrick. Lisa Terasa Purcell, "'The Metamorphosis Must Take Place': The Construction of Female Identity in the Writings of Jane Bayard Kirkpatrick (1772–1851)," honors thesis, Dept. of History, Rutgers University, 1995.

2. Linda Kerber, *Women of the Republic: Intellect and Ideology in Revolutionary America* (New York: Norton, 1980). Important expansions of Kerber's thesis include Jan

Lewis, "The Republican Wife: Virtue and Seduction in the Early Republic," *William and Mary Quarterly* 44, no. 4 (October 1987): 689–721; Margaret Nash, "Rethinking Republican Motherhood: Benjamin Rush and the Young Ladies' Academy of Philadelphia," *Journal of the Early Republic* 17, no. 2 (summer 1997): 171–91. For representative accounts of women's involvement in political and print culture, see Catherine Allgor, *Parlor Politics: In Which the Ladies of Washington Help Build a City and a Government* (Charlottesville: University of Virginia Press, 2000); Susan Branson, *These Fiery Frenchified Dames: Women and Political Culture in Early National Philadelphia* (Philadelphia: University of Pennsylvania Press, 2001); Jan Lewis, "Politics and the Ambivalence of the Public Sphere: Women in Early Washington, D.C.," in *A Republic for the Ages*, ed. Donald Kennon and Barbara Wolanin (Charlottesville: University of Virginia Press, 1999), 122–51; Rosemarie Zagarri, *Revolutionary Backlash: Women and Politics in the Early American Republic* (Philadelphia: University of Pennsylvania Press, 2007).

3. John Bayard (1738–1807) and Margaret Hodge Bayard (d. 1780) had eight surviving children born between 1760 and 1779; the couple also adopted three children from John's brother's marriage to Margaret's sister. For background material on the Bayard family, see James Grant Wilson, "Colonel John Bayard (1738–1807) and the Bayard Family of America," *New York Genealogical and Biographical Record* 16, no. 2 (April 1885): 49–72; James Grant Wilson, *Memorials of Andrew Kirkpatrick and His Wife* (New York: Privately Printed for Mrs. Dr. How, 1870).

4. For background material on Jane Bayard Kirkpatrick's childhood, see Wilson, *Memorials of Andrew Kirkpatrick,* esp. 63–68. Wilson based his account on Jane Bayard Kirkpatrick's unfinished, unpublished autobiography, from which he quoted extensively. The full manuscript of Jane's autobiography has not been located.

5. Jane Bayard to Sally Wister, February 1, 1790, Eastwick Collection, American Philosophical Society (APS), Philadelphia; John Pierce to Lucy Pierce, March 27, 1816, Poor Family Papers, Box 2, Folder 14, Schlesinger Library, Radcliffe Institute, Harvard University. The Eastwick Collection contains a handful of letters written by Jane Bayard to Sally Wister before Jane's marriage in 1792. Sally Wister is most noted for her Revolutionary-era journal; Kathryn Zabelle Derounian, ed., *The Journal and Occasional Writings of Sarah Wister* (Rutherford, N.J.: Fairleigh Dickinson University Press, 1987).

6. Jane Bayard to Sally Wister, February 1, 1790, Eastwick Collection. At the time that the Bayard sisters attended the Moravian Seminary, the school typically accepted new students between the ages of eight and twelve years, and most students completed their studies by age sixteen. At seventeen, Jane was most likely considered "too old" to begin a new course of study. See William H. Bigler, *A History of the Rise, Progress, and Present Condition of the Moravian Seminary for Young Ladies, at Bethlehem, PA with a Catalogue of Its Pupils, 1785–1858,* 2nd ed. (Philadelphia: J. B. Lippincott & Co, 1874).

7. Wilson, *Memorials of Andrew Kirkpatrick,* 56; Jane Bayard to Sally Wister, June 17, 1792, and May 20, 1791, Eastwick Collection. Jane's father married his second wife, Mary Grant Hodgson, in 1781, but she died in 1785. In 1788, John Bayard married his third wife, Johannah White (d. 1834); Wilson, "Colonel John Bayard."

8. Jane Bayard to Sally Wister, May 20, 1791, Eastwick Collection.

9. Wilson, *Memorials of Andrew Kirkpatrick,* 69; Jane Bayard to Sally Wister, August 30 [1792], Eastwick Collection. Jane's misgivings may have, in part, been

related to the differences in age between her and Andrew. At the time of their wedding, Andrew was thirty-six, whereas Jane was just twenty.

10. Jane Bayard to Sally Wister, August 30 [1792], Eastwick Collection.

11. Andrew Kirkpatrick, quoted in Wilson, *Memorials of Andrew Kirkpatrick,* 38; How, *Tribute of Filial Affection,* 10.

12. Genealogical records indicate that Jane gave birth to seven children; Sarah and Charles Martel died in infancy. In his *Memorials of Andrew Kirkpatrick* (published in 1870), Wilson omits Sarah from his list of Andrew and Jane's children, but in an 1885 genealogical record, Wilson lists Sarah (without any additional information) as born sometime between Elizabeth (b. 1802) and Charles (b. 1810). Wilson, *Memorials of Andrew Kirkpatrick,* 74–75; James Grant Wilson, "Descendants of Colonel John Bayard," *New York Genealogical and Biographical Record* 16, no. 2 (April 1885), 70–72. A distant family record also includes Sarah as one of Jane and Andrew's children; Joseph Gaston Baillie Bulloch, *A History and Genealogy of the Families of Bayard, Houstoun of Georgia: and the Descent of the Bolton family from Assheton, Byron and Hulton of Hulton Park* (Washington, D.C.: J. H. Dony, Printer, 1919), 5–7.

13. For demographic trends and average age of marriage, see Michael R. Haines, "Long-Term Marriage Patterns in the United States from Colonial Times to the Present," *History of the Family* 1, no. 1 (March 1996): 15–39; Susan E. Klepp, *Revolutionary Conceptions: Women, Fertility, and Family Limitation in America, 1760–1820* (Chapel Hill: University of North Carolina Press, 2009).

14. Samuel Miller to Fanny Martel, July 27, 1807, Boudinot Family Collection, Box 1, Folder 17, Manuscripts Division, Department of Rare Books and Special Collections, Princeton University Library, Princeton, N.J.

15. Samuel Miller to Fanny Martel, July 27, 1807, Boudinot Family Collection.

16. Cogswell, *Light of Other Days,* vii; Jane Bayard Kirkpatrick, journal, February 16, 1824; April 13, 1824; and January 8, 1829, Special Collections and University Archives, Rutgers University Libraries, New Brunswick, N.J. All further citations from Jane Bayard Kirkpatrick's journal will be cited as "Jane Bayard Kirkpatrick" with the date of entry.

17. Benjamin Ward to Linda Raymond, November 16, 1820, Gertrude Foster Brown Additional Papers, Carton 5, Folder 117, Schlesinger Library, Radcliffe Institute, Harvard University; Margaret Manigault, diary, June 21, 1805, in Joseph P. Monigle, "The Diaries of Mrs. Gabriel Manigault, 1793–1809," MA thesis, University of Delaware, 1959, 66; Harriet Margaret Wharton, journal, September 1813, Thomas and Henry Wharton Papers [Collection 2047a], Historical Society of Pennsylvania (HSP), Philadelphia; "Portrait from Life, of an Amiable Female," *Weekly Visitor, or Ladies' Miscellany* (New York), January 15, 1803.

18. Harriet Margaret Wharton, journal, April 18, 1813, Thomas and Henry Wharton Papers.

19. Martha Hazeltine, "Corresponding Secretary's Digest and Circular," in *Second Annual Report of the Young Ladies' Association of the New-Hampton Female Seminary, for the Promotion of Literature and Missions; with the Constitution, Etc. 1834–5* (Boston: Printed by Freeman and Bolles, 1836), 27; Martha Hazeltine, "Circular," in *Fourth Annual Report of the Young Ladies' Association of the New-Hampton Female Seminary, for the Promotion of Literature and Missions; with the Constitution, Etc. 1837–8* (Boston: Printed by Freeman and Bolles, 1838), 65. This model of womanhood made no men-

tion of woman's roles in the bedroom, illustrating a prescriptive effort to redefine middle-class women's expressions of sexuality within cultural models of chastity and passivity. For an examination of this reconfiguration of women's sexuality, see Claire A. Lyons, *Sex among the Rabble: An Intimate History of Gender and Power in the Age of Revolution, 1730–1830* (Chapel Hill: University of North Carolina Press, 2006).

20. [Sarah Pierce], "Dialogue between Miss Trust and Her Pupils," in *Chronicles of a Pioneer School from 1792 to 1833, Being the History of Miss Sarah Pierce and Her Litchfield School,* ed. Emily Noyes Vanderpoel (Cambridge, Mass.: The University Press, 1903), 214–15; Joseph Emerson, *Female Education. A Discourse, Delivered at the Dedication of the Seminary Hall in Saugus, January 15, 1822* (Boston: Samuel T. Armstrong, and Crocker & Brewster, 1823), 8–9.

21. [Pierce], "Dialogue between Miss Trust and Her Pupils," in *Chronicles of a Pioneer School from 1792 to 1833, Being the History of Miss Sarah Pierce and Her Litchfield School,* ed. Emily Noyes Vanderpoel (Cambridge, Mass.: The University Press, 1903), 214; Daniel Parker to Anne Parker, November 2, 1824, Parker Family Papers [Collection 1802], HSP. For overviews of nineteenth-century ideals and experiences of fatherhood, see Stephen M. Frank, *Life with Father: Parenthood and Masculinity in the Nineteenth-Century American North* (Baltimore: Johns Hopkins University Press, 1998); Shawn Johansen, *Family Men: Middle-Class Fatherhood in Early Industrializing America* (New York: Routledge, 2001).

22. Daniel Parker to Anne Parker, May 31, 1826; November 5, 1824; and April 21, 1825, Parker Family Papers; Anne Parker to Daniel Parker, February 21, 1825, and May 3, 1825, Parker Family Papers. The book referenced by Daniel Parker was M. Maigne, ed., *The Private Journal of Madame Campan, Comprising Original Anecdotes of the French Court: Selections from Her Correspondence, Thoughts on Education, Etc.* (London: Printed by Henry Colburn, 1825). Campan (1752–1822) was an educator who served in the court of Marie Antoinette of France.

23. Abigail Bradley Hyde to Mr. and Mrs. Bradley, April 5, 1829, Bradley-Hyde Family Papers, Box 1, Folder 3, Schlesinger Library, Radcliffe Institute, Harvard University.

24. Jane Bayard Kirkpatrick, January 25 1825; Jane Bayard Kirkpatrick, "Extract from Letters," in Cogswell, *Light of Other Days,* 81.

25. Cogswell, *Light of Other Days,* v.

26. Jane Bayard Kirkpatrick, in Cogswell, *Light of Other Days,* 8, 25. Jane's novella was based on the family of Reverend John Rodgers, a family friend who served as pastor of the Presbyterian Church on Wall Street in New York. Throughout her manuscript, Jane referred to Rodgers as "Dr. R." and her father as "Col. B." "Mary" was the second wife of John Bayard and the daughter of Mary Grant, Dr. Rodgers's second wife. See Samuel Miller, *Memoirs of the Rev. John Rodgers, D.D.* (New York: Whiting and Watson, 1813), esp. 112–13; Wilson, "Colonel John Bayard." Andrew Kirkpatrick and Jane Bayard married at Rodgers's church in 1792; "Records of the First and Second Presbyterian Churches of the City of New York," *New York Genealogical and Bibliographical Record* 13, no. 1 (January 1882), 44.

27. Jane Bayard Kirkpatrick, in Cogswell, *Light of Other Days,* 32.

28. Ibid., 36–43.

29. Ibid., 9–10, 48.

30. Ibid., 49.

31. Margaret Bayard Smith to Mrs. [Jane] Kirkpatrick, March 13, 1814, in Gaillard Hunt, ed., *Forty Years in Washington: Portrayed by the Family Letters of Mrs. Samuel Harrison Smith* (London: T. Fisher Unwin, 1906), 97. For an analysis of women's roles in Washington, D.C., see Allgor, *Parlor Politics.*

32. Margaret Bayard Smith, commonplace book, September 17, 1806, in Cassandra Good, "'A Transcript of My Heart': The Unpublished Diaries of Margaret Bayard Smith," *Washington History* 17, no. 1 (fall/winter 2005), 74–75. I am indebted to Fredrika Teute for her expertise on the Bayard sisters' correspondence and relationship. Although the Margaret Bayard Smith Papers contain numerous letters written from Margaret to Jane, unfortunately Jane's letters to Margaret have not been located. For accounts of Margaret Bayard Smith's literary career, see Fredrika Teute, "In 'the Gloom of Evening': Margaret Bayard Smith's View in Black and White of Early Washington Society," *Proceedings of the American Antiquarian Society* 106, no. 1 (April 1996): 37–58; Fredrika Teute, "The Uses of Writing in Margaret Bayard Smith's New Nation," in *The Cambridge Companion to Nineteenth Century Women's Writing*, ed. Dale M. Bauer and Philip Gould (Cambridge, UK: Cambridge University Press, 2001), 203–20.

33. Jane Bayard Kirkpatrick, February 2, 1824; February 5, 1824; June 20, 1824; July 29, 1824; April 16, 1825.

34. Gertrude Meredith to William Meredith, June 30, 1798, and September 2, 1800, Meredith Family Papers [Collection 1509], HSP. For a brief account of Gertrude Meredith, see Susan Branson, "Women and the Family Economy in the Early Republic: The Case of Elizabeth Meredith," *Journal of the Early Republic* 16, no. 1 (spring 1996): 47–71.

35. Jane Bayard Kirkpatrick, January 19–28, 1824.

36. Jane Bayard Kirkpatrick, January 3–23, 1827.

37. For a discussion of the use of the pronoun *we* to inscribe a "collective narrative," see Cynthia A. Huff, "Reading as Re-Vision: Approaches to Reading Manuscript Diaries," *Biography* 23, no. 3 (summer 2000): 504–23. For other accounts of women's self-fashioning through diary writing, see Heather Beattie, "Where Narratives Meet: Archival Description, Provenance, and Women's Diaries," *Libraries and the Cultural Record* 44, no. 1 (February 2009): 82–100; Susanne L. Bunkers and Cynthia A. Huff, eds., *Inscribing the Daily: Critical Essays on Women's Diaries* (Amherst: University of Massachusetts Press, 1996).

38. Jane Bayard Kirkpatrick, November 14, 1827; November 19, 1827; September 22, 1828; April 14, 1826.

39. Martha Tomhave Blauvelt, *The Work of the Heart: Young Women and Emotion, 1780–1830* (Charlottesville: University of Virginia Press, 2007), 161–76.

40. Margaret Bayard Smith to Mrs. [Jane] Kirkpatrick, December 6, 1805, in Hunt, *Forty Years in Washington,* 47; Sarah Ripley Stearns, journal, October 13, 1816, Sarah Ripley Stearns Papers, Schlesinger Library, Radcliffe Institute, Harvard University (accessed through *History of Women Microfilm Series,* Reel 992); Margaret Manigault, diary, July 8, 1794, and January 31, 1806, in Monigle, "Diaries of Mrs. Gabriel Manigault," 35, 113.

41. Eliza Perkins to Weltha Brown, December 10, 1821, Hooker Collection, Box 1, Folder 10, Schlesinger Library, Radcliffe Institute, Harvard University; Sarah Tappan Pierce to Elizabeth Tappan, March 5, 1807, Poor Family Papers, Box 1, Folder 11;

Lowry Wister to Hannah Foulke, March 23, 1803, Eastwick Collection; Cynthia W. Pease to Lydia Clark Abbott Flint, June 7, 1821, Lydia Clark Abbott Flint Papers (Ms S 171), Andover Historical Society, Andover, Mass.

42. Jane Bayard Kirkpatrick, February 11, 1824; February 13, 1824; and July 21, 1826; Sarah Bancker to Charles Bancker, May 4 [1805], Charles Nicoll Bancker Papers, APS; Gertrude Meredith to William Meredith, August 31, 1800; February 9, 1811; and September 4, 1800, Meredith Family Papers. For an analysis of how prescriptive ideology obscured the nature of women's domestic work, see Jeanne Boydston, *Home and Work: Housework, Wages, and the Ideology of Labor in the Early Republic* (New York: Oxford University Press, 1990). For a compelling example of how to analyze the "dailyness" of women's diary writing, see Laurel Thatcher Ulrich, *A Midwife's Tale: The Life of Martha Ballard Based on Her Diary, 1785–1812* (New York: Vintage, 1990).

43. Anna Maria Bayard to Sarah Wister, May 16, 1803, Eastwick Collection; M. Menhaus to Maria Frelinghuysen, January 29, 1796; Maria Cornell to Margaretta Cornell, December 20, 1817; Maria Cornell to Margaretta Cornell Demund, January 29 [1828?], Cornell Family Papers, Special Collections and University Archives, Rutgers University Libraries, New Brunswick, N.J.; Gertrude Meredith to William Morris Meredith, May 25, 1813, Meredith Family Papers.

44. Jane Bayard Kirkpatrick, April 20, 1825.

45. Jane Bayard Kirkpatrick, December 6, 1827. For an analysis of the relationship between dream interpretation and self-fashioning, see Mechal Sobel, *Teach Me Dreams: The Search for Self in the Revolutionary Era* (Princeton: Princeton University Press, 2002).

46. Jane Bayard Kirkpatrick, July 12, 1831; Catherine Frelinghuysen to Maria Cornell, January 30, 1810, Cornell Family Papers. For infant mortality rates, see Klepp, *Revolutionary Conceptions;* Robert V. Wells, "Demographic Change and the Life Cycle of American Families," *Journal of Interdisciplinary History* 2, no. 2 (autumn 1971): 273–82. For discussions of mother-child bonds and attitudes toward infant death, see Nancy Schrom Dye and Daniel Blake Smith, "Mother Love and Infant Death, 1750–1920," *Journal of American History* 73, no. 2 (September 1986): 329–53; Wendy Simonds and Barbara Katz Rothman, *Centuries of Solace: Expressions of Maternal Grief in Popular Literature* (Philadelphia: Temple University Press, 1992).

47. Elizabeth Bowne to Jane Bowne Haines, November 5, 1816, Wyck Association Collection, Series II, APS.

48. Jane Bayard Kirkpatrick, "Elizabeth," in Cogswell, *Light of Other Days,* 61–62; Gertrude Meredith to William Meredith, August 31, 1805, Meredith Family Papers. On the doctrine of resignation, see Max Cavitch, *American Elegy: The Poetry of Mourning from the Puritans to Whitman* (Minneapolis: University of Minnesota Press, 2007); Allison Giffen, "'Till Grief Melodious Grow': The Poems and Letters of Ann Eliza Bleecker," *Early American Literature* 28, no. 3 (December 1993): 222–41; Gary Laderman, *The Sacred Remains: American Attitudes towards Death, 1799–1883* (New Haven: Yale University Press, 1996).

49. Kirkpatrick, "Elizabeth," 62; Sarah Connell Ayer, quoted in Blauvelt, *Work of the Heart,* 168.

50. Jane Bayard Kirkpatrick, January 12, 1824; January 12, 1825; January 8, 1824; August 24, 1824.

51. Jane Bayard Kirkpatrick, April 21, 1824; January 25, 1825; April 6, 1825; November 21, 1832.

52. Cogswell, *Light of Other Days*, v; How, *Tribute of Filial Affection*, 11.

53. [Sarah Sleeper], "To the Active Members of the Association," in *First Annual Report of the Young Ladies' Association for the Promotion of Literature and Missions in the "Collegiate Institution for Young Ladies"* (Philadelphia: Printed by William Geddes, 1839), 38. The historiography on women and reform work is vast. See Bruce Dorsey, *Reforming Men and Women: Gender in the Antebellum City* (Ithaca: Cornell University Press, 2002); Lori Ginzberg, *Women and the Work of Benevolence: Morality, Politics, and Class in the Nineteenth-Century United States* (New Haven: Yale University Press, 1990); Nancy A. Hewitt, *Women's Activism and Social Change: Rochester, New York, 1822–1872* (Ithaca: Cornell University Press, 1984); Julie Roy Jeffrey, *The Great Silent Army of Abolitionism: Ordinary Women in the Antislavery Movement* (Chapel Hill: University of North Carolina Press, 1998); Beth A. Salerno, *Sister Societies: Women's Antislavery Organizations in Antebellum America* (DeKalb: Northern Illinois University Press, 2005).

54. Dorcas Society and Day Nursery School of New Brunswick, New Jersey, *Constitution* (New Brunswick, N.J.: Printed by Lewis Deare, 1814); Dorcas Society and Day Nursery Society of New Brunswick, New Jersey, *Records,* Vol. 1, esp. November 17, 1813; May 1, 1820; and February 15, 1823, Special Collections and University Archives, Rutgers University Libraries, New Brunswick, N.J.

55. Dorcas Society, *Constitution;* Dorcas Society, *Records,* esp. November 17, 1813; December 13, 1813; December 27, 1813; November 1825.

56. Dorcas Society, *Records,* December 13, 1813, and December 27, 1813.

57. Ibid., August 22, 1814; Jane Bayard Kirkpatrick, June 15–16, 1829. Jane's address for the infant school has not been located.

58. Jane Bayard Kirkpatrick, July 11, 1829; July 15, 1829; and July 16, 1830.

59. Jane Bayard Kirkpatrick, January 2, 1826, and January 7, 1826.

60. Jane Bayard Kirkpatrick, August 27, 1826. For published tributes to Jane Bayard Kirkpatrick, see How, *Tribute of Filial Affection;* Cogswell, *Light of Other Days;* Lydia H. Sigourney, "Death of a Christian Lady," 1851, reprinted in Wilson, *Memorials of Andrew Kirkpatrick,* 72–73; James Grant Wilson and John Fiske, eds., *Appleton's Cyclopædia of American Biography,* Vol. 3 (New York: D. Appleton and Co., 1887), 556.

61. Martha Hazeltine, "To the Honorary Members," in *Third Annual Report of the Young Ladies' Association of the New-Hampton Female Seminary, for the Promotion of Literature and Missions; with the Constitution, Etc. 1835–6* (Boston: Press of John Putnam, 1837), 42.

Conclusion

1. Miss A. M. Burton, "Introductory Address," *Boston Weekly Magazine,* October 29, 1803, 2.

2. "Present Mode of Female Education Considered," *Lady's Weekly Miscellany* (New York), June 11, 1808, 103–4; "On the Happy Influence of Female Society," *American Museum* (Philadelphia), January 1787, 63. The second article was excerpted from William Alexander, *The History of Women from Earliest Antiquity to the Present Time* (London: Printed for C. Dilly and R. Christopher, 1782).

3. "For the *Lady's Miscellany:* From *Segur's Influence of Women in Society,*" *Lady's Weekly Miscellany* (New York), November 22, 1806, 28.

4. Mary W. Hale, "Comparative Intellectual Character of the Sexes," *Godey's Lady Book* (Philadelphia), June 1840, 273–75.

5. Ibid.

6. For overviews of these trends in women's educational history, see David F. Allmendinger, "Mount Holyoke Students Encounter the Need for Life-Planning, 1837–1850," *History of Education Quarterly* 19, no. 1 (spring 1979): 27–46; Helen Lefkowitz Horowitz, *Alma Mater: Design and Experience in the Women's Colleges from Their Nineteenth-Century Beginnings to the 1930s* (New York: Knopf, 1984); Mary Kelley, *Learning to Stand and Speak: Women, Education, and Public Life in America's Republic* (Chapel Hill: University of North Carolina Press, 2006); Margaret Nash, *Women's Education in the United States, 1780–1840* (New York: Palgrave Macmillan, 2005); Jo Anne Preston, "Domestic Ideology, School Reformers, and Female Teachers: School-teaching Becomes Women's Work in Nineteenth-Century New England," *New England Quarterly* 66, no. 4 (December 1993), 543–45; Barbara Miller Solomon, *In the Company of Educated Women: A History of Women and Higher Education in America* (New Haven: Yale University Press, 1985).

7. "Review of the Cultivation of Female Intellect in the United States," *Literary and Evangelical Magazine* (Richmond), May 1827; "Elvira," "The Ladies' Diary," *Album and Ladies' Weekly Gazette* (Philadelphia), August 9, 1826, 5.

8. Elizabeth Lindsay to Apphia Rouzee, May 24, 1806, Hunter Family Papers, Series III, Virginia Historical Society, Richmond, Va.

9. Elizabeth Cady Stanton, *Declaration of Sentiments and Resolutions,* July 19–20, 1848, *The Papers of Elizabeth Cady Stanton and Susan B. Anthony,* http://ecssba.rutgers.edu/docs/seneca.html (accessed June 2011).

10. The idea that the early national period provided space for experimentation in gender roles and identities that were ultimately foreclosed is supported not only by my inquiries on women's intellectual equality but by recent studies of women's sexuality and political activity. See Claire A. Lyons, *Sex among the Rabble: An Intimate History of Gender & Power in the Age of Revolution, Philadelphia, 1730–1830* (Chapel Hill: University of North Carolina Press, 2006); Rosemarie Zagarri, *Revolutionary Backlash: Women and Politics in the Early American Republic* (Philadelphia: University of Pennsylvania Press, 2007).

11. Hannah More, *Essays on Various Subjects, Principally Designed for Young Ladies* (London: Printed by Whittingham and Rowland, 1810), 12–13.

12. M. H. S. Brown, in *Seventh Annual Report of the Young Ladies' Literary and Missionary Association of the New-Hampton Female Seminary, with the Constitution, Etc., 1840–41* (Concord, N.H.: Printed by Asa McFarland, 1841), 61.

❧ INDEX

Abbot, Ephraim, 94, 101, 103, 107–8
Abbott, Lydia Clark, 30, 45, 49
Aikin, John, 121
Alden, Timothy, 32, 35
American Lady's Preceptor, The, 10, 56–57
American Revolution, 3, 69–71, 140
Ancient History, 62
Ann Smith Academy, 24
Appleton Cyclopaedia of American Biography, 162
arithmetic (field of study), 25, 32
astronomy (field of study), 28, 77
Ayer, Samuel, 92, 95

Bache, Sarah, 41
Bacon, Mary Ann, 25, 30, 37
Bancker, Charles, 38, 74, 103, 126, 128–29, 154–55
Bancker, Sarah, 128–29, 154–55
Bancker, Violetta, 18–19, 26, 29, 40–41, 74
Bayard, Anna, 143–44, 155
Bayard, Jane. *See* Kirkpatrick, Jane Bayard
Bayard, John, 140–41, 143
Bayard, Margaret. *See* Smith, Margaret Bayard
Bayard, Martha Hodge, 140–41
Bayard, Samuel, 79
Beecher, Catherine, 23, 167
Bennett, John, 61
Beverley, Rebecca, 28–29, 35
Biddle, Thomas, 96, 120
Binney, Horace, 76
Binney, Susan, 103, 118
Blauvelt, Martha Tomhave, 127, 153
Bloch, Ruth, 91
Boston Weekly Magazine, 34, 163
botany (field of study), 121
Boudinot, Eliza Pintard, 31–32, 35–36
Boudinot, Rachel, 128
Bowne, Eliza, 124–25
Bowne, Jane. *See* Haines, Jane Bowne

Brace, John, 35–36, 119
Bradford Academy, 23, 33, 45
Bradley, Abigail, 27, 30, 54
Brewer, Anne, 30
Bride of Lammermoor, The, 104–5
Brown, M. H. S., 170
Brown, Weltha, 49–50, 65, 154
Bryan, Daniel, 9
Burnap, Lucy, 24, 33
Burnham, Harriet, 54
Burton, A. M., 163
Burton, John, 4, 6, 10, 70, 95, 136
Byfield Academy, 43
Byron, Lord, 100

Callender, Eunice
  domesticity, 64–65
  education, role of, 44, 46–47, 53–54, 57, 60
  emotional bonds, 42–43, 46, 53, 66
  history, reading of, 62–63, 66
  letter writing, 42, 45–48, 52, 55–56, 61–66
  novel reading, 60–61
  poetry, use of, 53
  shared reading, 53–55, 58–59
  social activities, 44
  youth, 44
  See also friendship
chemistry (field of study), 25, 74
Chester, Caroline, 30
Chester, Mary, 23, 26
Coelebs in Search of a Wife, 60, 62
Cogswell, Mary, 46, 78, 84
College of New Jersey, 69
composition (field of study), 25, 32
Connell, Sarah, 31, 45, 82, 84, 92, 95, 153
Cook, Sarah Crawford, 31
coquetry, 9, 12–16, 119–20, 167
Coquette, The, 13, 170
Cornell, Margaretta, 20–21, 27, 29, 38, 40, 74